A SCHOOL HISTORY OF INDIA

A SCHOOL HISTORY OF INDIA

BY

HARAPRASAD SASTRI

GYAN

Published by

GYAN

Gyan Publishing House
5, Ansari Road
Daryaganj, New Delhi-110002
Phone: 011-47034999, 9811692060
E-mail: books@gyanbooks.com

Distribution Network
gyanbooks.com
India, USA, Canada, UK, Australia

ISBN: 978-93-6280-208-8 (PB)
First Published, 1896

2nd Impression 2024

Printed at: Gyan Press, Delhi.

A SCHOOL HISTORY OF INDIA
Author: HARAPRASAD SASTRI

SCHOOL HISTORY OF INDIA

BY

HARAPRASÁD S'ÁSTRÍ, M. A.

SENIOR PROFESSOR OF SANSKRIT, PRESIDENCY COLLEGE, CALCUTTA
JOINT-PHILOLOGICAL SECRETARY, ASIATIC SOCIETY OF BENGAL
FELLOW OF THE CALCUTTA UNIVERSITY
MEMBER OF THE ROYAL ASIATIC SOCIETY OF GREAT BRITAIN AND IRELAND

NEW EDITION—THOROUGHLY REVISED.

Calcutta:
SANSKRIT PRESS DEPOSITORY
1899

DEDICATED

TO

The Hon'ble C. E. Buckland, C.S., C.I.E.,

IN RECOGNITION OF

THE INTEREST HE TAKES IN EVERYTHING CONCERNING

INDIA, ANCIENT AND MODERN.

PREFACE.

AN attempt has been made in the present work to give, within a short compass, the most important results obtained from the decipherment of inscriptions, from numismatics, and from the labours of oriental scholars generally, in India as well as in Europe. An endeavour has been made to construct a political history of the Hindu Period from the time of Buddha's birth to that of Muhammad Ghori's conquest, and in the Muhammadan period, to give a history of the various kingdoms, which arose out of the ruins of the Patháṇ empire and which really initiated that policy of toleration and sympathy with the Hindu population which, in the hands of Akbar, brought such an accession of strength to the Mughal empire. The period intervening between the fall of the Mughal empire and the rise of the British Power has been called the period of Hindu Revival, and a whole book has been devoted to its history. This book contains the history not only of the Márháttás but also of the Sikhs and the Gurkhás. The small space to which the author has been obliged to limit himself, has not admitted of his giving the details of Jat and Rájput history.

A short history of this nature, to be useful, ought to be written in English. The difficulty of writing in a foreign language long deterred the author from undertaking it ; and he is not sure that it would have been undertaken at all, if he had not been so fortunate as to receive the kind help of that accomplished English writer, Mr. James W. Furrell, the distinguished Editor of the *Calcutta Review* , in the execution of this part of his work.

No one is more sensible than the author himself of the numerous shortcomings of his work. Some of these shortcomings are inseparable from a historical construction like the present, and for the others the author alone is responsible

NOTE ON TRANSLITERATION.

Sir William Hunter's admirable system of transliteration of Indian names has been adopted in the present work, with this exception that the palatal "S" (श) has been represented by "Ŝ". In such Geographical names as Calcutta, Allahabad, Bombay &c., the spelling of which may be said to have acquired a historic fixity, no alteration has been made.

PREFACE TO THE REVISED EDITION.

MANY important discoveries have been made in Indian Archæology since the publication of the first edition of this book—some of them of very great historical value. The work has been carefully revised with a view to incorporate the results of these discoveries, as well as to remove some of the less important details. As the method of transliteration of Indian names in Roman characters is not generally understood, an Index in Devanágari characters has been appended for the convenience of students.

TABLE OF CONTENTS.

Introduction.

Book I. The Hindu Empire.

Book II. Small Hindu Kingdoms.

Book III. Early Muhammadan Invasions and the Patha'n Empire.

Book IV. Independent Muhammadan Kingdoms.

Book V. Independent Hindu Kingdoms.

Book VI. The Mughal Empire.

Book VII. Revival of the Hindus.

Book VIII. British Period.

A

SCHOOL HISTORY OF INDIA.

INTRODUCTION.

THE VEDIC AGE.

CHAPTER I.

THE VEDAS.

Materials for the history of Ancient India.

THERE is no work giving a connected history of Ancient India. Hindu sages have left but few records of contemporary events. Much historical information may, however, be gathered from a careful study of Indian literature, which is of vast extent and goes back to remote antiquity. Of this literature, the most ancient works are the Vedas. These are four in number, namely, the *Rigveda*, *Yajurveda*, *Sâmaveda*, and *Atharvaveda*; each Veda containing one *Samhitâ* and many *Brâhmanas*. The Rigveda Samhitâ contains much valuable information about the ancient Hindus, and European scholars regard it as the earliest great national work of the Aryans in India. The historian of India has, therefore, to treat of the Rigveda Samhitâ in the very beginning of his work.

The Rigveda.

The Rigveda contains more than a thousand *súktas*, or hymns, associated with the names of various *Rishis* (seers), or sages, and pronounced in honour of various *Devatás*, or deities (literally, objects of praise. The Hindus believe that the *súktas* were not composed by the *Rishis*, but revealed to them in virtue of their supernatural power. The Rigveda makes mention of Agni (fire), Indra (strength), Savitá (the sun), Váyu (air), Varuna (the sky), the Ásvins (divine physicians), the Maruts (storms) and various other deities, of whom Agni, Váyu, and Savitá are the chief.

The Rishis

The Rigveda speaks of various *Rishis*, such as Vaśishtha, Viśvámitra, Vámadeva, Atri, Agastya, Gritsamada of the family of Bhrigu, Kanva, Jamadagni, and others. The eight *Rishis* from whom the Bráhmans claim to trace their descent, are to be found among the persons to whom the *súktas* of the Rigveda are said to have been revealed.

The age of the Rigveda.

It is difficult to ascertain when the Rigveda was compiled. Some think that it was compiled between 2780 and 1820 B. C.; but the most recent theory on the subject is that the period of Vedic civilisation extended from about 4500 to 2500 B. C.; and it would not be far wrong if the collection of hymns which has come down to the present day, were put down to the second half of this period. This refers to the *compilation* of the Rigveda; the *composition* of the various hymns, therefore, must be of much greater antiquity.

Its Geography.

The rivers mentioned in the Rigveda mostly belong to Afghanisthán and the Punjab, or their vicinity. It speaks of seven rivers collectively as the Saptasindhu. The name of the first of these is the Sindhumátá and that of the last the Sarasvatí. The Sindhumátá is the modern Indus; the Sarasvatí has disappeared in the sands of the deserts of Rájputána.

The *Rishis* were constantly engaged in hostilities with a dark race, supposed to have been the aborigines of the land, and their prayers for victory over these enemies are still extant in the Rigveda. It is supposed that the aborigines who did not submit to the *Rishis*, are represented by the wild tribes of the hills and forests of the present day, while those who submitted are now represented by the lowest ranks of Hindu society, the *Śúdras* and *Antyajas*.

The dark Aborigines.

The *Rishis* called themselves and their followers *Áryya*. The words *Bráhman*, *Kshattriya*, *Vaiśya* and *Śúdra* are rarely met with in the Rigveda, from which many have concluded that the caste system was not well established when the hymns of the Rigveda were composed. Mention is made in the Rigveda of various powerful chiefs, who often advanced beyond the limits of the Punjab and made war on people living on the Sarayú (the Gogra) and even in Magadha (South Behar).

Rigvedic Social Organization.

The *Rishis* sometimes used animal food. They sacrificed horses, sheep and goats. They prepared a drink by mixing milk with the juice of a certain creeper called *soma*, which had intoxicating properties; and they offered libations of the *soma* juice to their *Devatás*. Their boats often descended the Indus to the sea. They used chariots drawn by horses; wore bright ornaments of gold and silver, and prayed to their gods for a progeny of brave and hardy warriors.

The Rigveda is written in various metres. The majority of the verses used to be chanted or sung. These songs were known as *sámas*, and a collection of *sámas* is known as the Sámaveda Samhitá. The Yajurveda is written in prose and verse. The verses are mostly taken from the Rigveda, and the prose sentences contain directions for the performance of sacrifices. The Atharvaveda, too, is written in prose and verse. It contains a few *sámas* also.

Other Vedas.

CHAPTER II.

THE BRÁHMANAS.

The Bráhmanas.

BESIDES the Samhitás, there are the Bráhmanas included under the name of the Vedas and regarded as a part of the revealed literature. They are written in prose and are like commentaries on the Vedas, though not commentaries in the modern sense of the word, explaining a work from beginning to end. The Bráhmanas, written in a less ancient language, explain the details of various sacrifices from their very commencement to the end; discuss why a particular article is wanted, why a particular libation is offered, why a particular hymn is uttered, what the meaning of the hymn is; and treat of other cognate matters. While discussing these and similar topics, the ancient *Rishis* have made mention of various events, contemporary as well as ancient, from which much valuable historical information may be gathered.

Spread of Aryan colonisation.

From these works we come to learn that the Aryans advanced from the banks of the Sarasvatí to Kurukshetra (Karnál), Panchála (Rohilkhund), Matsya (Jaypur), Súrasena (Mathurá), Káśí (Benares), Kośala (Oudh, Magadha (South Behar), Videha (North Behar), and even to Kalinga, or the territory bordering on the Bay of Bengal, where they established their colonies, their influence, and their sovereignty. But they had not as yet advanced to the south of the Vindhyas, and their influence was confined to the country between those mountains and the Himálayas.

Vedic classification of the Bráhmans.

Sacrifices were performed with great pomp and ceremony. They often took a long time, and various classes of priests were employed in their celebration. Those who recited the hymns of the Rigveda were called the *Hotri* priests. They studied the Rigveda, and, with their descendants, were known as *Rigvedi* Bráhmans. Those who loudly chanted the Sámaveda were known as *Udgátri* priests. They studied the Sámaveda and became *Sámavedí* Bráhmans. Those who performed other offices in connection with the sacrifice, were known as *Adhvaryu* priests. They studied the Yajurveda and were known as *Yajurvedí* Bráhmans. The Atharvaveda was studied only by a limited number of Bráhmans who were known as *Atharvavedí* Bráhmans. Besides these, there were Bráhmans who studied two, three, and sometimes even four, Vedas, and were known as *Dvivedí*, *Trivedí*, and *Chaturvedí* Bráhmans, respectively. Even to the present day the Bráhmans are classed as the *Rigvedí*, *Sámavedí*, *Yajurvedí*, *and Atharvavedí*. The words *Duve*, *Tewari*, and *Chauve* are mere Hindí corruptions of the names *Dvivedí*, *Trivedí*, *and Chaturvedí*.

The four Castes.

Those amongst the Aryans who were engaged in sacrifices became Bráhmans; those who were engaged in war were known as Kshattriyas, while the rest of the Aryan population went by the name of Vaiśyas. The conquered dark population became the Śúdras. The country between the Sarasvatí and the Drishadvatí was regarded by the Aryans in India as a region of the greatest sanctity and was called Brahmávartta. Many think that the four castes were fully organised there. As the new community advanced, the countries inhabited by it came to be regarded as sacred countries. Brahmarshideś, consisting of Kurukshetra, Panchála, Súrasena, and Matsya, was next in holiness to Brahmávartta. Madhyadeś, lying between the Sarasvatí and the confluence of the Ganges and the Jamuná, occupied the third place. The Áryyávartta, bounded on the north by the Himálayas, on the south by the Vindhyas, and on the east and west by the ocean, occupied the fourth place. All other countries besides these were looked upon as Mlechchhadeśas, or 'impure countries.' In the Bráhmanas of the various Vedas, the inhabitants of the Punjab and Sindh are often mentioned as a degenerate race.

Where formed.

CHAPTER III.

THE KALPASÚTRAS.

BESIDES the Samhitás and Bráhmanas, there are certain other treatises entitled *Kalpasútras*, which are also regarded as portions of the Vedas, but not as revealed. Their authorship is attributed to the *Rishis*. In order to ascertain under what circumstances these *Kalpasútras* were composed, it is necessary first to understand the origin of the various *Śákhás* branches) of the different Vedas. As the Bráhmans migrated to different countries, after the compilation of the Samhitás and the revelation of the Bráhmanas, opinions began to vary as regards the reading, pronunciation, and interpretation of the Vedas ; the further they wandered from their original home, the more marked became the differences of opinion, while the mode of performing sacrifices also varied greatly. The distinction of the *Śákhás* had its origin in these differences of opinion. Many *Śákhás* had distinct Bráhmanas, and almost all had different *Kalpasútras*. Different *Śákhás* prevailed in different countries. The religious, social, and domestic polity of the Hindus is fully explained in these *Sútras*.

The Kalpasútras.

From these *Sútras* we learn that the Aryans had already crossed the Vindhya mountains, and established their supremacy not only in the Deccan, but also in Southern India. Monarchy was the prevailing form of government. The Bráhmans were the advisers of the kings in matters relating to religion and government. The caste system prevailed in every part of India, and many mixed castes had sprung up. The proportion of the Śúdras and mixed castes in a community increased according to the distance of the country inhabited by it from the original home of the Hindus on the Sarasvatí.

Aryan colonies in the South.

The *Sútras* speak of the four stages of a Bráhman's life, namely, *Brahmacharyya*, the student life; *Gárhasthya*, the householder's life; *Bánaprastha*, the life of a recluse in the forest, and *Yati*, the mendicant life. Even in so remote an age, some Bráhmans used to enter upon a mendicant life from childhood. About a thousand years before the Christian era, the Rishi Gautama, one of the writers of the *Sútras*, laid down special rules for the guidance of mendicants. The following were the five principal duties of a mendicant as laid down in his work:—(1) not to destroy life; (2) not to steal; (3) not to lead an incontinent life; (4) not to tell a lie, and (5) not to drink intoxicating liquors. The ancients thought that these five duties could not be strictly observed by a householder, so the Rishi Gautama reserved them for the *Sannyásis*, or mendicants.

The four stages of a Bráhman's life.

The Sannyásis.

When the *Sútras* were written, the Hindus had already made considerable progress in Geometry and Astronomy. Their knowledge of the science of Grammar has not yet been surpassed in any part of the world. About this time, the foundation of Metaphysics was laid in the *Upanishads*, which were treatises on philosophical subjects; works on the sciences of Medicine and War began to be composed; the language of the Vedas, after various phonetic changes, took the form of modern Sanskrit; and Pánini's inimitable grammar and the great epic of the Mahábhárata were composed. Another great epic, the Rámáyana, also is said to have been written during this period. It was the first composition in a dialect and metre differing widely from those of the Vedas. It is for this reason that the poet of the Rámáyana is regarded as the first poet; but many of the events which are referred to in the Rámáyana and the Mahábhárata, can be traced to the Vedas and the Bráhmanas.

Literature and Science

BOOK I.

THE HINDU EMPIRE.

CHAPTER I.

India before the Sixth Century B. C.

Political divisions of India.

TOWARDS the close of the remote period of time mentioned in the Introduction, India was divided into many small independent kingdoms. Centuries of incessant hostilities were occupied in conquering Northern and Southern Hindusthán from the dark aborigines. Some of the chiefs of the various small Hindu kingdoms established a supremacy over others, and ruled extensive territories, under such titles as *Chakravartí* (the head of a circle of kings), and *Mandaleśvara* (the lord of a circle of kings). They used to perform great sacrifices, like the *Rájsúya* (a sacrifice in which the king had to press out the juice from the *soma* creeper with his own hands), and the *Aśvamedha* (a sacrifice in which a horse was killed).

The Kurus.

We come to learn from the Mahábhárata that the kings belonging to the family of Kuru, at Hastinápur, in the country of Kurukshetra, were anxious to establish such a supremacy as this by conquering various kingdoms. We also learn from the Vishnupurána that changes in the bed of the river Ganges brought about the destruction of Hastinápur, and that, consequently, the Kurus removed their capital to Kauśámbí, the modern Kośám, on the Jamuná, thirty miles to the west of Allahabad.

Ikshvákus and Śiśunágas.

The same authority tells us that, after the fall of the Kuru empire, the Ikshvákus of Kośala became the paramount power in Northern India. They were supplanted in their turn by the descendants of Śiśunága of Magadha.

Foreign invasions of the Punjab.

Subsequently to the establishment of the Aryan settlement on the banks of the Sarasvatí, very little is known of the Punjab, the original home of the *Rishis* of the Rigveda. But we are told in the histories of western countries that the Egyptian god, Osiris, the Egyptian Pharaoh (king), Rameses, and the Assyrian queen Semiramis, invaded the Punjab. These may not be facts; but it is certain that in the sixth century B. C., Darius, king of Persia, conquered a great portion of Western India. It is said that nearly a third of his revenue was derived from his Indian provinces and that it was paid in gold.

CHAPTER II.

The Buddhists and Jainas.

The Bráhman is regarded as the only religious teacher among the Hindus. In the *Sútra* works, the Hindus are enjoined by the *Rishis* to look upon the Bráhmans as terrestrial divinities. But from these *Sútras*, again, we come to learn that there were many Kshattriyas, as well as Vaiśyas, who devoted themselves from childhood to study and meditation, and that they often had many followers to whom they imparted spiritual instruction. Thus, gradually, there grew up amongst the Hindus two distinct classes of teachers, who often disagreed in the very fundamental doctrines of their faith. In the religious works of the Jainas, the Buddhists, and even of the Hindus, mention is often made of religious teachers, of various denominations, who renounced the world and lived on alms. These were known by the general name, *Yati*, or *Sannyási*. Their number was the largest in places near the Himálayas, in the northern part of Kośala. The Naimishâranya of the Hindus, where the *Rishis* used to perform their sacrifices, was situated in this part of the country, and many are of opinion that the first great Hindu thinker, Kapila, was born there. In the sixth century B. C., various religious sects were formed here. Of these, six are mentioned in Buddhist works. Two sects, one at Śrávastí, the modern Set, in Oudh, and the other at Vaisálí, the modern Besár, in North Behar, came into existence in Buddha's time. One is named the Ájívaka, and the other the Nirgrantha, or Jaina. The Vaishnavas and Śaivas existed for a long time. The father of Buddha himself was a Śaiva. On his birth Buddha was taken to a temple of Śiva outside Kapilavástu.

Sannyásís in the North.

Of the Sannyásí teachers, Gautama Buddha was pre-eminently the greatest. Born in 557 B. C., he lived for eighty years. He obtained "the highest knowledge" at the age of thirty-nine, and devoted the rest of his life to the propagation of his religion in Magadha and in Kośala. He died in the year 477 B. C, and the Buddhist era dates from his death. Kapilavástu, his birthplace; Bodh Gya, where he obtained the highest knowledge; Váránasí, where he "turned the wheel of law" (first began to preach), and Kuśínagara, where he obtained *Nirvána* (emancipation from all human passions), are regarded as great places of pilgrimage by his followers. He was the son of Suddhodana, a prince belonging to the great Ikshváku family. His mother also was a princess. But he renounced the rich inheritance of a kingdom for the sake of spiritual advancement. Prasenajit, the Ikshváku king of Kosála, and Ajátaśatru, the king of Magadha, having embraced his faith, a large number of disciples from among their subjects flocked round him.

Buddha.

His religion is mainly based on the principles of the Hindu religion. He knew, from personal experience, that severe austerities injured the health of both body and mind; and therefore he prohibited

His religion.

such austerities. For this reason the Bráhmans derided him as a sensualist, devoted merely to pleasure. But he taught his disciples to follow a middle course; that is, he prohibited severe auterities, on the one hand, and pleasures and amusements, on the other. Buddha's greatest credit lay in the fact that he, for the first time in the history of the world, organised on a grand scale those monastic orders which, in various forms, exercised so marvellous an influence for all subsequent ages both upon Europe and upon Asia. The Rishi Gautama, long before Buddha, had enjoined five special duties on ascetics. Buddha made these obligatory on all his followers, and added five more severe rules for his monks, *viz.*,—(1) not to eat at forbidden times; (2) not to dance, sing, or act in a play; (3) not to use garlands, scents, unguents, or ornaments; (4) not to use a high or broad bed, and (5) not to acquire or receive gold or silver.

It has been already stated that it was considered difficult for a householder to observe the five duties enjoined by the Rishi Gautama. But Buddha, without softening their rigour in the least, obliged householders to observe them. There was one provision, however, in his system, namely, the doctrine of the MIDDLE PATH (that is, of avoiding extremes), that enabled them to discharge such hard obligations.

The Jaina religion.

The Jainas agree with the Buddhists in the matter of the five duties of laymen and the ten duties of monks; but they often fall into extremes. If a fire is kindled, there is an apprehension of insects falling into it; and, therefore, many a Jaina lives in darkness at night. Some Jainas cover their faces when they stir out, to prevent insects from falling into their mouths and so losing their life. But happily the majority of the Jainas allow themselves great liberty in these matters.

The Buddhist Sacred Books.

Mahávíra, the founder of the Jaina religion, was a contemporary of Buddha. Neither of these two great men left any writings of his own. After the death of Buddha, five hundred aged monks are said to have assembled at the

Saptaparní cave in Rájagriha, the Kshattriya capital of Magadha. This was the first *Sangiti,* or Council of the Buddhists, and the sayings of Buddha were chanted at this assembly. The Buddhist Scriptures were divided into three parts. The philosophical writings were named *Abhidharma;* the rules and regulations for the conduct of *Bhikshus,* or Buddhist monks, *Vinaya;* and the beautiful parables by which Buddha attracted the multitude, *Sútras.* Each part was called a *Pitaka,* or basket, and so the Buddhist Scriptures went by the name of *Tripitaka,* or "the three baskets."

The Jaina Sacred Books.

Mahávira had died one hundred and fifty-five years before Chandra Gupta, the founder of the Maurya dynasty, ascended the throne, that is, in 467 B. C. The Jaina Scriptures were collected together during Chandra Gupta's reign under the name of the *Púrvís.* These are now lost; but they were replaced by another collection, entitled the *Angas,* in a more modern language, about 500 A. D. In the same reign, Bhadrabáhu, a great monk, on account of a severe famine in Magadha, led a vast number of Jaina monks to the Karnáta country. In the first century of the Christian era, two sects were formed amongst the Jainas, named *Śvetámbaras,* who wore white garments, and *Digambaras,* who went about naked. These two sects are still to be found in India.

CHAPTER III.

THE NANDA FAMILY.

Pátaliputra.

DURING the reign of the Śiśunága family, the Kshattriyas from Videha often invaded Magadha; and the king of that country was consequently obliged to erect a strong fort at the confluence of the Ganges and the Sona, or Hiranyaváha, the Erannoboas of the Greeks. Buddha is said to have prophesied that the fort would be the nucleus of a great city, a prophecy that was literally fulfilled.

The Śúdra kings of Magadha made it their capital, probably because they found Rájagriha, the ancient capital, very inconvenient, owing to the strength of the Kshattriya element there; and thus Pátaliputra, as this fort was named, became the chief city, not only of Magadha, but of all India.

The Nandas.

The founder of the Śúdra dynasty was Nanda. He is said to have extirpated the Kshattriya race. He had eight children, and the dynasty ruled for about one hundred years.

Alexander's invasion.

During the reign of the last of the Nanda kings, in the year 327 B. C., Alexander the Great, king of Macedon, invaded India. The Kshattriyas of the Punjab, after having expelled the Persian conquerors, had established their supremacy in that country. The king of Taxila submitted to Alexander; but a king belonging to the Puru family made a vigorous, though vain, resistance. Brought before Alexander as a captive, he was asked how he desired to be treated. The king answered haughtily: "Like a king." Pleased with this dignified answer, the mighty conqueror not only restored him to his kingdom, but extended its boundaries by adding other conquered countries to it. Alexander remained one year in the Punjab and advanced as far as the Sutlej. He had to fight hard with the tribes of the Málavas and Kshaudrakas, the Greek Malii and Oxydrakæ, and, in the war with the former, he was on the point of losing his life. He was anxious to conquer the Práchí the Greek Prasii), that is, the eastern kingdom, or Magadha; but his soldiers refused to undergo further fatigue and hardship in a foreign country, and clamoured to return to their homes, and Alexander was accordingly obliged to retrace his steps. During his stay in the Punjab, he had built a powerful flotilla, on board of which he despatched a portion of his army, while with the other portion he crossed the great desert of Baluchisthán. His fleet, in its voyage down the Indus, through the Arabian Sea and the Persian Gulf, is said to have discovered many new countries for the Greeks.

CHAPTER IV

The Maurya Dynasty

Chandra Gupta.

While Alexander was in the Punjab, Chandra Gupta was with him for some time, and learnt the Greek mode of warfare, and thus laid the foundation of his future greatness But he soon offended the great conqueror by his haughtiness and was expelled from the Greek camp On the departure of Alexander, Chandra Gupta proceeded to Pátaliputra, and, with the assistance of the Bráhman, Chánakya, afterwards his minister, succeeded in overthrowing the Nanda dynasty and making himself master of the whole of Northern India He was formally crowned in 312 B C, five years after he came to power The dynasty which Chandra Gupta founded was known as the Maurya dynasty, from Murá, his mother, or as some say, his grandmother

Seleucus

Alexander died in 323 B C, and his vast empire was parcelled out by his generals after a considerable period of anarchy during which Chandra Gupta succeeded in annexing the whole of the Punjab to his empire Seleucus, one of Alexander's generals, founded, in B C 312, a new Greek kingdom, with Babylon for its capital After establishing peace in Persia and other eastern provinces, Seleucus made a persevering attempt o regain Alexander's Indian conquests, but he was repeatedly defeated by Chandra Gupta, and was at last obliged to sue for peace From this time forward the Mauryas and the Seleucidæ remained at peace A Greek ambassador, named Megasthenes, was deputed by Seleucus to report on the manners and customs of the Indians and their political and social condition Megasthenes lived for five years at the court of Chandra Gupta and wrote his great work on India, which is now lost, but from which subsequent writers derived much information about the country

Bindusára

Chandra Gupta reigned for 24 years and was succeeded by his son, Bindusára, who reigned for 28 years Bindusára had three sons,—Sushíma, Aśoka, and Vításoka Sushíma and Aśoka were so turbulent that the king, acting under the advice of his ministers, sent Sushíma as governor to Taxila, and Aśoka to Ujjayini, in order to keep them away from the Court Subsequently he sent Aśoka to Taxila and brought Sushíma to Pátaliputra While at Taxila, Aśoka contracted a great liking for Antiochus, a Greek king. He was always friendly to the Greeks, who are known in his inscriptions as *Yona*, or "Ionians," and were subsequently known in India as *Yavanas*

Aśoka

Sushíma soon quarrelled with Rádha Gupta, the prime minister of his father, and Rádha Gupta contrived to send Sushíma away to Taxila and bring Aśoka to Pátaliputra About this time, B C 264, Bindusára died, and Rádha Gupta placed Aśoka in power, and, in order to secure his safety, destroyed every scion of the royal family—lopped off the tallest trees in the royal garden,—as the Buddhist historian has graphically put it Asoka's brother, Vítáśoka, saved himself by adopting a monastic life in the city of Paundravardhan in Bengal, but even there he was not safe.

CHAPTER V

Asoka

War in Kalinga

On ascending the throne of Magadha, Aśoka's first object was to extend his empire He was the undoubted lord of Áryyavartta, or Northern India, while his nephew reigned over the whole of Guzerát Recent investigations have shown that he was master of the greater part of the Deccan also But Aśoka was ambitious of making further conquests He accordingly invaded the Kalingas, or the countries bordering on the Bay of Bengal, and succeeded in conquering them, after a protracted and obstinate war extending over a period of three years The Kalingas were already, to a great extent, civilised before their annexation to the Magadha empire, and their kings were favourably disposed towards the Buddhists They used to construct *vihâras*, or monasteries, for the accommodation of

Buddhist monks, by improving natural caves in mountains; and they dug tanks and wells for their use, and improved their condition in various ways.

Aśoka's Conversion to Buddhism.

The sufferings entailed by the war, in which several hundreds of thousands of men are said to have been killed, wrought a wonderful change in the character of Aśoka. He, who on account of the ferocity of his nature was known as Chandáśoka, began from this time to be regarded as Dharmáśoka (Aśoka "the pious"). His inscriptions breathe a spirit of righteousness which extorts admiration. He made pilgrimages regularly almost every year. In the twentieth year of his coronation, in the course a pilgrimage, he put up a stone pillar at the spot at which Buddha was born, which has recently been discovered in the Nepal Tarái, about 25 miles to the north of Bridgmanganj Railway Station, on the Bengal North Western Railway, in British territory. But Aśoka was not yet a Buddhist. It was late in life that he became a convert to Buddhism; and his *guru*, or preceptor, was Upagupta, a noted name in the history of the Buddhist religion.

Spread of Buddhism.

It was in his reign that a great Council of Buddhist Elders was held at Pátaliputra. This Council classified the Buddhist religious literature and reduced it to writing. Aśoka's veneration for the Buddhist faith was so profound that he induced those very dear to him, Mahendra, his son, and Sanghamitrá, his daughter, to embrace a monastic life, and sent them to Ceylon to preach Buddhism there. He also sent Bhikshus (Buddhist mendicants) to preach the same religion in every country then known to the people of Magadha. Káśmir, Gándhára (Afghanisthán), Mahisa (countries bordering on the Godávarí), Vanavásí (Western Maisur), Aparántaka (the Konkan and Malabar), Yonadeśa (Greek countries), Himavanta (Tibet), and Subarnabhúmí (Lower Burma) received their first Bhikshus from king Aśoka. Some of these Bhikshus were Bactrian Greeks. The important works of Aśoka's reign were the propagation of Buddhism and the establishment of hospitals for men and animals. His inscriptions are to be found scattered all over northern India and the Deccan on rocks and stone pillars. He was formally crowned king in 260 B. C. and died in 223 B. C. His vast empire enjoyed profound peace during his long reign ; and he lived on good terms with the kings of Southern India. Many Greek kings were his friends, and his preachers made their way even to the Indo-Chinese Peninsula. It was during his reign, however, that the seeds of future disasters to India were sown in Bactria, where in 256 B. C., Diodotus established an independent Greek kingdom on the ruins of that founded by Seleucus.

Administration of Aśoka.

The way in which Aśoka governed his vast Empire is a subject well-worth study. His father and grandfather had a large body of officers of various grades employed in the administration. Their general name was *purusha*, men, or officers. To the highest grade belonged the *Mahâmâtras*, or ministers. They were employed in all sorts of responsible business ; in guarding the frontier, in advising the king in matters of importance ; in executing his orders, and even in superintending the palace. Princes royal were generally employed as governors of important provinces, as we have already seen in the case of Aśoka and his brothers. Aśoka employed his sons in a similar way.

Some of the innovations which Aśoka introduced relate to religion and morality. He appointed *Dhammamahâmâtras*, or over-seers of religion, to keep watch not only over his own co-religionists, the Buddhists, but over the Bráhmans, Ájívakas, and others. He employed a large body of *Rajuks*, or writers, whose business it was to take note of the religious and moral progress of the community ; but the most important of the innovations introduced by Aśoka and one which had an abiding effect on the Indian people was the convening of periodical Assemblies for the purpose of rewarding merit. Grand Assemblies were held at Pátaliputra every fifth year, but on the frontiers they were held every third year. In these Assemblies difficult points of law were settled; experiments on various subjects were made, and rewards and prizes were given for proficiency in any branch of learning or in any of the fine arts. In Buddhist countries, assemblies of this sort are now confined to the priest-hood alone held at various intervals.

CHAPTER VI.

The Greeks in India.

Greek kingdoms in India.

The Bactrian kingdom founded by Diodotus did not last long. Rude nomad hordes from Central Asia poured in upon it from the western boundary of China and compelled the Bactrians to seek shelter in India and Afghánisthán, where these fugitives founded various kingdoms, great and small, on the ruins of the empire of Aśoka. Recent investigations have shown that not only the Scythians of various tribes, but the Parthians, too, made many settlements in India. The Parthians, however, could scarcely be distinguished from the Greeks, as they were thoroughly imbued with Greek civilisation. Menander, the Greek king of Sákala, in the Punjab, advanced, about 141 B. C., as far as the city of Sáketa, in Ayodhyá, but had to retrace his steps on account of the stubborn resistance he met with from Pushpamitra, the founder of the Sunga, or Mitra, dynasty. The Greek and Parthian kingdoms in India lasted for two hundred years after this event; for coins of a Parthian king of the Punjab named Gondopherus were issued about the fiftieth year of the Christian era.

Their influence on India.

The intercourse between the Greeks and the Indians subsisted for four centuries, from the time of Alexander the Great to that of Gondopherus. The Greeks used to come to India; but the Indians rarely went beyond their own territories. The Greeks who visited India did not belong to the celebrated cities of Greece, but were inhabitants of border kingdoms like Bactria, and had been barbarized, to a great extent, by their constant intercourse with the Barbarians. The people of India freely acknowledge their obligations to the *Yavanas* in the science of Astronomy; and it is said that the Indians owe the arts of architecture and sculpture to the same source; but this does not appear to be true, as the Greek and Indian styles differ greatly. The Indians certainly got new ideas from the Greeks in matters relating to science and art, in which the Greeks excelled. The Greeks, too, obtained much light from the Hindus in religion and philosophy, in which the Indians then held, as they still do, a high position. This is evident from the conversation which king Menander held with Nágasena, a Buddhist reformer, and which forms the subject of an extensive Páli work entitled *Milinda-prasna*, or the questions of Menander. Menander's questions relate to *nirvána*, which Nágasena expounds to him. The work is still extant in Ceylon.

CHAPTER VII.

THE SUNGA, KÁNVA, AND ANDHRA DYNASTIES.

Pushpamitra.

In the course of fifty years after the death of Asoka, his descendants lost much of their power. Outlying provinces under their relatives became virtually independent. The central power passed into the hands of ministers. One of these, Pushpamitra, held a grand review of the imperial army at Pátaliputra in the presence of the last king, Vrihadratha, and there treacherously killed him. Thus the foundation of the Sunga dynasty was laid. Pushpam itra, however, contented himself with the title *Senápati*, or commander-in-chief, and raised his son, Agnimitra, to the throne in 180 B. C. Pushpamitra was a great general and a patron of learning. His wars with the Greeks have already been noticed. He invaded Vidarbha and made the river Varadá the boundary between it and Málava. Pátanjali, the great commentator on Pánini, flourished during his reign.

The Mitras.

Some of the kings of this dynasty were very powerful. They are said to have transferred their capital from Pátaliputra to Vidisá, the modern Vilsá. But in course of time they lost their prestige. One of these Kings was of a licentious character, and his Bráhman minister, Vasudeva, sent a low-born girl, dressed as the chief queen, to him, and had him killed by her hand (111 B. C.). Vasudeva was a descendant of the great Rishi Kanva, and so the dynasty founded by him is known in history as the Kánva dynasty.

The Kánvas.

The Kánvas do not appear to have done away with the family of their masters; for there are statements in the Puránas that the Andhra kings from the Deccan annexed not only the kingdom of the Kánvas, but also what yet remained to the once powerful Sunga dynasty.

The Andhras.

There were twenty-four kings of the Andhra dynasty. Besides their capital, Dhankataka, the Andhras had another very important city in the Eastern Márháttá country, *viz*, Pratisthán, known to the Greeks as Paithana, a great emporium of trade. The Andhras began to reign some time before 71 B. C., when they destroyed the northern empire of the Sungas; and their rule lasted till 218 A. D. The cradle of the Andhra empire was the eastern Márháttá country. It was one of the latest Aryan acquisitions, and was the birthplace of Ápastamba, a writer of the *Sútras*, who is said to have flourished in the fifth century B. C. In the first and second centuries of the Christian era, when north-western India was overrun by barbarian hordes from Central Asia, the Andhras sustained the reputation of the Indian nation. Nearly the whole of civilised India was included in their empire. The Andhra kings of Southern India were Buddhists, and the remains of their religious architecture are still to be found in various places in the Deccan.

The Kshattriyas of Málava.

Some scholars are of opinion that the Kshattriyas of Málava never acknowledged the supremacy of the Andhras, but, as a sign of independence, started a local era, from 56 B. C., which may be called the *Málava* Era. This era gradually rose into importance, and in the ninth century came to be known as Vikramsamvat.

Political condition of India.

The Indo-Scythians and Greeks seem to have held sway in western and central India, about the beginning of the Christian era. The Greeks advanced as far as Kauśámbí, thirty miles to the west of Allahabad. The Andhras ruled in the Deccan and the greater part of Aryyávartta. The Pallavas ruled in Southern India, with Kánchí for their capital.

CHAPTER VIII.

THE SCYTHIAN EMPIRE IN INDIA.

The Scythians.

CENTRAL Asia was known to the Indians under the name of Śakadvípa. The Greeks called it Scythia. Powerful nomad hordes from this vast region often poured in upon the civilised countries of western Europe and southern Asia, and destroyed their civilisation. In the second century B. C., one of these hordes destroyed the Greek kingdom of Bactria and compelled the Greeks to seek shelter in India. The Scythians followed close upon them, and gradually occupied Kabul, Kandahár, Peshawar, Káśmír, and the Punjab. They even advanced as far as Mathurá and the Márháttá country. Tribe after tribe came in and conquered the country occupied by their predecessors. The most powerful of these were the Kushanas, known in Sanskrit as the *Devaputras*.

Kanishka

Kanishka was the greatest prince among the Scythian rulers of India. He was a Kushana. He ascended the throne in the year 78 A. D., at Purushapur, the modern Peshawar, which was his capital; and an era known as the Śaka era dates from his accession. The Scythians and Greeks were in those days the best astronomers; and, because they accepted the new era, it soon obtained a much wider currency than the other Indian eras. Many Hindu kings established their own eras; but most of them have disappeared, and it seems strange that an era started by a Scythian barbarian should still be in undisputed currency.

The Śaka Era.

The last Buddhist Council.

The empire of Kanishka was of vast extent, and probably stretched from the Vindhyas to the Altai mountains. The religion professed by the Scythians is not known; but Kanishka himself was a Buddhist. He called together the last and greatest Buddhist Council, or *Sangíti*, which settled the creed of Northern Buddhism, subsequently known as the *Mahâyâna* (High path) school. The Northern Buddhist works are written in Sanskrit, and they make a nearer approach to Bráhmanism than those of the Southern Buddhist, or the *Hínayâna* (Low Path) school. The preachers of Northern Buddhism converted China, Tartary, Tibet, and other northern countries of Asia.

The Śakas after Kanishka.

Kanishka was succeeded by Huvishka, and Huvishka by Bazdeo (Vasudev). The dynasty reigned for 190 years. On their coins they described themselves as *devaputras*, or sons of celestial beings. The *Kshatrapas*, or Viceroys, of Mathurá and Maháráshtrá were probably their dependents. The first Kshatrapa of Maháráshtra was Nahapána, who established his capital at Junair (Jírna-nagar). He attempted to further the interests of Buddhists and Bráhmans alike; but a branch of the Andhra dynasty defeated him and destroyed his power. Chastana, another Kshatrapa, conquered Ujjayiní and Guzerat. He and his son were reduced to great straits by the Andhra king, Pulumáyi. The people of Guzerat elected his grandson, Rudradáma, as their king. He was a powerful ruler and succeeded in keeping the Andhras at a distance from his country. With two more kings the family of Chastana came to an end.

It would be undesirable to leave the history of the Andhra and Śaka period without mentioning the name of one of the greatest sages India ever produced. This is Nágárjuna, the physician, magician, occultist, philosopher, and reformer, revered by Hindus and Buddhists alike. Born in Central India, he was a contemporary of the Sátaváhanas, or Andhras. He is regarded as the real founder of the *Maháyána* School, which, scorning the restrictions imposed upon religious teaching both by the Hindus and early Buddhists, determined to spread the saving knowledge to all human beings. He has edited and enlarged the medical work, *Suśruta.* The earliest Buddhist lexicography is attributed to him. The Tantriks, both Hindu and Buddhist, look upon him as their chief exponent. He has temples dedicated to him even up to the present day, and is regarded by the Buddhists of all sects as second only to the great founder himself.

CHAPTER IX.

The Gupta Empire.

The Guptas.

The accession of the Gupta dynasty to power is the greatest event of the fourth century of the Christian era. The Guptas appear to have been generals of some great Scythian king against whom Gupta, the founder of the family, headed a successful rebellion.

To place himself as far as possible from the Scythians and to be beyond the range of their influence, he seems to have made Kusumpur, *i.e.*, Pataliputra, his capital. Firmly established there, he began to extend his power in all directions. His son, Ghatotkach, followed his example, and, during a long and prosperous reign, greatly added to his dominions. Chandra Gupta, the grandson of Gupta, assumed the title of *Mahárájádhirája* (supreme king of great kings). He married Kumáradeví, the daughter of the king of Nepal, who belonged to the Solar dynasty. Chandra Gupta was proud of his connection with such a noble family, and he is said to have introduced in India the local era of Nepal, started by Jay Sinha in 319 A. D. This era is known as the Gupta era. The establishment of a new era of their own is an indication of the complete severance of the Guptas from their over-lords.

The Gupta Era.

Samudra Gupta, the son of Chandra Gupta, was a very powerful king. There is a posthumous inscription of his on the Asoka stone pillar at Allahabad, which records the extent of his dominions. He is said to have conquered and restored to their position the kings of Dakshina Kośala (Gondwána), Kerala (Malabar coast), Kánchí, and other southern countries, and to have conquered all the kings of Aryyávartta and annexed their dominions to his empire. The kings of East Bengal, Nepal, Kámrúp, and other border countries, as well as those of Málava and Khándeś, acknowledged his supremacy; and the Devaputras and other Scythians submitted to him. Since the time of the Mauryas, no empire had been so extensive in India. Chandra Gupta II., the son of Samudra Gupta, ascended the throne towards the end of the fourth century and reigned for twenty years.

Samudra Gupta.

During the reign of Skanda Gupta, the grandson of Samudra Gupta, the Húnas began to pour in upon India from their desert home in Central Asia. They soon overran the Punjab and the neighbouring countries, and fell upon the Gupta empire. Skanda Gupta made great efforts to check their advance;

The Húna Invasion.

but they came in like swarms of locusts and utterly destroyed the Gupta empire. The last mention of Skanda Gupta is dated 468 A. D.

Gupta Civilisation.

The Guptas were worshippers of Vishnu, and the image of Lakshmí figures on their coins. They were great patrons of learning, and from this period Sanskrit began to be extensively used in all the transactions of life, in place of various dialects of Prákrit (the vernaculars of the period). Hinduism began to revive about this time, and Buddhism declined. Arts, manufactures, and commerce flourished during the long peace which India enjoyed during the ascendency of this dynasty. An inscription records that the guild of silk-weavers of Daśapur, the modern Mandasor, in Málava, erected and maintained a grand temple to the Sun-god by raising subscriptions among themselves.

CHAPTER X.

The Húnas and Yaśodharmadev.

The Húnas.

The Húnas were the most powerful of the various barbarian tribes inhabiting Central Asia. By the end of the fourth century they had destroyed the Western Roman Empire, and in the middle of the fifth they fell upon India, carrying ruin and devastation in their train. The ancient Gupta empire was unable to withstand the shock and fell to pieces. The Húnas established their capital at Sákala, in the Punjab, and annexed the whole of Central India and the greater portion of Málava to their dominions, which extended to Persia and Tartary.

On the death of Skanda Gupta, the direct line of Gupta kings came to an end. Buddha Gupta, belonging to another branch of the same family, made a desperate attempt to avert the ruin of the empire. But Torâman, the Húna chief, defeated him and wrested from him even the eastern portion of Málava. The last king, Bhánu Gupta, however, reigned till 510 A. D. in that portion of the Gupta empire which the Húnas either could not, or did not take. There is nothing to show that Torâman ever crossed the eastern boundary of Málava. Torâman's son, Mihirakula, too, was a great conqueror, and the people of India trembled at the very mention of his name. He is mentioned even in the history of Káśmir.

Torâman.

Mihirakula.

But Mihirakula was checked in his victorious career by the rising genius of Yaśodharmadev, the king of Ujjayiní, in Málava. Málava was a dependency of the Guptas, though it appears not to have been annexed to their empire, but to have been ruled by a feudatory. After the conquest of the country by Torâman, anarchy prevailed for some time, till Yośodharmadev drove Mihirakula away from Málava. It was now a life and death struggle for the Húnas. If they were not able to check the rising power of Yaśodharma, they must be prepared to leave India. A desperate war ensued. The last battle was fought at Korur, between Multan and Luní, in the year 533 A. D., and in it the Hú nas were utterly defeated. In one of the inscriptions of Yaśodharmadev, the extent of his empire is given. It was bounded on the north by the Himálayas; on the south by the Eastern Gháts; on the east by the Brahmaputra; and on the west by the Arabian Sea. It is said that it included some countries which the Guptas, and even the Húnas, had failed to conquer, and Mihirakula himself acknowledged the suzerainty of Yaśodharma.

Yaśodharmadev.

His empire.

Oriental scholars have come to the conclusion that Yaśodharmadev is the same as the great Vikramáditya of Indian legends. One of the titles of Vikramáditya was Śakári, or the enemy of the Scythians, and Yaśodharmadev expelled from India the most powerful of the Scythian hordes that ever invaded it. The legends ascribe to Vikramáditya the era dated from 56 B. C., so well known as Vikramasamvat. It is never mentioned as the Vikrama era before the ninth century A. D. previously to which date, the era was known as the *Málava* era.

The Vikrama-samvat.

The celebrated Navaratna, or nine gems (*i. e.*, nine famous men in science and literature), flourished at the court of Vikramáditya about this period. Indian life put forth, at this important crisis, a vigour and activity unknown in earlier or later ages and surpassed only by those of modern European life. The great poet, Kálidás, was one of the Nine Gems. The world will always appreciate and admire the dramas, epics, and lyrics of Kálidás; the boldness of Varáhamihira's speculations in astronomy and cognate sciences; the accuracy of Amarasinha, the great lexicographer of India, and the genius of Vararuchi, the poet. Yaśodharma himself was a worshipper of Śiva; but he tolerated every religion, and one of his principal Gems was a Buddhist. The people of India will always look back with pride on this period of their history. Yaśodharma was the greatest of Hindu kings, and the Hindus have made his capital one of the seven great places of pilgrimage. It is a matter of regret that next to nothing is known about Yaśodharma's successors in Málava, which, however, retained its independence even after its imperial position had been lost.

The Navaratna.

CHAPTER XI.

The Kingdoms of Valabhí, Magadha, Maukhari, and Thánesvar.

The empire of Yaśodharmadev included many dependent kingdoms. Of these four were more prominent than the rest, namely, the Valabhí kingdom of Guzerat; the Gupta kingdom of Magadha; the Maukhari kingdom of western Magadha; and the kingdom of Sthánviśvara (Tháneśvar).

The Valabhí Kingdom

When the Gupta empire was in the zenith of its power, one of its generals, Bhatáraka, conquered Guzerat and held it as a dependency of the Guptas. The celebrated city of Valabhí was his capital. Bhatáraka's family reigned at Valabhí down to 744 A. D. They had assumed the title of *Mahárájá*, or great king, some time before 426 A. D. There were fourteen kings of this dynasty, seven of whom were named Śiláditya. Their influence never extended beyond Guzerat; and even within the boundary of that province there were other independent sovereigns. Though some of the Valabhi kings assumed the dignified titles of *Paramabhattáraka* (supreme lord) and *Mahárájádhirája* (supreme king of great kings), yet they always described themselves as dependents. They adorned and beautified their capital by the erection of various temples and palaces, and encouraged men of science and literature of all the various creeds that flourished in India—Hindus, Buddhists, and Jainas alike. They gave away much rent-free land to Bráhmans learned in the Vedas, and thus encouraged Hinduism more than any other creed.

The Gupta Kingdom of Magadha.

After the overthrow of their Empire the Guptas seemed to have retained power in three different parts of the Empire under three different dynasties, *viz.*, in Eastern Málava, Eastern Magadha, and Oudh, all claiming imperial dignity but none possessing any very great extent of territories. They had many rivals too. For a time the rise of Yaśodharmadev cast them all into shade. By the end of the sixth century we find many of the Guptas taking service under the dynasty of Tháneśvar. Two of them were known as kings of Málava. Of the three Gupta Kingdoms, that of Eastern Magadha founded by Krishna Gupta was the most important. Eleven kings of this family reigned in Magadha. The eighth king, Ádityasen, declared himself independent in 672 A. D. His son was known as *Mahárájádhirája.* The kingdom extended eastward to Rárh, or Burdwan. Narendra Gupta, otherwise known as Sasánka, probably belonged to this family. They often came into contact with the Maukharis, either as friends or enemies.

The Maukhari Kingdom.

The Maukharis were a very ancient race, whose power was confined to western Magadha. For a long time their capital was Kányakubja (Kanauj). They lost their ascendancy through their constant hostilities with the Guptas of Magadha, which extended over four generations. Some of the Maukhari kings assumed the titles of *Paramabhattáraka* and *Mahárájadhirája,* and it was for this reason that they came into hostile contact with their relations, the Guptas of Magadha.

The Kingdom of Tháneśvar.

Mahárájá Narendravardhan, belonging to the family of Pushpabhúti, reigned at Tháneśvar. For three generations the family did not rise into importance; but in the fourth generation Pravákaravardhan assumed the title of *Mahárájádhirája.* He fought with the Húnas in the North, and with the Gurjaras in the South. A Maukhari king of Kanauj, Grahavarmá by name, was his son-in-law. Prabhákara sent his eldest son, Rájyavardhan, to oppose the Húnas in the north; but shortly after this, Prabhákara dying, Rájyavardhan, on his return to the capital after the complete subjugation of the Húnas, ascended the throne. The king of Málava, taking advantage of the confusion of the times, invaded Kanauj and killed Grahavarmá. But Rájyavardhan, on his return, defeated the king of Málava, and re-conquered Kanauj. After this expedition, he led an army into Karnasuvarna, in western Bengal, to punish king Śasánka, said to have been the last representative of the Eastern Guptas, the great persecutor of the Buddhists, who had cut down their Bodhi tree (the tree under which Buddha attained Bodhi, or "perfect" knowledge). He was very treacherous; for, having submitted to Rájyavardhan, he made a treaty of friendship with him, and afterwards, inviting him to his camp, assassinated that unsuspecting and benevolent king. Harshavardhan, the younger brother of Rájyavardhan, loved his brother tenderly. To avenge his death, he led an army into Bengal and destroyed the power of Śasánka. In a short time Harshavardhan made himself master of the whole of Áryyávartta, and removed his capital from Tháneśvar to Kanauj. He was ambitious of conquering the Deccan and Southern India; but Satyáśraya, the great Chálúkya king, checked his advance and defeated him in battle. He was a great patron of learning. Vána Bhatta, the author of Kádamvarí, lived at his court. Harshavardhan was a Buddhist; and it was during his reign that Hiouen Thsang, the great Chinese monk, came to India and travelled all over the country for fifteen years. Following the example of Aśoka and other great monarchs, he used to hold a quinquennial assembly of all the learned men of India, and to reward them according to their learning. Harshavardhan ascended the throne in 607 A. D., and reigned for about 50 years. With his death his vast empire came to an end.

The Maukharis and Guptas of Magadha began to contend for supremacy, and in the end both were ruined. In the midst of these disturbances the seventh century of the Christian era came to a close, and with the eighth a new order of things arose in India.

BOOK II.

SMALL HINDU KINGDOMS.

CHAPTER I.

The First Muhammadan Invasion.

In the beginning of the eighth century A. D., a new foreign enemy appeared in India. This was Muhammad Bin Kásim, the general of Khalífa Walid, of Baghdad. But, before giving a history of his invasion, it will be necessary to furnish a brief account of the rise and spread of the Muhammadan religion and empire.

Muhammad.

Muhammad was born in 570 A. D., at Mecca, where, at the age of forty-three, he began to preach; but the people, far from accepting the new faith, began to persecute him and sought to take his life. He fled to Medina in 622 A. D., and the Muhammadan era dates from his flight. The era is named Hijira, which, in Arabic, means 'flight.' The religion of Muhammad was very favourably received at Medina. The powerful Arab tribes, inspired with enthusiasm by his preaching, conquered, in a short time, the whole of northern Africa, from the Isthmus of Suez to the Atlantic, and wrested the rich provinces of Asiatic Turkey from the Eastern Roman Empire. The effete monarchy of the Fire-worshippers in Persia fell to pieces on their approach, and the vast majority of the Persians accepted the new faith. The more resolute spirits among them, however, fled to the mountainous districts on the Caspian, or to Guzerat in India, where their descendants are known as the Parsis, and where they still retain their old religion and worship Fire.

Conquest of Sindh by the Arabs.

After the overthrow of the Persian monarchy, the Muhammadans began to think of conquering the rich Indian kingdoms On a slight pretext, an expedition was sent against the Rájá of Sindh, who had his capital at Alor Muhammad Bin Kásim, who was the leader of this expedition, crossed the desert of Baluchisthán, and, after severe fighting, made himself master of the country and destroyed the rich cities of Alor and Bráhmanábád (711 A. D) Thus one fair province of India passed into the hands of the Muhammadans, who retained its possession for more than three centuries Towards the latter end of this period the kingdom was divided into two portions with Multan and Mansura as their capitals. Mahmúd of Ghazní included both in his Empire The Muhammadan rulers of Sindh treated the Hindus almost on equal terms, and many Hindus rose to the position of great nobles of the kingdom The Sauviras, one of these noble Hindu families, succeeded, in the thirteenth century, in making themselves independent rulers of Sindh In a few generations the family became converts to Muhammadanism and claimed their descent from the prophet

CHAPTER II.

The Kingdom of Magadha

By the middle of the ninth century a change had arisen No one was now regarded as *Mahárájádhirája*, or *Paramabhattáraka* Different parts of the country adopted different forms of religion and polity under different dynasties There was incessant fighting, and, though the existence of independent kingdoms was favourable to the growth of science and literature, it weakened the political power of the Hindus and made them unfit for resisting foreign invasions

The Pál Dynasty.

About the middle of the ninth century, Gopál founded a kingdom in Magadha, with Odantapurí for its capital. The kings of the Pál family were Buddhists; and, though Buddhism was on the decline in every other part of India, it was still flourishing in Magadha. There were two grand monasteries, one at Nálanda and the other at Vikramaśila ; while a third at Benares was also in a flourishing condition. Students from China, Tartary, Anam, Siam, and other countries flocked to these monasteries for the purpose of receiving religious instruction. About the year 1066, Dípankara Śrijnána, a Bhikshu from Vikramaśila, crossed the lofty, snow-clad ranges of the Himálayas at the age of seventy, in order to propagate the Maháyána doctrines of Buddhism in Tibet, the people of which country grovelled in the grossest superstitions and were exceedingly given to demon-worship. A large number of Indian Buddhist Pandits went with him and helped him in the translation of many Buddhist Sanskrit works into Tibetan.

Conversion of Tibet.

The extent of the Pál Empire.

There were seventeen kings of this dynasty, some of whom were very powerful. King Dharmapál, the second of the dynasty, conquered Kámrúp and founded a new branch of the dynasty there; and Devapál is said to have carried his conquests as far west as Delhi. Benares formed a part of their kingdom; northern Bengal fell early into their hands, and they were always proud of the title of Gaureśvara (lord of Gaur). They constructed extensive public works, and some of the tanks excavated by them still excite wonder. They built magnificent monasteries, and the Tibetan monasteries of the present day are constructed after the pattern of the Pál monastery at Vikramaśila. Every branch of learning received encouragement at their hands, and of the sciences none more than that of Medicine. The great medical author, Chakrapáni Datta, nephew of the kitchen-superintendent of king Nayapál, flourished about 1060 A. D.

Encouragement of the Hindus.

Though Buddhists themselves, the Pál kings always held the Bráhmans in the highest respect, and members of a Bráhman family were their hereditary prime ministers.

The fall of the Páls.

The greater part of Bengal and Mithilá was wrested from the Pál dynasty by the Sen kings of Bengal in the twelfth century, and the dominion of the former was confined to southern Behar, and, perhaps, to Benares. In the year 1197 A. D., Bakhtiyár Khiliji defeated Govinda Pál, the last king of this dynasty, and destroyed Odantapuri, where he is said to have massacred all the Buddhist Bhikshus assembled in the local monastery during the rainy season. Govinda Pál survived the Muhammadan conquest and was honoured as king by the Buddhists, though his kingdom had been destroyed.

CHAPTER III.

The Kingdom of Bengal.

The earlier history of Bengal is involved in obscurity. One glimpse is obtained from the history of Ceylon. About the beginning of the sixth century B. C. the son of a Bengal King, Vijay Sinha, by name, expelled from his country by the order of his father, established himself in that island—a circumstance owing to which the island is still known as Sinhala, or Ceylon.

The earlier history of Bengal.

It was first inhabited by the Poundras and Pulindas—the modern Punros and Pods, who form the lowest strata of Hindu society in Bengal,—and it formed a part of the Magadha empire. Samudra Gupta conquered nearly the whole of the country. Its first civilisation was Buddhistic; some of the greatest Buddhist philosophers and reformers, such as Silábhadra and Chandrakírtti, were born here, and Mongolia is said to have received its Buddhism hence. The first famous Hindu king of Bengal was Adisúr. His capital probably was in Western Bengal. But his history, with that of his descendants, is enveloped in obscurity. He brought five Bráhmans from Kolánch, in Kanauj, for the purpose of propagating Bráhmanism in Bengal. As the families of these Bráhmans increased, their descendants spread on both sides of the Ganges in Rárh and in Varendra. It was some time before the Bráhmans of these two places, though descended from the same five ancestors, became so distinct in their character that matrimonial alliances between them were prohibited; and by the middle of the ninth century, the Rárhís and Várendras had become absolutely distinct. Varendra was held by the Pál kings; but Rárh does not appear to have ever been under their sway. Many of the descendants of these five Bráhmans also received grants of villages from the kings of Rárh, as also the Pál kings of Magadha, as early as the days of Dharmapál, and, from this fact, they and their descendants are known as Grámínas, or Gáins (owners of villages).

Adi Śúr.

By the end of the eleventh century, however, a new power had arisen in Bengal. Sámanta Sen, a feudatory Rájá of Karnát, after being repeatedly defeated by his over-lord, fled thither, and founded a small colony on the banks of the Bágírathí. This new colony was probably founded at Navadvíp; for the islands which composed Navadvíp, "or the nine islands," were a likely place for a refugee to live in with a small body of retainers. Sámanta Sen's grandson, Vijay, was a great conqueror, and is said to have defeated Nányadev, the king of Nepal. He certainly left a large kingdom to his son, Ballál Sen, who is reputed to have re-organised the caste system in Bengal and introduced *Kulinism*, a system of nobility, among the Bráhmans, Vaidyas, and Káyasthas of the country. Mithilá is said to have been conquered by him. He is reputed to have divided Bengal into five

The Sen dynasty.

provinces, namely, Rárh (Western Bengal), Varendra (North Bengal), Bágri (the Gangetic delta), Banga (East Bengal), and Mithilá. There is an era current in Mithilá which goes by the name of his son, Lakshman Sen, and which commences from 1119 A. D. Lakshman Sen is said to have been a great king in the earlier part of his life; but, when he was about eighty years of age, his kingdom was invaded by Bakhtiyár Khiliji, who took possession of Gour and Navadvíp (1199).

The Lakshman Sen Era.

Lakshman Sen fled with his family to Víkrampur, where his descendants reigned for 120 years more. Many Bráhmans from Rárh and Varendra fled with their king to Víkrampur, which became from that time the great seat of Bráhmanism in Bengal. Mithilá long remained semi-independent, but was eventually absorbed into the rising Muhammadan monarchies of Bengal and Jaunpur, in the fifteenth century.

The Sen kings in East Bengal.

CHAPTER IV.

THE KINGDOM OF KANAUJ.

NOTHING is known of Kanauj for a century after the death of Harshavardhan. In the eighth century, Yaśovarmadev was the king of Kanauj, and the celebrated poet, Bhavabhúti, was an ornament of his court. Lalitáditya, the king of Kásmír, defeated Yaśovarmadev, and made peace with him only on one condition, namely, that Bhavabhúti should undertake a journey to that country.

Yaśovarma and Bhavabhúti.

During the reign of Rájya Pál, Sultán Mahmúd of Ghazní invaded Kanauj. The king was not prepared for war, and was, therefore, obliged to enter into a treaty with him. Rájya Pál was succeeded by two more kings, after whom came the Ráshtrakútas,

Mahmúd's invasion.

or Ráthors, who were the rulers of Kanauj for seven generations. One of them, Govinda Ráj, wrote a commentary on Manu; and, under the patronage of this king, Lakshmídhara wrote one of the earliest and most comprehensive digests of Hindu Law, entitled Smriti Kalpataru.

The Ráthors of Kanauj.

During the reign of Jay Chandra, the seventh king of this dynasty, Muhammad of Ghor invaded Kanauj and conquered it. Śivají, one of the descendants of Jay Chandra, led a small band of his followers into the desert, where he founded the kingdom of Márwar of which Jodhpur is the present capital.

Their fall.

CHAPTER V.

The Kingdom of Kálanjara.

About the middle of the ninth century, the Kshattriya tribe of the Chandrádityas, or Chandels, who claimed descent from the Lunar dynasty, founded an extensive kingdom in Bundelkhund and its neighbourhood. At one period of its existence it extended from the Jamuná to the Narmadá and from Gwalior to the fort of Kálanjara. Dhánga, one of the Chandel kings, fought hard against Subaktigin, as an ally of Jay Pál, king of Lahore; and Ganda, his son, killed Rájya Pál, the king of Kanauj, because he had made peace with Mahmúd. During the reign of his great-grandson, Kírttivarmá, the great poet, Krishna Miśra, wrote the excellent allegorical drama entitled Probodha-chandrodaya. At the close of the twelfth century Prithvíráj Chauhán, of the united kingdom of Delhi and Ajmir, wrested the greater portion of Kálanjara from Paramardídev. Kuthuddín conquered the whole kingdom; but Trailokyavarmá, the son of Paramardídev, recovered the greater part of it. Trailokya's descendants

The Chandels.

Paramardídev and his successors.

reigned at Kálanjara for three hundred years more. Sher Sháh invested and captured the fort of Kálanjara in 1545 A. D. Durgávati, the daughter of the last king Kírtti Sinha, was married to Dalapati, the king of Garamandal. She afterwards became famous for the heroism she displayed against the generals of Akbar.

CHAPTER VI.

MÁLAVA.

Nothing is known of Málava under the successors ot Vikramáditya, except the fact that, after its conquest by Rájyavardhan of Kanauj, it formed, about the beginning of the seventh century, a part of Harshavardhan's empire and shared its destinies for about one hundred years.

The Paramáras.

In the beginning of the ninth century, however, the Paramáras came from their ancient citadel of Achalgarh, near Mount Abu. Upendra was the first Paramára king who established himself in Málava and he made the famous city of Dhárá its capital. Munja, the sixth in succession from Upendra, was himself a poet and a great patron of learning. Illustrious writers like Dhanika, Dhananjaya and Haláyudha adorned his court. He defeated Tailapa, the Chálúkya king of Kalyána, sixteen times in battle, but on the seventeenth occasion he was himself defeated and taken captive. He made an attempt to escape, but was detected and put to death, in 993 A. D. His successor in Málava was his brother, Sindhuráj, who maintained the reputation of the family. The great Rájá Bhoj, so well known in Indian legends, succeeded Sindhuráj.

Bhoj.

Bhoj was a poet and an author, and a large number of works on Rhetoric, Astrology, Hindu Law, and Yoga were composed under his patronage. He is said to have fought a great battle against Mahmúd of Ghazní, when that conqueror invested Kálanjara. He, too, like Munja, after repeated successes against the Chálúkyas, met with a reverse of fortune at their hands when, in league with the king of Guzerat, they invaded his territories and occupied his capital. He died in great distress in 1042. A.D.; but his son, Udayáditya, succeeded in defeating his father's enemies and clearing his hereditary kingdom of them, Later on, the Paramáras became so powerful that Lakshmandev, son of Udayádita, invested Tripurí, the capital of a neighbouring king dom, in 1104 A.D. Sultan Altámsh invaded Málava and destroyed Ujjayiní in 1232 A.D.; but the Paramáras continued to reign at Dhárá. The last Hindu king of Málava made war against Sárangadev, one of the kings of Guzerat. It appears that Málava was annexed to the Pathán empire in the reign of Aláuddín Khiliji.

CHAPTER VII.

The Kingdom of Guzerat.

The Valabhí kingdom came to an end about the middle of the eighth century, and its last inscription is dated 744 A. D. Banaráj founded, in 746 A.D., the celebrated city of Anahilpattan, now known as Pattan. Banaráj was the first king of the Chaurá, or Chápotkata, dynasty, which ruled Guzerat for one hundred and ninety-six years under seven kings. Under their rule Anahilpattan rose to be a magnificent city. During their ascendency in northern and western Guzerat, Govinda III., of the Ráshtrakúta dynasty of Mahárashtra, led a powerful military expedition into Guzerat and annexed Baroach (Bhrigukachcha.)

The Chápotkatas.

Sámanta Sinha, the last Chaurá king of Pattan, lost his life in 943 A.D. at the hands of his sister's son, Múlráj, who belonged to the Chálúkya family of Mahárashtra. Múlraj became king of Guzerat and enjoyed a long and prosperous reign. Early in the next century, Guzerat

The Chálúkyas.

was invaded by Mahmúd, the king of Ghazní. Chámundadev, Múlráj's son, was quite unprepared for the invasion and fled to the hills. Mahmúd easily made himself master of Pattan and plundered the celebrated shrine of Somanáth on the sea-coast. On Mahmúd's return, the Chálúkyas regained their kingdom; and Chámunda's grandson, Bhím, harassed Bhoj of Málava for a long time, during which he occupied Dhárá, the capital of Málava, and conquered a portion of Sindh. He is said to have rebuilt the temple of Somanáth.

The Muhammadan invasion repelled.

Kumárapál was the greatest sovereign of this dynasty. He successfully repelled an invasion led by Sultán Muhammad Ghori into Guzerat, and thus maintained the independence of the country for more than a century. Kumárapál's successors were weak and effeminate; and Kutbuddín Aibec, taking advantage of this, invaded Guzerat. He was opposed in the field by Lavanaprasád, the feudatory Rájá of Byághrapallí, and the Muhammadans had again to retire. Lavanaprasád, who belonged to the Chálúkya family, succeeded in deposing the ancient dynasty and raising his son, Vrihadvala, to the throne. The new dynasty was known from the place of its ancient residence, Byághrapallí, as Bághelás. It ruled Guzerat during the whole of the thirteenth century. Under Viśáladev the Bághelás rose to great power and maintained a large army, and Sárangadev, one of their last kings, is said to have overthrown the last Hindu king of Málava. Guzerat was annexed to the Pathán empire, in 1297 A.D., by Ulagh Khán, one of Aláuddín's generals, and the Bághelás retired to the inaccessible mountain regions in the east of Málwa, where their kingdom still exists. Many of the Chálúkya and Baghelá kings professed the Jaina faith and were very tender about the destruction of life. Kumárapál prohibited the sale of meat in the whole of Guzerat, and paid from the treasury to each butcher a sum equal to his income for three years. The kings of Guzerat erected magnificent temples for the benefit of Hindus and Jainas alike and patronised learned men of every creed.

CHAPTER VIII.

THE PUNJAB.

The Punjab.

Very little is known of the history of the Punjab after the dismemberment of the empire of Harshavardhan. The Hindu kings of Káśmír and the Muhammadan kings of Sindh often invaded, overran, and occupied the country. By the end of the tenth century, kings with the title of Pál had begun to rule in the Punjab. They had their capital at Lahore, and held Káśmír and Multan in subjection. It was during their rule that Subuktigín and his son, Mahmúd, founded a powerful Muhammadan kingdom at Ghazní. The frontier kingdoms of the Hindus and the Muhammadans came into collision with each other before the end of the tenth century, and after a continued struggle of more than twenty-five years the Hindu kingdom was annexed to that of the Muhammadans in 1023 A. D. Thus another province of India was permanently lost to the Hindus.

CHAPTER IX.

Delhi and Ajmir.

Delhi.

It is said that Yudhishthir, the hero of the Mahábhárata, founded the city of Indraprastha, the site of which coincides with a part of the city of Delhi. In the beginning of the Christian era, king Dilu founded a new city, close to Indraprastha, which he named Delhi, after himself. The Scythians are said to have destroyed it, and nothing is heard of it for nearly seven centuries. In 736 A. D., however, Anangapál, a Rájput chief of the Tomar family, restored the city and made it the capital of his small kingdom. Nineteen kings of this dynasty ruled at Delhi; but they were not very powerful, nor was Delhi an important city.

The Tomars.

The Chauháns of Ajmir.

Viśáladev, the Chauhán king of Ajmir, conquered Delhi in 1151 A. D. The last Tomar king, Anangapál, was compelled to give his daughter in marriage to Someśvár, the son of Viśáladev, and to enter into an agreement with his conqueror that Someśvar's son should succeed to the throne of Delhi. This son was the celebrated Prithví Ráy, who ruled the united kingdom of Delhi and Ajmir. He resided principally at Delhi, where he constructed an extensive fort, still known as Ráy Pithorá. Three great events happened during the reign of Prithví Ráy and are celebrated in the three parts of the famous epic, entitled *Prithví Ráy Rásau*, of the great Hindí poet, Chánd. The first of these events is the war between Prithví Ráy and Jay Chandra of Kanauj for the possession of Delhi. The second is the defeat of Paramardídev of Kálanjara and the conquest of the greater part of his kingdom. The third is the war with the Muhammadans, which resulted in Prithví Ráy's dethronement and death.

CHAPTER X.

SOUTHERN INDIA AND THE DECCAN.

THE sage Agastya is said to be the guardian of the Southern regions and is credited with the colonisation of India South of the Vindhyás. Examine the traditions of Southern India in any way, they all lead to one person, and that is Agastya. He is said even to have written a Grammar for his colony. Coming to historic times we find the Pándya and Chola kingdoms mentioned in the inscriptions of Aśoka. The western coast is said to have been colonised by Paraśurám, the celebrated Bráhman warrior, in remote antiquity, and to have been ruled by the Náyars, who had no kings, but governed through a *Perumal* (governor), brought from the Chera kingdom Western Maiśur) at the end of every fifth year. It is said that many *Perumals* ruled the Malabar coast, and that the last *Perumal* became a Buddhist and went to Mecca. A very large number of Christians and Jews are to be found in this part of the country. It is said that, after the destruction of Jerusalem in 70 A. D., the Jews fled in large numbers to Southern India. Saint Thomas, one of the Disciples of Christ, converted many of the people to Christianity. He is said to have died in India, and his reputed tomb, which is still shown at Mailapur, Madras, was a place of pilgrimage to the early Christians of the country. It is a matter of fact that, from very remote antiquity, the people of Arabia, Egypt, Greece and Syria maintained commercial intercourse with Southern India; and Pliny, the celebrated Roman geographer, mentions several places of note in this part of the country about the second century A. D.

The Christians and Jews.

The Pallavas established themselves in the regions north of the Kaveri about the beginning of the Christian era, founded the great city of Kánchí, the temples of which still excite admiration, and made it one of the greatest places of pilgrimage in India.

The Pallavas.

The Chinese traveller, Fa Hian, regarded it as the grandest city in the world in the fifth century.

The Chálúkyas.

Their great enemies were the Chálúkya Kshattriyas, belonging to the Lunar race. The Muhammadans called them Solánki. The founder of this family was Jay Sinha. His grandson, Pulikeśí, conquered Vátápi, the western capital of the Pallavas, and made it the capital of the Chálúkya empire. During the wars between the Chálúkyas and the Pallavas, Vátápi was several times razed to the ground; but the Chálúkyas, though they often made themselves masters of Kánchí, never ventured to destroy it. Satyáśraya preserved the independence of the Decean by compelling the great conqueror, Harshavardhan of Kanauj, to withdraw his invading army to the north of the Narmadá. Though victorious abroad, Satyáśraya had very great trouble with the Pallavas, and, in order to keep these ancient enemies in check, he created a new Chálúkya kingdom between the rivers Godávarí and Krishná, with his brother, Kubja Vishnuvardhan as its first king. This kingdom lasted from the middle of the seventh to the end of the eleventh century.

Satyáśraya repels Harsha.

A new Chálúkya kingdom.

Śankaráchárya.

With the prosperity of the Chálúkyas, the Pallavas began gradually to decline, and their kingdom came to an end in the eleventh century. But, as long as they existed, they never ceased to trouble the Chálúkyas. It was during the period of the ascendency of the early Chálúkyas that Śankaráchárya preached his celebrated *Vedánta* philosophy. The revolution brought about by his disciples throughout India was the greatest after the Buddhist reformation, and the followers of this doctrine gained from this time an ascendency which they have not yet lost. This great revolution checked the progress of Buddhism, Jainism, and the different schools of Tántrikism (mysticism) in various parts of India; and it was from this period that Hindu kings began to build splendid monasteries for the accommodation of Hindu monks, who were for the first time organised and brought under discipline by Śankaráchááryya.

CHAPTER XI.

The Ráshtrakúta Kingdom.

The Ráshtrakútas.

The Rattas were a powerful tribe of Kshattriyas in the Deccan; and one of their clans assumed the Sanskritised name, Ráshtrakúta, and began to give great trouble to the Chálúkyas in the eighth century. The capital of the Ráshtrakútas was Mányakheta, the modern Málkhed. They annexed some of the small States of the Deccan and Southern India, and made for themselves a powerful empire. One of their kings, Dantidurga, defeated Kirttivarmá, the last of the Chálúkyas of Vátápi, in 752 A.D, and reduced him to the condition of a feudatory. How Govinda III., the greatest of the Ráshtrakúta kings, conquered a portion of Guzerat and founded a new Ráshtrakúta kingdom there, has already been mentioned. The family held undisputed sway, in the Deccan for more than two hundred years. In the eleventh century, they made themselves masters of Kanauj, and a branch of the family is still reigning in Jodhpur, where they are known under the corrupt name of *Ráhthor*. The Ráshtrakútas were worshippers of Śiva and Vishnu, and some of the best cave temples of Ellora were excavated by them.

The Chálúkyas of Kalyána.

Thirteen kings of this family reigned at Mányakheta. They became degenerate with long possession of power; and in 972 A. D. their last king, Kokalla, was killed by Tailapa, a scion of the Chálúkya family, who about this time founded a new empire with its capital at Kalyána. During this time many of the feudatories of the great Maháráshtra kingdom became independent, and many rose to great importance. The history of these feudatories forms an important chapter of the history of the Deccan. Two of them survived the second Chálúkya dynasty, founded by Tailapa, and were powerful potentates when the Muhammadans invaded the Deccan.

The second Chálúkya dynasty rose to great eminence and power. Several of its kings assumed the title of Vikramáditya, 'sun of prowess,' and one of them started a new era entitled the Chálúkya Vikramasamvat. The celebrated commentary on Hindu law entitled the Mitákshará was composed under their patronage. One of the Vikramádityas of this dynasty included Málava and the Chola country within his vast empire. These kings were mostly Hindus, and did much to advance the cause of the Hindu religion.

The Chedis of Kalyána.

Vijjvala, a scion of the Chedi dynasty, dethroned Tailapa III. in the year 1157 A.D., and made himself master of Kalyána. His great minister was Vásava, who founded a new sect called Lingáyats, for the extension of which he spent enormous sums of money from the treasury. The king protested against such wasteful expenditure, whereupon Vásava had him assassinated. The sons of Vijjvala reigned for twenty years more, when the kingdom fell an easy prey to Ballál II., the Hoyśála king of Karnát.

Vásava and the Lingáyat sect.

Someśvar IV., of the second Chálúkya dynasty, made a desperate attempt to regain his ancestral kingdom with the assistance of his feudatory, Bomma, of the Kákateya family. But Ballál II. succeeded in compassing the death of both of them.

Cholas.

Orientalists have not yet been able to obtain a connected history of the Chola kings belonging to the Solar dynasty. These rose to power on the ruins of the Pallava kingdom of Kánchí, in the eleventh century A.D. They annexed the small Chálúkya kingdom, founded by Kubja Vishnuvardhan. In the beginning of the eleventh century, one of them, Rájendra Chola, not only overran with a victorious army the Pándya and Chola kingdoms of Southern India, but also levied contributions from the kings of Bengal and Magadha.

CHAPTER XII.

THE YÁDAVA KINGDOMS.

The Yádavas of Devagiri.

THE Yádavas claimed descent from Krishna, so well known in the Mahábhárata. They considered Mathurá in Hindusthán to be their first, and Dváraká in Guzerat, their second capital. Drirhapraháṛa, one of their chiefs, founded in the Deccan a small kingdom, which remained for eighteen generations feudatory to the Ráshtrakútas and the Chálúkyas. The nineteenth king, Bhilloma, conquered Kalyána in 1189 A.D., extended the boundaries of his kingdom, and removed his capital to Devagiri. After a contest with the Hoyśála Yádavas that lasted for three generations, the supremacy of the Yádavas of Devagiri over the Deccan was acknowledged. Seven princes of this dynasty reigned in the Deccan. They were great patrons of learning. Vopadeva, the author of *Mugdhabodha*, a Sanskrit grammar, and Hemádri, the great writer on modern *Smriti*, or Hindu Law, flourished under their patronage. Bháskaráchāryya, the great Astronomer, lived under the patronage of the Nikumbhas, who were feudatories of the Yádava dynasty.

The Yádavas of Dvárasamudra.

The Hoyśála Balláls, who had their capital at Dvárasamudra, the modern Halebidu, also belonged to the Yádava family. They rose into importance as feudatories of the second Chálúkya empire; but Ballál I. declared himself independent. His successor was Vishnuvardhan, who reigned from 1113 to 1137 A.D. and extended the boundaries of his kingdom in every direction. Rámánuja, the great preacher of Vaishnav doctrines, flourished about this time, and Vishnuvardhan embraced his religion. On the fall of the Chálúkyas, the Hoyśála Ballála annexed Maisúr and other provinces to their kingdom. Ballál II. of this dynasty assumed the title of *samrát* (emperor . Five kings reigned after him, and the kingdom was destroyed by Káfur, the general of Aláuddín.

The Kákateyas of Orangal.

It has already been said that the feudatory king, Bomma, helped to regain the lost prestige of the second Chálúkya empire. He belonged to the Kákateya family and became independent after the fall of the Chálúkya kings. The Kákateyas had their capital at Orangal, where they reigned for several generations. They were great patrons of learning, and the great commentator, Mallináth, flourished under their patronage. Aláuddín did not succeed in destroying their kingdom. They waged war for a century against the kings of the Bahmaní dynasty. Their great king was Pratáprudra, who lost his kingdom and his life in a battle with Ahmad Sháh Bahmaní. Even after this, Orangal continued to be a Hindu capital for a further period of one hundred and fifty years. It was destroyed by the Kutb Sháhí kings of Golkonda.

CHAPTER XIII.

Hindu Civilisation.

The Indo-Aryans and Perso-Aryans.

It is said that the Hindus were the last of the Aryans to leave their original abode and that they possess the largest stock of Aryan ideas. Some European Vedic scholars think that they find in the Rigveda traces of a time when the Indo-Aryans and the Perso-Aryans lived together as brethren, and that there are indications of a schism which separated these two branches of the Aryan people and made the Hindus the worshippers of Devas, and the Persians the worshippers of Asuras; both of which terms are applied in the Rigveda to Divine beings. Leaving these speculations aside, we find in the Rigveda traces of a state of society and civilisation hardly inferior to those of Egypt or Babylonia. The Hindus had already domesticated various species of animals and had made considerable advance as an agricultural people. They were acquainted with the use of boats, chariots, the precious metals, and medicinal herbs. Some of the bold philosophical speculations in the Rigveda afford evidence of the intellectual activity of the people, which is especially exhibited in the melody, variety, and richness of the Vedic prosody. They were an eminently religious people and performed frequent sacrifices.

Vedic civilisation.

It would be exceedingly interesting to trace in detail the origin and development of the various Hindu sciences, from their first inception in the Rik and the other Vedas to their consummation in numerous and exhaustive treatises. But it would be out of place to attempt such a task in a work like this. An endeavour, however, will be made to describe the principal features of the literature and science, and of the social, religious, and educational institutions of the ancient Hindus.

Religious poetry.

Poetry had its origin in the Vedas, some of the hymns of which are conspicuous for their poetical excellence. The Bráhmanas, though often written in prose, abound in lofty poetical conceptions and grand flights of imagination. But nowhere does Hindu religious poetry display greater vigour than in the Purânas, which, however, are not works of art, and so contain much that is rank, wild, obscure, and unmethodical.

The Rámáyana and the Mahábhárata.

The Mahábhárata and the Rámáyana, though they seem to have been originally designed as works of art, have, to a very great extent, changed their character, and are now regarded as religious poems. Among the great poets of the world, Válmíki, the author of the Rámáyana, and Vyása, the compiler of the Mahábhárata, stand pre-eminent for the simplicity and boldness of their conceptions and the epic grandeur of the characters they paint. The morals they teach are of the most catholic character, and the ideals they set forth are the highest to which humanity can aspire. The Mahábhárata and the Rámáyana are national Hindu epics.

The Rámáyana.

The story of the Rámáyana runs thus:—Daśaratha, of the Solar race of kings reigning at Ayodhyá, had four sons, Rám being the eldest. The king was anxious to invest Rám with the office of *yuvarája*, or heir-apparent; but his second queen, to whom he was bound by promise to grant two requests, asked him to banish Rám for fourteen years and to give the kingdom to her son, Bharata. The king had no choice but to comply with her requests, though the absence of his favourite son, Rám, cost him his life.

Rám and his wife, Sítá, roamed over various places, and lived for a long time at Panchavatí, the modern Násik, in the Dandaka forest, the modern Márháttá country, from which place Rávan, the king of Ceylon, stole away Sítá and carried her to his capital. Rám formed an alliance with the monkey-king of Kishkindhyá (in Bellary District), and, with his aid, recovered Sítá, after killing Rávan, with all the male members of his family. The character of Rám as an ideal man, of Sítá as a chaste and virtuous wife, and of the whole family of Rám as a model Hindu family, appeal to the admiration and sympathy, not only of the Hindus, but of all nations.

The Mahábhárata.

The Mahábhárata tells the tale of a family quarrel. On the death of a king of the Lunar race, the elder of his two sons, Dhritaráshtra, was disqualified from succeeding, because he was blind. The younger, Pándu, died within the life-time of his disinherited brother; and the children of the brothers began to quarrel. Duryyodhan, the son of the blind man, tried various expedients to destroy the Pándus; but, though he failed in all his endeavours, the Pándus were often put to great trouble by his wicked machinations. Yudhishthir, the eldest of the Pándus, was a god-fearing man; but, when all endeavours for an amicable settlement failed, he declared war. All the Kshattriya kings of India joined either one or the other party, and a great battle, which lasted for eighteen days, was fought at Kurukshetra. The Pándus were victorious and Yudhishthir ascended the throne. As representing the cause of justice, the Pándus were strongly supported by Krishna, who is regarded as an incarnation of Vishnu. Most of the Hindu ruling families of India trace their descent from Krishna and other chiefs who figure in the war of the Mahábhárata.

Kálidása and Bhavabhúti.

Among purely non-religious poets, Kálidás and Bhavabhúti stand pre-eminent. Both attempted to write on the subjects treated of in Válmíki's work. Kálidás produced the *Raghuvansa*, in which he sets the character of Rám in the boldest relief, with Rám's eminent predecessors and successors as a background. Every character is drawn with a masterly hand, and in the midst of a group of such characters stands that of Rám, the ideal man, the model of virtue, the divine in the human. The effect produced by the whole work is grand and sublime. A similar desire to rival Válmíki induced Bhavabhúti to produce the *Mahávíracharita* and the *Uttaraŕámacharita*, on the character and achievements of Rám, which have not yet been surpassed in their delineation of the tenderest and noblest feelings of the human heart or the lofty Bráhmanic purity of their sentiments.

Origin of the Hindu Drama.

The Hindu theatre appears to have been of Indian growth. It shows no trace of foreign origin; scenes in Hindu dramas are often separated by scores of years and by hundreds of miles, and there is so little of the lyric element in them that it is difficult to trace them to the Greek drama.

History.

Indian literature is singularly wanting in histories. Kings and conquerors have, however, often left pompous records of their own achievements in inscriptions, and merchants belonging to the Jaina religion accurate dates of their great preachers, while Buddhists and others have left wild legends in connection with the history of their own faith. In some instances kings have been represented as employing historiographers at their courts to compose proper histories, such as the *Rájatarangini* of Kásmír and the *Rásamálá* of Guzerat.

Coins.

It will not be out of place to give here some account of the Indian coins and inscriptions from which the chronology and history of India may be, to a certain extent, constructed. The most ancient coins of India were punch-marked. At first, there was only one circular punch-mark in the middle; but subsequently the marks increased and covered the entire surface of the coins, and there was variety in the shape of the marks. The next variety of ancient coins contained one letter in the centre, surrounded on all sides with punch-marks. What the import of this letter was, it is impossible to say. Orientalists conjecture that it was the initial letter of the name of the country, for, in the next class of coins, names of various countries are to be found in the middle of punch-marks. Next in order of time are the coins of Greek kings, the richness and variety of which have extorted admiration from numismatists all over the world. They bore the heads of kings and were finely executed. The Indo-Scythian coinage was based on the Greek model, and contained four human figures.

The Gupta coins bore the figure of Lakshmí, the goddess of wealth, on one side, and those of the king and queen on the other. After the time of the Guptas there were various mints all over India, from which coins were issued, stamped according to the fancy of the kings issuing them.

Inscriptions.

The most ancient inscriptions in India are all in Pálí; Sanskrit began to be used from the fourth century of the Christian era, which, in fact, was a period of revival of Hindu national and religious life. In Upper India foreign kings were driven out by Indians professing the Bráhmanic religion, and in Southern India Buddhist kings were replaced by Bráhmanic sovereigns. The most ancient Indian inscriptions are the edicts of Asoka, inscribed on rocks and stone pillars all over India, of which more than fifteen have been discovered. These are written in Bráhmi characters, the most ancient in India. This is a finished alphabet. At the end of the fourth century A. D. we find the Gupta character, in Northern, and the ancient Grantha character in Southern, India. The Gupta character developed, in three or four centuries, three distinct groups of characters, known as the Sáradá in the west, the Srîharsha in the centre, and the Kutila in the east; while the Grantha developed the modern Grantha character of Karnát, along with the Tailangí, Drávirí, and other characters not of Aryan origin. The Kutila group developed into the Bengali, Uriya, Assamese, Maithilí, and Nepalí characters. The Srîharsha gave rise to the various Nàgarí characters prevailing in the North-Western Provinces, Màlava, Guzerat and the Maháráshtra countries. One well-developed character of this group is known as either the Devanàgara, or the Sàstrí character. The Sáradá has produced the modern Kásmirí, the Gurumukhí and the modern Punjabí characters.

Bráhmi character.

Gupta character.

Various modern characters.

The biographical literature of India is equally poor with the historical. The Buddhists and Jainas—in fact, all the different religious sects of India—attempted to give accounts of the lives of their great preachers; but they mixed them up with much that is marvellous and miraculous. The first purely biographical work is the *Harshacharita*, by Vána, giving an account of Harshavardhan, the great conqueror of the seventh century; but it reads more like a poem than a biography, though written in prose.

Biography.

The language in which the Vedas are written appears to have been the spoken language of the Indo-Aryan people; for it shows all the life, the variety, the richness, and the adaptability of a spoken language. It gradually softened down in India and produced

Languages.

the various spoken dialects. The first series of these dialects was known as Páli, and the second series as the Prákrits. The dialect which assumed the highest importance as a literary language was Sanskrit, or "the purified speech." Many other dialects rose, from time to time, to the position of literary languages; but none of these assumed the same importance as Sanskrit. The Prákrits are the sources of the modern vernacular languages of India. The vernaculars have, however, borrowed much directly from Sanskrit, especially when they have risen to the importance of literary languages.

The Bráhmanas abound with speculations on Grammar. These speculations were the first beginnings of four of the six *Vedángas*, or sciences subsidiary to the study of the Vedas, namely, *Śikshá* (Pronunciation); *Vyákarana* (Etymology); *Nirukta* (Derivation); and *Chhandah* (Prosody).

Grammar and Philology.

In these subjects two names stand pre-eminent, namely, those of Pánini in Grammar and Yáska in Philology. They wrote their treatises on a thoroughly scientific method. The fact that the entire Aryan speech was resolvable into about 1964 primitive roots, was known to Sanskrit grammarians even before Pánini. Yáska's *Nirukta*, being confined to the derivation of Vedic words and proper understanding of Vedic works, is not much studied at the present day. But Pánini's grammar, written in *Sútras*, or aphorisms, is very widely studied. The Bráhmans wrote grammars, not only of the Sanskrit language, but of almost every literary language derived from Sanskrit, such as Páli and the various Prákrits.

Pánini and Yáska

Of the other two Vedángas, *Yotisha* (Astronomy) falls under the head of science; *Kalpa*, that is Law and Ritual, may be conveniently treated of here. The *Kalpas* are written in the aphoristic form. There are *Kalpa* works for almost every *Sákhá* of each of the four Vedas. In theory the *Kalpasútras* of each *Sákhá* are divided into three branches, the *Grihyasútras*, treating of domestic ceremonies,

Hindu Ritual.

the *Srautasútras*, treating of great national sacrifices, and the *Dharmasútras*, treating of social and political organisation. The *Grihyasútras* are still studied by a limited number of persons, as the performance of many of the domestic rites is still considered to be obligatory on every good Hindu.

The old aphoristic works, are very much neglected, their place being supplied by small hand-books for different ceremonies. The *Srautasútras* are so little known that very few manuscripts of them are to be found.

Hindu Law.

The *Dharmasútras* have, with very few exceptions, disappeared, their places being supplied by numerous metrical treatises, of which Manu, Atri, Hárita, Yájnavalkya, Ushaná, Angirá, and Yama, are regarded as authorities, Manu being considered the chief. Some are of opinion that any *Smriti*, or metrical treatise on law, that contradicts Manu, is of no authority. Commentaries on these metrical treatises began to be written from the ninth century of the Christian era. It was only after the Muhammadans had obtained a permanent footing in India, that voluminous compilations from these *Smriti* works, their commentaries, *Grihyasútras* and *Puránas*, began to be written, regulating every action, however minute and unimportant, of a Hindu's life. The authority of these compilations has, in the absence of political power, saved the Hindus from being absorbed into the conquering races.

Schools of Hindu Philosophy.

The earliest philosophical speculations of the Hindus begin almost with the Rigveda, and the entire Vedic literature is full of speculations on the origin of the world, the nature of the human soul, the destiny of man, and the nature of the Supreme Being. At the end of the Vedic period, these speculations were brought into some shape in works entitled the *Upanishads*. These contain bold speculations on many philosophical subjects; and, as they were the latest works of the Vedic literature, they were collectively called the *Vedántas*. But these Vedánta works are not systematic treatises on metaphysics; and different schools of philosophy have drawn upon them in support of their peculiar theories. The Tírthikas, or Philosophers, who had no regard for the *Upanishads*, entered upon speculations after newer methods. The Jainas, the Buddhists, the Ájívakas, and the numerous Tírthikas mentioned in their works were all bold thinkers. They produced numerous schools of Philosophy, of which six were prominent. These six, according to very ancient Buddhist and Jaina works, were the Buddhist, Jaina, Nástika Atheistic), Śaiva (worshipping Śiva), Sánkhy , and Mímánsaka. But, with the disappearance of Buddhism and the decadence of Jainism, the term 'six schools' came to mean the six Hindu schools of Philosophy, *viz.*, Sánkhya and Pátanjala, Mímánsá and Vedánta, Nyáya and Vaiśeshika, attributed to Kapila, Pátanjalí, Jaimini, Vyása, Gotama, and Kanáda respectively. A brief account of these schools is given below.

What they aim at.

According to the *Śástras,* man is bound to bear the consequences of his own actions. This is an inexorable moral law, from which there is no escape. This is known as the doctrine of *Karma*. But it is often seen that, in this world, people do not feel the consequences of their deeds, and the causes of human happiness or misery often cannot be explained by ordinary modes of reasoning. So the *Śástras* teach that the human soul undergoes an infinite number of transmigrations, from the meanest insect to the highest divinity, in order that it may thus reap the harvest of its own works. Transmigration means new birth; birth implies old age, and decay; thus three kinds of misery,—birth, old age, and decay—are inevitable. How to get rid of these miseries, was the problem which the Rishis set before themselves, and they invariably came to the conclusion that, if they could attain *tattvajnána* ("real knowledge"), they would not be born again. Real knowledge involves knowledge of what, 'I am', as distinguished from what 'I am not.' In the investigation of this matter, the Rishis displayed remarkable originality and boldness. As a matter of course, each speculator differed from the rest ; but each displayed a wonderful power of close reasoning and firmness of grasp in maintaining his position.

The Sánkhya system.

Kapila appears to have been the first great Indian philosopher. He is said to be the *Ádividván* (the first thinker). Kapila thinks that the self is absolutely distinct from the external world The doctrines attributed to him may be traced even to the oldest Upanishads. He was the first to fix metaphysical conceptions by number, and so his system is known as the *Sánkhya,* or enumerative philosophy. Buddha seems to have derived from Kapila his system of fixing ideas by numbers.

What little of Sánkhya is known, is from two Vedántist commentators. Of really Sánkhya works there remains only a small treatise, containing seventy-two verses.

The Yoga system.

In the Sánkhya philosophy there is no speculation about I'śvara, or the supreme soul, and so a new system of Philosophy, based on the Sánkhya method, attempts to supply this deficiency. It is called *Yoga,* because it gives detailed rules for the concentration of mind, or *Pátanjala,* from the name of the author. There is a collection of aphorisms of this school, on which various commentaries have been written. The oldest of these is written by Vyása, and the most popular is attributed to Rájá Bhoj.

Jaina and Buddhist systems.

After the Sánkhya, the Buddhist and Jaina systems of philosophy rose into importance. Very little is known of Jaina philosophy ; for, though there are a large number of works on the subject, these are unfortunately still sealed books to the public, as the Jaina monks guard their manuscript treasures with extreme jealousy. The Buddhists placed mind and matter side by side, and, by a process of reasoning similar to that followed in Europe during the last two centuries, they first denied the existence of matter, then that of the various attributes of mind, which they reduced to a mere collection of ideas. Following up this line of reasoning, they came on

Súnya, or Void, and this they called *Nirván* (extinction). Just as the lamp is extinguished, so is the soul extinguished. This was Buddha's doctrine. Buddhist philosophical works are written in Sanskrit and in Páli.

The Mímánsás.

The most important of the Hindu systems are the *Mímánsá* and the *Vedánta* (called also *Púrva* and *Uttara Mímánsá* respectively), which profess to interpret the ritualistic and philosophical portions of the Vedas. They are both written in the aphoristic form. Of these two, again, the Mímánsá rose into importance earlier than the Vedánta. The Mímánsá asserts that the Vedic rituals are the only *Karma* that begets merit, by which one may get rid of 'the three miseries.' The Mímánsá aphorisms were commented on by Savarasvámí; and his commentary, again, is commented on by one of the greatest names in Indian history, Kumárila Bhatta, who successfully controverted the Buddhists and laid the foundations of modern Hinduism. As the Mímánsá lays down rules for the interpretation of the Vedas, and as these rules also apply to the interpretation of *Smritis*, or works on Hindu Law, there are numerous handbooks and summaries, some of which are still studied.

Kumárila Bhatta

The Vedánta system.

There are various commentaries on the Vedánta aphorisms, and some of them are text-books of large sects of *Sonnyásis*. The first great commentary is by Sankara, who says that there is one Supreme Being, who is true, and everything else is mere illusion. He was the first to organise Hindu monastic life; and the majority of *Sannyásis* are still his followers. Sankara's commentary is the source of other commentaries, to the third, fourth and even fifth remove, and it has numerous handbooks and abridgements.

Sankarácháryya.

Rámánuja.

No less voluminous are the works belonging to the sect of Rámánuja, who evolved, from the Vedánta aphorisms, the system of Vishnu-worship. He believes that Vishnu is the only true being, and that his worshippers are simply emanations from him. Rámánuja is said to be the great preacher of *Bhakti Śástra*, or the doctrine of devotion, and many Vaishnava sects have been founded by his followers. Rámánanda, Chaitanya, and Kavíra were followers of Rámánuja. But they went further, in displaying their spirit of devotion, than the great founder of their sect.

The Nyáya System.

The Nyáya and Vaiśeshika systems of philosophy came into importance last of all. They are regarded as forming one and the same school, though there are two distinct works in the aphoristic form. They perfected Hindu Logic, and displayed great acumen in analysing sentences and defining the meanings of grammatical roots, words, and terminations. They inculcate a belief in the existence of the soul and of matter, in a personal God, and in the eternity of the human soul. They attribute the formation of the world to ever-existing atoms, and with them *mukti*, or emancipation, means the complete annihilation of happiness and misery. The school flourished in eastern India, first in Mithilá, then the Bengal. There are many works of this school which have commentaries to the sixth or seventh remove.

Mathematics.

The Hindus are credited with having invented the decimal system of notation, which has been adopted all over the world, and which has contributed so much to the simplification of arithmetical calculations. They were aware that almost all arithmetical sums could be solved by the process of the Simple Rule of Three. They could extract square and cube roots, and they reduced many calculations of every day occurrence to simple formulæ, which were known even to the lowest classes of men. In Algebra, the Hindus solved their Equations by various ingenious methods. They knew all the different laws of Proportion, and could work sums in Permutation and Combination. In Trigonometry, too, they were acquainted with every rule except those requiring Logarithmic calculations.

The science of Geometry had its origin in the *Śúlvasútras*, which are considered as a part of the *Śrautasútras*, and which treated of the shape and size of the various altars required at great national festivals.

Astronomy.

The sixth Vedánga, entitled Jyotisha, designed for the determination of the time for the various sacrifices, is the origin of Hindu Astronomy. That the Indians made great progress in astronomical science, is admitted on all hands. In the sixth century after Christ, Áryyavata not only determined that the earth is round, but also discovered that it has a diurnal motion on its axis. Bháskaráchároyya proved by convincing arguments that the earth is round; that it is self-poised in space; and that it has the power of attracting things to it. The Hindus admit that they have learnt much from the Greeks in Astronomy, and the presence of Greek terms in Hindu astronomy proves this.

Medical Science.

The Hindu science of medicine has its origin in the Vedic literature. The earlier works on medicine treated only of medicinal herbs; but the later works introduced the use of mineral substances, especially of mercury, gold, and copper. They had many different instruments for surgical operations and knew a good deal of the pathology of diseases. They examined almost every plant within their reach for the purpose of ascertaining its medicinal properties. The oldest school of medicine was at Kámpilya in Panchála, that is, in Rohilkhund. There are six or seven original Samhitás, written in prose and verse, by Charaka, Suśruta, Hárita, Agastya, and others; but these treatises have been revised again and again by subsequent professors of medicine. Later on, however, several medical compilations were prepared, the oldest of which was written by Chakrapáni Datta in the eleventh century A. D. Even before Chakrápani, there were small handbooks, of which one has been lately recovered from Central Asia, written in the character of the fifth century A. D.

The Indian people treated not only the diseases of human

beings, but those of the lower animals also. Aśoka encouraged the establishment of hospitals for the treatment of diseases, not only of men, but also of animals. It is said that a Sanskrit work on the diseases of horses, written by an inhabitant of Śálihotra in the Punjab, was translated into Persian, and that all modern works on the subject have been derived from the Persian translation. There are other treatises on horses and their diseases. The elephant, too, received much attention from the Hindus, and there is an extensive work on elephants, their life-history, and their diseases, by Pálakápya.

Veterinary Science.

In order to add to the conveniences and comforts of life, the Hindus invented sixty-four Fine Arts. These comprehend the arts of dancing, singing, tinging the teeth, dressing the hair, carpentry, painting, portrait-painting, sculpture of images of gods, architecture in stone and in bricks, the writing of inscriptions, engraving on gold, silver, and stone. Architecture is still a living art, and it dates from great antiquity. The Chálúkyas and Ráshtrakútas encouraged the system of cave temple architecture which, in Ajanta and in Ellora, extorts the admiration of visitors from all parts of the world. The ancient temples of Kánchí and the temples of Jagannáth, Bhuvaneśvar, and Konárak testify to the architectural skill of the Hindus. The sculptors and engravers of Bengal were famous all over India, and some of the stone images produced by them are inimitable. Some of the paintings in ancient manuscripts from Nepal still look fresh, though seven or eight centuries have elapsed since they were written. The art of sculpture received great encouragement at the hands of the Buddhists. Their stúpas and temples were surrounded with stone railings, on which were sculptured the stories of Buddha's previous existences. These stories are the origin of the parables and fables for teaching popular morality all over Asia, and these, being represented in stone on the Buddhist

The Fine Arts.

railings, afforded to ignorant people an easy means of learning moral lessons of inestimable value.

The influence of Bráhmans.

The king was the nominal head of Hindu society; but the real head was the Bráhman. Legislation in India was, once for all, fixed in the Kalpa-sútras and in the Smriti Samhitás; and the king had no legislative functions to perform. The power of interpreting the law rested with the Bráhmans and not with him. He was not even the head of the judicial department of the State; for the Bráhman was the chief judge. Though he received his appointment from the king, yet he was not a paid servant. The king was the head of the executive and of the military. He protected the lives and properties of his subjects from foreign as well as domestic enemies, and punished crime. The entire education of the higher classes was in the hands of the Bráhman. He was the head of religion. He was the interpreter between gods and men. He was. in fact, the head of Hindu society, the king being entrusted with inferior functions. It was owing to the existence of this strong, learned, and intellectual body of men in Hindu kingdoms, that Hindu kings could not assume absolute power and exercise it according to their will; and it is owing to the existence of this body that Hindu society still remains intact after so many centuries of subjection. Immediately after the loss of their political independence, they compiled those great *Smriti* works which regulate the minutest acts of a Hindu's life, and so governed Hindu society, even without the help of kings. Yet the Bráhman was not wealthy. He did not live by agriculture, or by commerce, nor was he the proprietor of the soil. The secret of his success was his wonderful education.

The cause of this influence.

From the fifth year of his age, he was trained to do those things which contribute to the health and activity of mind and body; and he was not allowed to stop until he had thoroughly mastered them. His education often occupied nearly a third of his life. He devoted himself to the study of literature and science and acquired a wonderful habit of concentration of mind. It is this power which has raised him to the foremost rank among intellectual races. Though, by the ordinary rules of *Smriti*, a Bráhman was bound to devote a very large number of years to study, yet his thirst for knowledge was so great, that he often led an unmarried life in the family of his preceptor, devoting himself to the unravelling of the deepest mysteries of science and literature. Even if he married, he could not devote himself to pleasure, or to the acquisition of wealth or power. He had to perform sacrifices and officiate at their performance by others. He had to teach, as well as to learn ; to make gifts as well as to receive them. His life as a householder came to an end when he reached his fiftieth year. He had then to make over his household property to his son and to retire, with other men of his age, to some place beyond the reach of city-life, there to spend his time in religious conversation and religious speculation. There he had to procure his food and raiment. But when, in extreme old age, he had no power to do this, he returned to the city and there lived on alms. In cities he had to impart the knowledge he had acquired, during a long and meritorious life, on domestic, social, religious, and other matters, to younger people. It is the lectures of these venerable old people, cast into the shape of books, that have come down to us, after many a revision, as Puránas and Upapuránas.

The Caste System.

The wonderful power of organisation of the Bráhmans was nowhere displayed to greater advantage than in the organisation and development of the caste system. Each caste had a government of its own, with a headman and councillors, working under the general superintendence of the king and the Bráhmans. As, with the exigencies of the times, mixed races and mixed castes sprang up, and the non-Aryan races began to be incorporated into Hindu society, they were formed into distinct castes, and given distinct governments and distinct occupations, contributing to the better economy of the social system and making all the different parts of that system work harmoniously, with the sole object of rendering the people contented and happy.

The Kshattriyas developed a system of war, in which they disdained to take any unfair advantage of their enemies. Their chivalric notions of honour, their high-mindedness in dealing with fallen enemies, and their noble resolution not to submit to an enemy, have won the admiration of the European historians of India. The Vaiśyas developed the resources of the country and perfected the fine arts which made ancient India so famous. The Káyasthas were professional scribes and accountants. They performed all the functions of clerks, and their assistance was always sought by kings and Bráhmans. The mixed castes were traders and artisans. The Śúdras were labourers and agriculturists. The work of watching and guarding villages was entrusted to sturdy aboriginal races who came within the pale of Hinduism. Thus every one did the duty allotted to him, and the principle of the division of labour was known and acted upon in these remote times.

The Hindu village community.

The organisation of the Indian village communities is another instance of the insight of the Bràhmans into human nature. Each village was so organised as to become a self-acting social unit, containing representatives of all the arts and professions that are requisite to enable a Hindu to lead a happy life in a village. Groups of these villages were placed under officers of various grades, with the king at their head. The various revolutions of the last three thousand years have not in the least degree affected the structure of these communities.

Religious organisation.

The Bráhmans were the absolute heads of the religious systems of India, and they frequently organised great national sacrifices, such as the Ŕájsúyá and the Aśvamedha, which often occupied several years in their performance. But, in the course of time, the Buddhist monastic orders and the Jaina Gachchhas, literally "trees," which resulted from the increase in the number of Sannyásís, became their rivals. The inherent defect of the monastic orders was that, as soon as they obtained wealth and power, they degenerated into ignorance and vain display; and so, after some centuries of struggle, the Bráhmans regained their ascendency. But monastic orders again arose amongst the Bráhmans themselves organised by superior Bráhmanic monks like Śankaráchâryya. The religious headship of India was thus permanently divided between Bráhman housholders and Bráhman monks. Both courted popularity by pompous religious displays; the Bráhmans by organising annual worship and pilgrimages to holy places, and the Sannyásís by organising periodical and annual *melás* fairs). The most pompous worship of the Bráhmans has been the Durgá Púja in Bengal, and the greatest Melá held by the Sannyásís has been the Kumbha Melá, held four times in every twelve years at Haridvár, at Prayág (Allahabad), at Ujjayiní, and at Gautamí near the mouth of the Godávari. The interests of the Sannyásís and the Bráhmans are not always the same, and their rivalry is one of the causes of the political weakness of the Hindu community. In Bengal, the Sannyásís have little influence; but they are looked upon with great favour in the North-Western Provinces and in the Punjab. In the Mahárâshtra country and in Southern India the Bráhmans are generally in the ascendant, but the Sannyásís too, are powerful.

Pújás and Melás.

The Rishis of the Vedic period had secular and religious education under their entire control. But, with the rise of the monastic orders, religious education fell, to a great extent, into the hands of the monks, and it remains in their hands even now. The Sannyásís of modern days, however, care to teach only the standard works of their sects, while the teaching of grammar, language, law, rhetoric, mathematics, and science is almost entirely in the hands of the Bráhmans. In Bengal, the Vaidyas study the science of medicine; but in all other parts of India medical science is entirely in the hands of the Bráhmans.

Educational institutions.

Students received education without the payment of fees. The duty of maintaining teachers and their families devolved on the community, while the kings granted lands to learned Bráhmans and to monasteries. Wealthy men often invited learned Bráhmans to be present at their religious and domestic ceremonies and sent them away with rich presents. People considered learned and pious Bráhmans the most deserving recipients of gifts on every appropriate occasion. Learned men, whether monks or Bráhmans, were never obliged to beg. A Bráhman teacher was bound to supply with food those of his students who came from a distance. In monasteries, young monks were maintained by the establishment, and other students procured their food as best they could.

Bráhmanic and monastic students.

Some of the Bráhman teachers are said to have taught more than sixty thousand students. The place where Pakshadhar Miśra taught his students, in the fifteenth century, in Mithilá, resembled a city. In the sixteenth century, Navadvíp, Benares, and Poona contained vast numbers of students, receiving instruction under celebrated Professors in all the various branches of knowledge. But none of these educational institutions was grander than that at Nálanda in the seventh century ot the Christian era. The monastery had ample accommodation for 10,000 students, and the revenue of one hundred villages was assigned for their support. The building was a four-storied one, and its ruins at Baragáon, in Behar, still attract the attention of the intelligent traveller and remind how munificent the Indians were in supporting education and how learned men ungrudgingly instructed large numbers of students of all nations in various Śástras without receiving anything in return.

Some notable Institutions.

BOOK III.

EARLY MUHAMMADAN INVASIONS AND THE PATHA'N EMPIRE

CHAPTER I.

The Ghaznaví Dynasty.

The Khalfás of Baghdad reigned in great splendour for about a hundred years, and their empire extended from the Atlantic to Afghanisthán. On its dismemberment, about the middle of the ninth century, several small independent kingdoms were formed. One of these was the Sámáni kingdom of Khorásán and Transoxiana, with its capital at Níśápur. One of the Sámánís was a great favourite with Khalífá Mámún, who appointed his sons to governments beyond the Oxus, where they gradually assumed independence. One of the Sultáns of this dynasty had a Turkish slave named Alptigín, who, on his master's death, was compelled to flee to the inaccessible country near Ghazní. He had 3,000 disciplined Turkish slaves with him, and with their aid he carved out a small kingdom for himself, bounded on the east by the Indus, and on the north and west by Balkh and Herát. Alptigín had a slave named Subuktigín, whom he made his son-in-law and successor. On Alptigín's death, in 977 A. D., Subuktigín ascended the throne of Ghazní.

The Sámání kingdom.

The Ghaznaví kingdom.

Annexation of Peshawar

The Hindus could not tolerate the establishment of a Muhammadan kingdom so near their frontier, and so Jaypál, Rájá of Lahore, led an expedition against him; but he was obliged to conclude peace. The quarrel was, however, renewed shortly after, and Jaypál, though assisted by the kings of Delhi, Ajmir, Kálanjara, and Kanauj, was defeated at Laghman, and Subuktigín annexed Peshawar to his kingdom.

Mahmúd of Ghazni

Subuktigín died in 997 A. D. and was succeeded by his son, Mahmúd, then only thirteen years of age. For two years Mahmúd was occupied with a civil war in his own kingdom and with disturbances on his western frontier. But, on their termination, he cast a wistful eye on the rich kingdoms in the plains of Hindusthán. He left Ghazní with 10,000 chosen horse, and was met by his father's old antagonist, Jaypál, in the neighbourhood of Peshawar, in 1001 A. D. He defeated Jaypál, pursued him down to the Sutlej, plundering many rich cities on the way, and took him prisoner, but released him on his promising to pay tribute. Jaypál, considering death better than disgrace, committed suicide. His son and successor, Anangapál, was true to his father's engagement to pay tribute. But Mahmúd had still to come twice to India, first in order to punish a refractory Hindu chief, dependent on Anangapál, and again to punish the Afghán chief, Abul Fateh Lodí, the Muhammadan ruler of Multan. Gradually the relations between Mahmúd and Anangapál grew more and more strained, and war became inevitable. Anangapál sent ambassadors to the neighbouring Hindu kings, who all resolved to make a final stand against the encroachments of the foreigner. Hindu women sold their jewels, melted their golden ornaments, and sent their contributions from afar to furnish resources for the holy war (1008). The Hindu army increased every day and surrounded the Muhammadan camp, which

His first invasion.

Second and third invasions.

Fourth invasion.

Mahmúd was at last obliged to entrench. A battle was fought with great ardour on both sides, and ended in the defeat of Anangapál. Mahmúd gave the Hindus no time to re-assemble, but pursued them vigorously all the way from Peshawar to Nagarkot in Kangra, where he plundered the celebrated temples situated near a natural flame called Jválámukhí, a place of great pilgrimage.

Fifth to Eighth invasion.

He returned to India and took Abul Fateh Lodí prisoner to Ghazní in 1010 A.D. The following year he planned a bold plundering expedition to Thánesvar, the capital of Harshavardhan, which proved to be immensely profitable. He next led two expeditions against Kásmír. His ninth expedition was directed against Kanauj. He made great preparations; and, taking a route close to the mountains, where the rivers are easily crossed, suddenly appeared before the gates of Kanauj, which was then ruled by Rájyapál, perhaps a scion of the Pál dynasty of Magadha. The king was taken unawares, and conscious of his helpless position, sought the protection of Mahmúd, which was extended to him with alacrity. Mahmúd spared Kanauj, but plundered Mathurá. For twenty days the city was given up to pillage; the idols were broken and the temples profaned; a part of the city was set on fire, and the miseries of a conflagration were added to its other calamities. The sight of the beautiful edifices, the triumphs of Hindu architecture, first excited in Mahmúd the desire to adorn his own capital with similar buildings.

Ninth invasion.

Tenth and Eleventh Invasions.

Mahmúd's tenth expedition was undertaken in 1023 A. D. to relieve the king of Kanauj, who was hard pressed by the Chandel king, Ganda, because of his allegiance to the Musalmans. Mahmúd could make no impression on the Rájá; but, on his way back to Ghazní, he deposed king Jaypál II., the son of Anangapál, for his constant rebellions, and annexed the Punjab. His eleventh expedition, too, was against Rájá Ganda; but it also was unsuccessful.

Twelfth invasion.

The twelfth expedition was planned for the purpose of plundering the temple of Somanáth, situated on an islet in the southern extremity of the kingdom of Guzerat. It was an important place of pilgrimage for Hindus, and was believed to be immensely rich. The Sultán left Ghazní in September 1024, with a large army, and, crossing the desert, came suddenly before Ajmir, the Rájá of which had no resource but in flight. Ajmir was plundered. Then crossing the Aravallí mountains, Mahmúd came before Anahilpattan, the capital of Guzerat, the king of which, Chámundadev, fled precipitately. Mahmúd reached Somanáth, his destination, without much trouble, but there he met with a stout resistance from the priests, who had armed themselves for its defence. The battle was raging with fury when the king of Guzerat arrived with a well-appointed army. In spite of this reinforcement, victory declared itself for the Musalmans, and 5,000 brave Rájputs lay dead on the field. Mahmúd entered the temple, plundered it, and destroyed the images (1026). He was so delighted with the situation of Somanáth that he seriously thought of making it his capital, but his ministers dissuaded him from carrying out his purpose. Mahmúd, during the rest of his life, had great trouble with the Seljuk Tartars on the western border of his empire, and consequently was unable to plan any further invasion of India. He died in 1030 A.D.

Mahmúd's successors.

After the death of Mahmúd, no king of the Ghaznaví dynasty led any important military expedition into India. Their power in the west gradually declined as the Seljuk Tartars advanced from the Caspian. While the successors of Mahmúd were deeply engrossed in war with the Seljuks, the Hindu kings made several attempts to recover Lahore. In these they were unsuccessful, but they succeeded in regaining Nagarkot. During the middle of the twelfth century, the Ghaznaví kings stirred up a fierce enemy at their door and brought about the ruin of their family. Maudúd, one of the successors of Mahmúd, treacherously seized the territory of Ghor, a small valley near Kandahár, inhabited by the Afghåns of the Sur tribe. Bairám, who succeeded Maudúd, killed two of the chiefs of Ghor under circumstances of great ignominy. Aláuddín, the next chief, vowing vengeance on the Ghaznaví family, swept down upon Ghazní from Firoz Koh, the Ghori capital. On his approach, Bairám fled, and Ghazní was given up to plunder and completely destroyed with fire and sword. The successors of Bairám made Lahore their capital, and the Punjab was the only territory that was left to the family. But in the course of forty years, they were driven even from this last retreat by Ghori family (1186).

CHAPTER II.

THE GHORI DYNASTY.

Muhammad of Ghor.

AFTER the death of Aláuddín, Ghiyásuddín and his brother, Muhammad, reigned jointly at Ghor for a long time. The Ghoris were at first engaged in wars with their Tartar neighbours in the west, the kings of Khwárasm. Muhammad conquered the town of Uch, near the junction of the five rivers of the Punjab, in 1176. Two years later he led an expedition to Guzerat, but had to return in disgrace. In 1186 A. D. he suddenly appeared before Lahore, took possession of it, and sent Khusru Málik, the last Ghaznaví king, a prisoner to Ghor. Thus secure in the Punjab, Muhammad began to mature his favourite plan of conquering Hindusthán.

Conquest of Delhi,

About this time Prithví Ráy Chauhán, king of Delhi, had conquered Máhobá from the Chandel king, and thus became the most powerful neighbour of Muhammad of Ghor. As soon as Muhammad advanced towards the east and laid siege to Bhatindá, Prithví Ráy marched with a powerful army to expel him. The armies met at Náráyan, on the Sarasvatí, and the Musalmans were completely defeated (1191). But Muhammad returned to Hindusthán after two years, and an obstinately contested battle was fought at Tiráori, near Tháneśvar, in which the Hindus were completely defeated. Their king was killed, and the kingdom of Delhi and Ajmir fell into the hands of Muhammad. He annexed Delhi to his own kingdom and appointed Kutbuddín Aibec its governor.[1]

Of Kanauj.

The next year Muhammad invaded Kanauj, and, in a battle fought in the neighbourhood of Etawa, defeated Jay Chandra, the Ráthor king of Kanauj, and annexed Kanauj and Benares.

Of Behar and Bengal.

Within three years of these events, Bakhtiyár Khiliji, a general of Muhammad Ghori, conquered Oudh and northern Behar, and advanced to the capital of Behar, in 1197. Soon after the conquest of Behar, Bakhtiyár pushed on to Navadvíp, the capital of Bengal; and Gaur and Navadvíp were occupied without a struggle (1199). Eastern Bengal retained its independence for one hundred and twenty years more, when it, too, was absorbed into the Muhammadan empire. Emboldened by repeated successes, Bakhtiyár led an army into Assam; but he could produce no impression on the Rájá, and during the rainy season, when the floods of the Brahmaputra covered the whole country, he had to retreat hurriedly to Bengal, with the loss of the greater part of his army.

The nature of his conquests.

On the death of his brother, in 1202 A.D., Muhammad Ghori was left the sole ruler of the country, which then extended from the Bay of Bengal to the borders of Persia. This vast territory was simply overrun, but not consolidated. Some of the large Hindu citites fell into the hands of the Musalmans, but the Hindus maintained their independence in all the outlying districts, and it took more than a century to subjugate the country completely.

Death and character.

The Gakkhars were a wild tribe of the hill regions of the Punjab. On his way back to Ghor, in the year 1205, Muhammad Ghori pitched his camp on the Indus; when, finding him off his guard, the Gakkhars suddenly fell upon his camp and killed him. Muhammad Ghori was an enterprising soldier, whom no misfortune could ever disconcert, and who clung to his purpose with extraordinary tenacity. Deafeated and disgraced several times, he, nevertheless, succeeded in conquering the whole of Hindusthán. His army was composed of adventurers, mostly belonging to the Afghán tribes, commanded by his slaves. Loyalty sat loosely on them; and, in a few years after his death, nothing of his vast kingdom remained to his family. Kutbuddín asserted his independence in Hindusthán, and Násiruddín Kubácha in Sindh and Multan. The rest of his kingdom, with the cities of Firoz Koh and Ghazní, was absorbed into the kingdom of Khwárasm.

CHAPTER III.

The Slave Kings (1206—1288).

Why called Slave kings.

Kutbuddín was the first Muhammadan Sultán who established his capital in India itself, his predecessors having been only invaders and conquerors. He was a slave of Muhammad Ghori. His son-in-law, Sultán Altamsh, was a slave, and Sultán Ghiyássuddín Bulban also was a slave of Altamsh, and these Sultáns and their immediate successors are therefore known in history as the Slave kings of Delhi, which was their capital.

Sultán Altamsh.

The Slave kings attempted the conquest of Guzerat and Kálanjara, but in vain. Sultán Altamsh defeated the Paramára Rájputs of Málava, sacked Ujjayiní, and detroyed the celebrated temple of Mahákála, famous for its sanctity, in 1232 A. D. After the death of Altamsh, his daughter, Rezia, ascended the throne of Delhi, the only instance of a female ruling there. During the reign of Bulban, Tughral Khán, the governor of Bengal, raised the standard of rebellion, but was defeated and killed.

Changíz Khán.

It was during the reign of Sultán Altamsh that Central Asia was visited by that scourge of humanity, Changíz Khán, who by his superior military genius, brought together all the nomad hordes of Mongolia, and, inspiring them with hopes of gain and glory, led them to a series of brilliant victories, which led the whole country from the Pacific Ocean to the Baltic Sea at his feet. He killed the entire families of those who had the audacity to oppose his arms, massacred their adherents, and razed their capitals to the ground. Khwárasm was a powerful kingdom in Western Asia, and Changíz attacked it. Jaláluddín, the king, after a signal defeat, fled precipitately from the Caspian to the Indus, hotly pursued by a Mughal horde, and placed himself under the protection of Sultán Altamsh. But he was peremptorily ordered to leave India. This disgraceful act of inhospitality saved India from an invasion by Changíz Khán. But, after his death, the Mughals led army after army into the country, and the Slave kings had great difficulty in repelling these fierce invaders. It is not known what their religion was; but probably they were Buddhists. They hated the Muhammadans and compelled the Slave kings not only to maintain a large army, but also to provide for the maintenance of many Muhammadan kings, dethroned and expelled by them from Western Asia. Bulban is said to have maintained thirty-two of these royal exiles.

The fall of the Slave kings.

On the death of Bulban, his grandson, Kaikobád, was raised to the throne. This young man was devoid of character, and had a number of profligate young knaves about him, who ruined him and his family. The veteran chief of the Punjab, Jaláluddín Khiliji, who, for fifty years had fought bravely against the Mughal invaders, was invited to depose Kaikobád and ascend the throne (1288).

CHAPTER V.

The Khiliji Dynasty, (1288-1321).

The Khiliji Dynasty.

The necessities of the times had already compelled some of the later Slave kings to take into their service not only a large number of Tartar adventurers, driven from their country by the Mughals, but many converted Mughal mercenaries also. The Khilijis pursued this policy and thus strengthened their position. Aláuddín Khiliji, the nephew of Jaláluddín, conquered a great portion of Bundelkhund and eastern Málava and paved the way for an invasion of the Deccan. At the head of 8,000 men, he crossed the Vindhya ranges and presented himself unexpectedly before Devagiri, the capital of Rám Rájá, the Yádava king of Maháráshtra, who submitted to him and paid him an immense sum of money. Flushed with success, Aláuddín returned to Hindusthán, assassinated his uncle, a wise and generous ruler, and ascended the throne of Delhi in 1295 A.D.

The story of the beauty of Padminí, the consort of one of the princes of Mewar, and Aláuddín's invasion of the place, are narrated further on, in Book V. Chap. III. Aláuddín's greatest general was Káfur. He was a Rájput by birth; but he embraced Muhammadanism, and, with the zeal characteristic of a convert, became an implacable enemy of Hinduism. He led an immense army into the Deccan, destroyed the Yádava kingdoms of Devagiri and Dvárasamudra, harassed the Kákateyas of Orangal, and overran the country down to Rámeśvar.

Aláuddín's conquest of the Deccan,

Of Guzerat.

Aláuddín sent an expedition to Guzerat in 1297, under his celebrated general Ulagh Khán, against Karnadev, the last king of that country, and annexed it, with its dependency, Málava. Aláuddín was pre-eminently the most successful conqueror amongst the early

Pathán rulers of Delhi, and he made his power felt from one end of India to the other. But he was a man altogether devoid of principle, and his reign was constantly disturbed by the rebellions of his officers and of the conquered Hindus, as well as by Mughal invasions. One of these invasions was headed by Kutlugh Khán, the ruler of Transoxiana. This was the first struggle between the Mughals and the Patháns for supremacy in India, and Aláuddín's vigour alone saved it for the Patháns. His last days were greatly embittered by intrigues at court for the succession and by rebellions of the Hindus at Chitor, Guzerat, and Maháráshtra. Chitor soon regained its independence. The rebellion in Guzerat was suppressed with a high hand; but Harpáldev was still in open rebellion in the Deccan when Aláuddín died, in 1316.

Káfur, who had already made away with Ulagh Khán, the conqueror of Guzerat, attempted to seize the government on the death of Aláuddín. But Mubárak, the third son of Aláuddín, procured his assassination and further secured his position by imprisoning his own brothers and by murdering a number of noblemen who might have been dangerous to him. He sent an army against the rebel, Harpáldev, and captured and executed him. Mubárak had a great favourite named Málik Khusru, a low caste Hindu who had embraced Muhammadanism; he raised this man to the highest offices of State, and everybody's life and property were at his mercy. Khusru was not without energy. At the head of a large army he marched to the south and conquered the Malabar Coast, while the king at Delhi led the life of a debauchee. On his return,

Fall of the Khilijis.

Khusru put him to death, together with all the survivors of Aláuddín's family, and assumed the Government. He made himself odious by persecuting Hindus and Musalmans alike, and Ghiyásuddín Tughlak, the governor of the Punjab, led an army into Delhi and put him to death (1321).

CHAPTER V.

THE TUGHLAK DYNASTY (1321-1412).

THOUGH Málik Káfur and Málik Khusru conquered nearly the whole of the Deccan and Southern India, yet they allowed the Hindu princes to rule the country. But Ghiyásuddín annexed Mahárásbtra to the Muhammadan empire. He was already an old man when he came to the throne, but he was a vigorous ruler and had for a long time defended the Punjab against Mughal invasion. He reigned for four years only and was then assassinated by his son, who ascended the throne under the title of Muhammad Tughlak. He reigned from 1325 to 1352. But in the course of these twenty-six years, the Muhammadan empire came to an end, and a number of small Muhammadan kingdoms arose out of its ruins. Firoz Tughlak and other successors of Muhammad did indeed assume the title of 'Emperor of Delhi.' But they were no longer emperors and ruled only a small territory around Delhi.

Ghiyásuddín Tughlak.

To understand the history of the dismemberment of the Muhammadan empire, it will be necessary to examine the constitution of the Muhammadan army. The Musalmans, who came with Muhammad of Ghor and his successors, almost all belonged to the Afghán or Pathán tribes. Afghánisthán is divided into a number of narrow valleys, each inhabited by one or other of the Afghán tribes, each tribe being ruled by a chief, with the title of 'Amir.' The Ghoris and the Khilijis were the rulers of the several valleys, of Afghánisthán; and their armies and those of the Slave kings were composed of these tribes. They conquered different parts of India and settled in them; but their loyalty to the Slave kings, who were of Turkish origin, was not very sincere; and they took every opportunity to rebel. This was one of the sources of weakness of the Slave kings; and it was owing to this that they were unable to push their conquests much beyond where Muhammad Ghori left them

Constitution of the Pathán army.

The Tartar adventurers and the converted Mughals who entered the service of the Delhi emperors, together with the converted Hindus, had been an additional source of strength and power to the Khiliji rulers of Delhi; and with their help Aláuddín succeeded in conquering India south of the Vindhya ranges. These adventurers belonged to various nationalities in Central and Western Asia. Any one who could bring together a number of adherents declared himself an Amir, and a very large number of such Amirs entered the service of Delhi and were known as the Amiráni Sada. They entertained no feeling of loyalty to the rulers of Delhi, and were kept together only by the hope of plunder and adventure.

The Amiráni Sada.

But Ghiyásuddín Tughlak was a Turkish slave himself, and could count neither upon the loyalty of the tribes, as the Khilijis did, nor upon that of the Amiráni Sada. It would have required great strength of character to keep these discordant elements together. But, unfortunately, Muhammad Tughlak was the very opposite of a strong ruler. He was capricious in the extreme; and, though he was a learned man and a linguist, a good Musalman and a good citizen, there was a taint of insanity in him, and he had no sympathy for the sufferings of others. The beautiful scenery of Devagiri struck him, and he at once ordered that its name should be changed into Daulatabad and that it should be made the capital of his empire. He ordered all the citizens of Delhi to remove to Daulatabad, with their families and effects, under pain of severe punishment. The sufferings of these poor people knew no bounds; but the project had to be given up, owing to the sheer impossibility of carrying it out. Again, he sent a large army to conquer China; but it perished in the jungles of Assam. He collected another immense army for the conquest of Persia; but he had no money to pay his soldiers. In order to replenish his treasury, wasted by these extravagances, he raised the taxes to such a pitch, that the cultivators between the Ganges and the Jamuná took refuge in

Muhammad Tughlak.

the jungles to escape paying him. But the jungles were surrounded by hunters, and the people were shot down like wild beasts.

Secession of Bengal.

In Bengal the Afghán tribes were very powerful. They had recently conquered East Bengal up to the borders of Tipárá and Assam. Muhammad divided the province into three parts. Bahádur Khán, his first governor of East Bengal, declared himself independent; and, though the emperor succeeded in crushing him, yet disorder and confusion increased, until, in the course of ten or twelve years, Háji Iliás united eastern, western, and southern Bengal and declared himself independent, under the title of Shamsuddin Ilíás Sháh, in 1345. Thus Bengal was lost to the Delhi empire, but the emperor was so much occupied in quelling numerous rebellions in western India and the Deccan that he was not in a position to make the least effort to regain his footing there.

It has already been stated that the Amiráni Sada were a turbulent, disaffected, and disloyal body of men, whose attachment to the Delhi empire was merely for the sake of their pay and the prospect of plunder. They never failed to profit by the disorders of the times and were a source of much trouble to their employers. Muhammad appointed Aziz Hamid, a worthless favourite, to the government of Málava in 1337; and enjoined him to keep the Amiráni under control. The wretch, however, immediately on his arrival at Dhárá, invited eighty of the Amiráni to a feast and there ruthlessly massacred them. Thereupon the Amiráni of Málava, Guzerat, and the Deccan raised the standard of rebellion. There were from thirty to forty of these chiefs in almost every city, and they expelled the imperial officers and occupied the cities. The emperor contended for fifteen years, with varying fortune, against these rebels. The Deccan declared itself independent in 1374. Guzerat, Málava, and Sindh were to a certain extent tranquillised. But the exertion imposed upon him by these troubles proved too much for the health of the emperor, and he died in 1351.

And of the Deccan.

CHAPTER VI.

TIMÚR.

Firoz Tughlak.

FIROZ TUGHLAK, the successor of Muhammad, at once acknowledged the independence of the Deccan and made several attempts to re-annex Bengal to the empire. He twice invaded that country, but had to return discomfited, and was at last obliged to acknowledge its independence also. Whoever was sent to govern Málava or Guzerat, strengthened his position by courting the favour of the inhabitants, and acted with perfect independence. One of his governors of Guzerat went so far as to build Hindu temples, in order to reconcile the Hindu subjects to his usurpation. Thus the only portion of the Muhammadan empire over which Firoz ruled in peace was from the west of Bengal to the Punjab. A very large number of Rájputs were converted to Muhammadanism during the course of this reign; and the religion of the Prophet spread in all parts of the country, especially, in Bengal, owing to the preaching of a large number of Pírs, or holy men. Firoz had the welfare of his subjects always at heart. He constructed roads, excavated tanks, and built *serais* (inns); and thus did much good to the country.

Conversion of the Hindus.

Loss of the remaining provinces.

At the very outset of the reign of Mahmúd Tughlak, Guzerat and Málava ceased to be dependencies of Delhi. His prime minister, Khauja Jahán, was appointed Màlik-us-Sharq, or Governor of the east, in 1394. He established his capital at Jaunpur, declared himself independent, and founded the Sharqi rule. Thus the Pathán empire was now confined to Delhi and its neighbourhood.

In 1398 a new scourge appeared in India and destroyed even the last vestiges of the Delhi empire. Timúr, with innumerable Tartar hordes, after overthrowing all the kingdoms of Central Asia, fell upon India. On his approach, Mahmúd left Delhi and sought the protection of the newly founded independent kingdom of Guzerat. Delhi was at that time torn by internal feuds, and there was no united action to check the progress of Timúr. It was Timúr's habit to massacre the inhabitants of any city to which he was obliged to lay siege; and, before reaching Delhi, he had already brutally put the inhabitants of six or seven Indian cities to the sword, so that, as he approached, the inhabitants of city after city fled precipitately with their property. The inhabitants of Delhi made a feeble attempt to oppose him, but in vain; and the citizens opened their gates on his assurance that no lives would be taken. On entering Delhi, Timúr proclaimed himself emperor; and immediately afterwards the sack of the place began. For five days human blood flowed in torrents; and the roads became impassable from the heaps of dead bodies left on them to rot. After a stay of fifteen days Timúr left the city; and, massacring the inhabitants of Meerut on his way, proceeded to Haridvár. Here the Hindus began to harass him, and he had to cut his way, sword in hand, through the jungles at the foot of the mountains. All the way to Jamu he was greatly harassed by the Hindus of this wild region. From Jamu he returned by the same road by which he had come. Famine, anarchy, and plague marked his route. Of all the enemies of humanity Timúr and Changiz were the greatest. They were on a par in cruelty; but Timúr was treacherous, too.

Invasion of Timúr.

Sack of Delhi.

After Timúr had left India, Delhi remained desolate for two months. Then Ekbál, the minister of Mahmúd, took possession of it. Internal feuds broke out afresh, and Ekbál was the first victim. Mahmúd returned to his capital and reigned there only in name in 1412. He had already ceased to coin money as emperor of Delhi and relinquished the imperial authority altogether.

The extinction of the Páthan empire.

BOOK IV.

CHAPTER I.

INDEPENDENT MUHAMMADAN KINGDOMS.

THE KINGDOM OF DELHI (1412-1526).

The Saiyyad dynasty.

THE death of Mahmúd Tughlak was followed by a period of anarchy, taking advantage of which, Khizir Khan Saiyyad, the governor of the Punjab, made himself master of Delhi. He never assumed the insignia of royalty, but gave himself out to be the viceroy of Timúr. He and his three descendants ruled at Delhi, and were known as the Saiyyad dynasty. During their reigns, the limits of the kingdom were narrowed down to the walls of the city. There was hereditary enmity between the Saiyyads and the Afghán Lodís. Bahlol Lodí made himself master of the Punjab, conquered Sirhind, and at last invaded Delhi. Aláuddín, the last of the Saiyyad kings, made over Delhi to him and retired to Badáon, where, in a small garden, he passed his days in religious contemplation worthy of a descendant of the prophet.

The Lodí dynasty.

On his accession, Bahlol assumed the title of Sultán. The first act of his reign was an expedition to Multan, which was an independent kingdom. But, before he reached that place, the Sharqi king of Jaunpur invaded Delhi and created a diversion, Bahlol was so much incensed at this, that he resolved to destroy the Jaunpur kingdom, and in this he succeeded, after a severe struggle which lasted twenty-six years, when the

Conquest of Jaunpur.

kingdom was annexed, in 1478. Behar still remained to the Sharqi kings; but in 1488, immediately after Bahlol's death, his son, Sikandar Lodí, invaded that province and annexed it, in 1494.

Foundation of Agra.

Sikandar held his court at Agra, which he founded about 1500 A.D. He is said to have prohibited pilgrimages of the Hindus throughout his dominions. He died in 1516, and was succeeded by his son, Ibráhim Lodí, a haughty and vainglorious prince who soon estranged the nobility by slighting and insulting them.

Rebellions followed in quick succession, and Jaunpur regained its independence. Daulat Khán Lodí, the governor of the Punjab, invited Bábar, the Sultán of Kábul, to invade India. Bábar responded to the call and took possession of Lahore. But, when he entered the province of Sirhind, he found himself opposed by Ibráhim Lodí at the head of a large army.

Battle of Pánipat.

An obstinately contested battle was fought at Pánipat, in which Bábar obtained a complete victory, and Ibráhim lost about 40,000 men and his life (1526).

CHAPTER II.

The Kingdom of Bengal (1345-1592).

The Iliás Sháhí dynsaty.

Shamsuddín Iliás Sháh declared himself independent in 1345, and Firoz Tughlak acknowledged his independence in 1355. He removed his capital from Gaur to Pánduá, where his son, Sikandar, built the celebrated Adína Masjid. Sikandar's successors were not very powerful, and Rájá Ganeś deposed them and made himself master of Bengal. He reigned for eight years, and was popular with both Hindus and Muhammadans. His son, Jadu, embraced Muhammadanism and assumed the title of Jaláluddín. His grandson, Ahmad Sháh, was

Rájá Ganeś and his family.

deposed and killed owing to his unpopularity. This dynasty reigned from 1405 to 1445, in the latter of which years, the Muhammadans restored the kingdom to the family of Shamsuddín Iliás Sháh. The princes of the second Iliás Sháhí dynasty, who reigned for 42 years, were weak, and were often tools in the hands of the Khaujas and Habshís, or Abyssinians, who became so powerful that, in 1488, they deposed the king and raised one of their number to the throne. The Hindu kings of Kamatpur and Tipárá extended their boundaries at the expense of the kingdom of Bengal; and the Sharqis, though dispossessed of Jaunpur, occupied Behar.

The second Iliás Sháhís.

Aláuddín Husain Sháh destroyed the power of the Khaujas and Habshís in 1494 and ascended the throne of Bengal. Husain had been, in early life, the servant of a Káyastha officer of the State, named Subuddhi Khán. He entertained great respect for the Hindus, two of whom, Rúp and Sanátan, held high offices under him. He destroyed the Kamatpur kingdom and made war on Orissa. He made an attempt to conquer Behar, but was opposed by Sikandar Lodí, and had to enter into a treaty with that monarch. He had two sons, Nasrat Sháh and Mahmúd Sháh, who reigned till 1536. The celebrated Sher Sháh deposed Mahmúd and became Sultán of Bengal. His descendants, expelled from Delhi, endeavoured to retain Bengal; but in this they were foiled by Sulaimán Kiráni, who became its undisputed master in 1563, and removed his capital from Gaur to Tándá, near Rájmahal.

Aláuddín Husain Sháh.

Sulaimán had a general named Kálápáhár. He was originally a Hindu, but embraced Muhammadanism and became a fierce iconoclast. He led an expedition into Orissa in 1565, conquered the country, deposed the usurping monarch, Telingá Mukunda-dev, and committed the image of Jagannáth to the flames. Sulaimán died in 1572 and was succeeded by his brother, Dáud. Dáud quarrelled with Akbar and in three years lost his kingdom,

The Kiránis conquer Orissa.

which was annexed to the Mughal empire in 1575. But the country was not finally subjugated till 1592; when Akbar's governors induced the Patháń chief, Isa Khán, the guardian of Osmán Kiráni, to accept a Jágir in Orissa and settle there.

CHAPTER III.

The Kingdom of Jaunpur (1394-1478).

The Sharqi dynasty.

The founder of this kingdom was Khauja Jahán, who held a high office at Delhi. Mahmúd Tughlak made him governor of his eastern provinces, with the title of Málik-us-Sharq, 'the lord of the East.' He immediately proclaimed himself independent and endeavoured to consolidate his power and extend his dominions (1394). He bequeathed his kingdom and his title to a young man, Mubárak Sháh, whom he had adopted as his heir and who was the real founder of the Sharqi dynasty. Including Khauja Jahán, the dynasty comprised six kings, and their kingdom extended from Bengal to Delhi. They beautified their capital, Jaunpur, with splendid palaces and mosques. Though Bahlol Lodí destroyed the kingdom and annexed it in 1478, the last king, Husain Sháh, reigned in Behar till 1494. There Sikandar Lodí defeated him, and he had to flee to Bengal, where he died in 1499. Thus the Sharqi dynasty came to an end. Sikandar Lodí destroyed many of the Sharqi edifices at Jaunpur.

CHAPTER IV.

The Kingdom of Sindh (1443-1572).

During the feebleness of the kingdom of Delhi Multan became independent under the Lunga dynasty, half Hindu and half

Muhammadan, which reigned for about thirty years, when the Arghúns from Sindh absorbed Multan in their dominions.

In the eleventh century the kingdom of Mansura fell into the hands of the Sauviras, a Rajput tribe. By the end of the fourteenth century they became Muhammadans and were replaced by another tribe of Rajputs, who, in their turn, were replaced by the Arghúns, claiming descent from Timúr.

CHAPTER V.

The Kingdom of Guzerat (1396-1572).

Muzaffar I, Sultán of Guzerat.

Farhatul Mulk, the governor of Guzerat, having attempted to gain the good will of the Hindus by building Hindu temples, the emperor sent Zafar, a converted Rájput, as governor, to Guzerat in 1391. Zafar signalised his advent in Guzerat by destroying Hindu temples and defiling places of Hindu pilgrimage. The temple of Somanáth, which had been rebuilt by Bhímdev in 1036, was again destroyed. Zafar is said to have proclaimed his independence in 1396, under the title of Muzaffar Sháh. He died in 1412, and his successor, Ahmad, removed the capital, from Anahilpattan to Ahmadabad, which he named after him-self. He adorned it with so many splendid edifices that it is still regarded as one of the most beautiful cities in India. Of the successors of Ahmad, Mahmúd Bigáráh was the most powerful. He succeeded in destroying two of the most ancient Hindu principalities in Guzerat, namely, Junágarh and Champánagar, hill forts, which had both hitherto been considered impregnable. Muzaffer II., another of the kings, invaded Málava and occupied Mándú,

Foundation of Ahmadabad.

the capital. He was a good naval commander and fought with the Portuguese at sea.

Of the Musalman kings of Guzerat, Bahádur Sháh, who ascended the throne in 1526, was the most popular. He was a brave and intrepid soldier and quite reckless of life. Immediately on his accession he invaded Málava, which he annexed to Guzerat in 1536. Ráná Sangrám Sinha having, on one occasion, assisted the king of Málava, Bahádur invested Chitor in 1529, after the death of that great king, and took it. Cannon were here used for the first time in siege operations in India. The Rájput ladies of Chitor preferred death to dishonour and burnt themselves.

Bahádur Sháh.

Málava annexed.

Karnávatí, the widow of Sangrám Sinha, in her distress, sent a 'rákhi,' to Humáyún, the emperor of Delhi: that is, sought his protection and fraternal affection. Humáyún, on receipt of the 'rákhi,' proceeded to Chitor for the protection of Karnávatí and succeeded in expelling the governor of Bahádur. Not content with his success at Chitor, Humáyún invaded Guzerat, and pursued Bahádur to Mandesor, where he had entrenched himself. Humáyún cut off his supplies, which alarmed him so much that he fled first to Mándú, thence to Cambay, and thence to the island of Diu. Humáyún stormed the fort of Champánagar, the walls of which he scaled in person, and annexed Guzerat to his empire. But, shortly after this, Humáyún's empire was itself destroyed, and Guzerat remained independent for thirty years more.

Humáyún in Guzerat.

The Portuguese had long been anxious to obtain possession of Diu, near Somanáthpattan; but Bahádur Sháh would never allow them to have it. When, however, he fled before Humáyún and sought the protection of the Portuguese, they compelled him to cede the place. On the fall of Humáyún's empire, Bahádur repented of what he had done and made several attempts to break off his engagement with the Portuguese. They, however, invited him to their ships, and there he was killed, either by accident or by design, in 1557.

Bahádur's death

Muzaffar III., the last king of Guzerat, made over the kingdom to Akbar and became a councillor of his court (1572). But, after nine years, he fled from Delhi, made many attempts to regain his kingdom, and passed the remainder of his unfortunate life under the protection of Ráy Sinha, a Hindu Rájá of Káthiawar.

CHAPTER VI.

THE KINGDOM OF MÁLAVA (1401-1567).

The Ghori dynasty

DILWAR KHÁN GHORI, a nobleman at the court of Firoz Sháh Tughlak, was appointed governor of Málava, and he took the earliest opportunity to assert his independence, in 1401 A. D. He removed his capital from Dhárá to Mándú, which his successors made a strong fort and a beautiful city. His son, Hushang, was of a warlike disposition and founded the city of Hushangabad. Shortly after Hushang's death, the Ghori family became extinct, and Mahmúd Khiliji obtained possession of the kingdom. He conquered Ajmir, Kerauli, and Ranastambhapur, and endeavoured to keep the Rájputs in check. Málava enjoyed unusual prosperity under the first three Khiliji kings; but, during the civil war which ensued after the death of Násiruddín Khiliji in 1512, a Rájput chief named Medinî Ráy obtained the ascendency at the court of Málava, and the weak king, Mahmúd II., was a mere tool in his hands. The Muhmmadans resented this, and compelled Mahmúd to take steps to send the Rájputs away from the court. This involved him in such difficulties that he was obliged to take refuge with Muzaffar II., king of Guzerat, who reinstated him in his capital. Medinî Ráy thereupon fled to Rána Sangram Sinha, and a protracted struggle ensued between

The Khiliji dynasty.

Medinî Ráy.

the Muhammadans and Rajputs for supremacy in Málava. During the progress of this struggle, Sultán Mahmúd was, on one occasion, severely wounded and made captive by Sangrám Sinha, who placed him under the best medical treatment available and sent him to Mándú with all the honours due to his rank. It was expected that Mahmúd would at least be generous to the family ofRáná Sangrám Sinha. But, immediately after the death of that brave prince, he attacked his son, who, in his distress appealed to Bahádur Sháh, and they both combined their forces to attack Málava. Mándú was taken, and the kingdom annexed to Guzerat in 1536. The subsequent history of Málava has been given in the account of Akbar's reign.

Annexation to Guzerat

CHAPTER VII.

THE KINGDOM OF KHÁNDEŚ (1399-1599).

THE first prince of Khándeś who threw off his dependence on Delhi, was Málik Rájá Fárúkí, who claimed descent from the Khalifá Omar, and had been governor of Khándeś for more than thirty years. He declared his independence in 1399, but died shortly afterwards. His son, Násir, treacherously seized the impregnable fort of Aśirgarh, which had long remained in the possession of Rájás belonging to the Ahiri caste. The Fárukís entertained the greatest reverence for the Molláhs, and, on the capture of Aśirgarh, two cities were founded in its vicinity to perpetuate the memory of two of these learned men. One of these was Jainábad and the other was Burhánpur. The latter became the capital of Khándeś, and is still a large city. Khándeś was annexed by Akbar in 1599.

The Fárúkí dynasty

Foundation of Burhánpur.

CHAPTER VIII.

THE BAHMANÍ KINGDOM (1347-1526).

The origin of the name 'Bahmaní.'

THE Amiráni Sada revolted in 1337, and the Deccan declared its independence, which was acknowledged by Firoz Tughlak immediately after his accession. Husain, the general who founded this kingdom, was originally the servant of a Delhi Bráhman, named Gangu, who, being an astrologer, predicted that he would become king and extorted from him a promise that the dynasty founded by him should be named after him and that he, Gangu, should be appointed prime minister. Husain was true to his word. He assumed the title of Husain Gangu Bahmaní, and appointed Gangu prime minister. This was the first appointment of a Hindu to such a high office under the Musalmans. The first capital of the Bahmaní kingdom was Kolburga, and the second, Bidar. The kingdom was bounded on the east by Telingána, on the south by the Krishná and the Tungabhadrá, on the west by the Konkan and the Sahyádri range, and on the north by Málava.

The Hindus and Musalmans in the Deccan

Husain Gangu died in 1358. His son, Muhammad, defeated Vináyak Ráo, the brother of the king of Orangal, and obtained possession of Golkonda. On a frivolous pretext, Muhammad insulted the Rájá of Vijaynagar, who, to avenge himself, invaded the Bahmaní kingdom with a large army, took possession of the Doáb, formed by the Krishná and the Tungabhadrá, and massacred the garrison of its chief city, Mukdul. The war was carried on with great tenacity on both sides; but the Hindus were at last defeated. The Musalmans advanced to the vicinity of the capital, and the king sued for peace. More than a hundred thousand Hindus are said to have perished in this war. Ahmad Sháh, the ninth king of this dynasty, subdued the Kákateya kingdom of Orangal in 1424, and annexed it to his dominions. But the capital and several outlying districts still

Annexation of the Kákateya kingdom.

maintained their independence by a sort of guerilla warfare. Ahmad removed his capital to Bidar, and died in 1435.

His son, Aláuddín, conquered the Konkan and compelled the petty chiefs to pay tribute. He married the beautiful daughter of the Konkan king and renamed her Parichehárá. Aláuddín was an excellent ruler. He established many hospitals and made great efforts to prevent the use of intoxicating drugs and liquors. His son, Humáyún, appointed as his chief minister Khauja Máhmúd Gáwán, one of the most prominent figures in the history of the Muhammadans in India.

Mahmúd Gáwán.

It was about this time that two strong parties with opposite interests were formed in the Bahmaní kingdom. One was the foreign, and the other the Deccani, party. The former was composed of foreigners from Arabia, Persia, Turkey, and Egypt; and the latter mostly of converted Hindus, converted Abyssinians, and the early Muhammadan settlers. Humáyún died after a short reign of three years, leaving the regency in the hands of the Queen-Mother, Mahmúd Gáwán, as representative of the foreign party, and Khauja Jahán Turk, as representative of the Deccani party. The Queen-Mother for a long time successfully administered the kingdom with the help of these two eminent men. But at last Khauja Jahán Turk sent Mahmúd Gáwán on a distant expedition, and attempted to usurp the sole authority. The king, Nizám Sháh, though still a minor, denounced him in open court as a traitor and put him to instant death; and from this time Mahmúd Gáwán became the chief adviser of the Bahmaní kings. Few characters so unselfish, so modest, so learned and so able are to be found in Indian history. He came to India as a merchant, and, by sheer force of ability and integrity, became the foremost man in the Bahmaní State. He spent all his wealth in public charities, in founding schools and colleges, in building mosques and hospitals, and in helping the learned and the distressed. He subjugated Telingána and made it a province of the Bahmaní kingdom. Up to this time the whole sea-coast from Bengal to Guzerat was in the hands of the Hindus. But Mahmúd Gáwán, by annexing the Konkan and the Northern Circars, extended the Muhammadan power from sea to sea, and thus separated the Hindu kingdoms from one another. It was about this time that the Musalmans invaded the holy city of Kánchí, which had hitherto remained in the undisturbed possession of the Hindus. Sultán Muhammad Sháh, the thirteenth Bahmaní king, was present at the capture of this beautiful Hindu city. The fiscal arrangements of Mahmúd Gáwán, some of which are still in force, were excellent, and so was his organisation of the educational, judicial, and military departments. But all his noble qualities and disinterested services to the State could not save him from the malignity of the Deccani party. Nizámul Mulk, the leader of that party, presented to the king what purported to be a treasonable correspondence between Mahmúd Gáwán and the king of Orissa. This so much incensed Muhammad Sháh, that, as soon as Gáwán appeared at court, he ordered him to be put to death (1481). The letter was a forgery, but the king discovered the fact too late. In 1489, Yúsuf Adil Sháh declared himself independent at Bijapur, and Imádul Mulk, at Berar. Nizámul Mulk now became the most powerful man at Bidar. At this time a war broke out in Telingána, and the fourteenth king, Mahmúd Sháh II., marched into the country at the head of his army. Nizámul Mulk took this opportunity of strengthening his position by distributing the royal treasure among his own partisans. When the news of this event reached Mahmúd, he ordered Nizámul Mulk to be killed, and thereupon Nizám's son, Málik Ahmad, retired to Junair, his father's jágir, and there declared himself independent, in 1490. Thus Bijapur, Berar, and the Márháttá country were lost to the Bahmanis. The Northern Circars and Telingána, acquired by the bloodshed of a century, separated themselves from the main kingdom in 1512; but the dynasty lingered on at Bidar for fourteen years more, when it was

His death.

brought to an end by Amir Bárid, the chief officer of the State. Thus, within forty years of the assassination of Mahmúd Gáwán, the powerful Bahmaní kingdom was completely dismembered, and five small kingdoms, Berar, Bidar, Ahmadnagar, Golkonda, and Bijapur arose out of its ruins.

Dismemberment of the Bahmaní Kingdom

CHAPTER IX.

The Kingdom of Berar (1489-1572).

FATEH ULLA IMÁD SHÁH established an independent kingdom in Berar in the year 1489. He was a converted Hindu from Karnát; and Mahmúd Gáwán, his patron, had appointed him governor of Berar. He made Gwailgarh, one of the most picturesque hill forts of India, his capital. The Bahmani kings made no effort to re-conquer Berar; but the kings of Ahmadnagar were their great enemies, and, to escape from their hands, the descendants of Fateh Ulla had to acknowledge the supremacy of Bahádur Sháh, the king of Guzerat. The Muhammadan and Hindu kings of the Deccan and Southern India often engaged in hostilities and entered into alliances with their neighbours on no fixed principle. In 1565, almost all the Muhammadan powers of the Deccan made common cause against the powerful Hindu king of Vijaynagar. But, on the destruction of that Hindu kingdom, the king of Bijapur tried his best to appropriate the whole of it, and, as a set-off, advised the king of Ahmadnagar to conquer and annex Berar. In this the king of Ahmadnagar succeeded, and Berar ceased to be an independent kingdom (1572). Turfán Khán, the minister of Berar, sought and obtained protection from Akbar, and thus brought about the absorption not only of Ahmadnagar, but also of the other kingdoms of the Deccan, into the Mughal empire.

The Kingdom of Berar.

Its annexation to Ahmadnagar.

There were five kings of this dynasty. Their capital was latterly removed from Gwailgarh to Ellichpur, where the ruins of the palaces and mosques built by them are still to be seen.

CHAPTER X.

The Kingdom of Bidar (1526-1609).

The kingdom of Bidar.

After the death of Mahmùd Gáwán, Kásim Bárid became supreme at Bidar, the capital of the Bahmaní kingdom. His son, Amir Bárid, expelled the Bahmaní kings from Bidar and made it an independent principality; and his son, Ali Bárid, assumed the title of Sháh. The Bárids were able but unprincipled rulers. Kásim and Amir were treacherous, intriguing, and of a restless disposition. The Bárid Sháhís brought ruin on themselves by their bad character, and soon became absolutely dependent on the powerful kingdom of Bijapur. The family lingered on for a long time, Bidar was finally annexed to the Mughal empire in Sháh Jahán's reign. There were seven kings of this dynasty, the last four of which were men of no note.

CHAPTER XI.

The Kingdom of Ahmadnagar (1491-1636).

Nizamul Mulk was born in the family of a well-to-do Bráhman, at Puttri, in Berar. He was made a captive and converted to Muhammadanism. Mahmúd Gáwán, who encouraged real worth wherever found, raised him to high office and made him governor of Junair. The Deccani party, on the death of Khauja Jahán Turk, made him their leader. How he brought about the death of his distinguished patron, has already been stated. He, too, died a violent death in the course of a few years. His son, Ahmad, retired to Junair and declared

The Kingdom of Ahmadnagar.

himself independent He removed his capital from Junair to Ahmadnagar, which he founded and named after himself. The Bráhman relations of Ahmad, hard pressed by the king of Berar, sought his protection, and this led to perpetual hostilities between the two kingdoms In 1527 Bahádur Sháh, king of Guzerat, in order to protect his new dependent, the king of Berar, invaded Ahmadnagar and compelled Burhán Nizám Sháh to acknowledge his supremacy But, in a short time, Burhán succeeded in throwing off the yoke, and entered into an alliance with the Rájá of Vijaynagar for the partition of the Bijapur State In this he was unsuccessful, and the king of Bijapur, in revenge, allied himself with the Hindu king and harassed Husain Nizám Sháh, Burhán's son and successor

Battle of Tálikot

In 1565 all the Deccani Musalman States jointly led a powerful army into Vijaynagar and completely destroyed it But the subtlety of Husain prevented any of the belligerent parties from profiting by the ruin of the Hindus As already related, he himself seized Berar The kings of Ahmadnagar conquered and annexed many of the Márháttá hill forts in the Konkan and the Sahyádri They appointed Hindus to high offices in the State for instance one Kumár Sen was for a long time Peshwa at Ahmadnagar In Ahmadnagar, as in the other Deccani kingdoms, there were two parties, one of foreigners, and the other of Deccanis During a civil war, consequent on the death of the eighth king in 1594, one of these parties applied for aid to Akbar, who sent a powerful army against Ahmadnagar, which invested the capital and was induced to retire only by the cession of Berar

Chánd Bibi.

Chánd Sultáná, a Princess of Ahmadnagar, married to one of the kings of Bijapur, displayed such heroism in the wars with the Mughals as astonished all India, and it was not until her death at the hands of her own troops that the Mughals succeeded in capturing Ahmadnagar, in 1603. Even after the capture of the capital, the dynasty continued to rule over a great portion of its territories and founded a new capital at Khirki, now Aurangabad Málik Ambar, an Abyssinian, supported the tottering fortune of this dynasty in its last days The fiscal arrangements made by him were admirable and are still in force in some places The family became extinct in 1636, and the country was annexed to the Mughal empire There were twelve kings of this dynasty, under whose fostering care the great Márháttá families which played so important a part in the subsequent history of India, rose to power

Málik Ambar

CHAPTER XII

The Kingdom of Golkonda (1512-1688)

Kutbul Mulk, appointed governor of Telingána by Mahmúd Gáwán, severed his connection with Bidar in 1512 His family ruled for a hundred and seventy-six years, and could boast of some unusually long reigns It is remarkable that none of the kings of this family died a natural death

The Kutb Sháhis of Golkonda.

The Kutb Sháhis did not, as a rule, mix much in the politics of the kings of the Deccan, but they quietly conquered one Hindu city after another and extended their power to the south and to the east, without exciting the jealousy of the neighbouring States They annexed Rájmahendri, the capital of the Drávira country, as well as the far-famed city of Orangal Their capital was Golkonda But, the place proving very unhealthy, the capital was removed to Hyderabad The Kutb Sháhis were of great help to the Deccani kings in their war with Vijaynagar in 1665 The fifth king, Abdullá, had a very powerful minister, in Mir Jumlá, who came to India as a trader and rose to the foremost position in the State of Golkonda. The king employed him in the conquest and subjugation of small Hindu principalities in Karnát, a task in which he achieved great success This excited the

Hyderabad made the capital

Mir Jumlá.

jealousy of his sovereign, who determined to ruin him. But Mir Jumlá sought the protection of Prince Aurangzeb, then engaged in the conquest of the southern kingdoms. The protection was granted, and Aurangzeb employed Mir Jumlá in weakening the Kutb Sháhì kings. The dynasty continued for thirty years more; the kingdom was annexed to the empire of Delhi in 1688.

CHAPTER XIII.

THE KINGDOM OF BIJAPUR (1489-1686).

OF all the kingdoms that arose out of the ruins of the Bahmaní empire, Bijapur was the most powerful. It was founded by Yúsuf Adil Sháh, a scion of the Imperial family of Constantinople. He had some claims to the throne, and would have been assassinated while an infant, had not his mother succeeded in sending him to Persia. India was then a field for the wildest adventure to the Muhammadans, and so Yúsuf came to India and sold himself as a slave to Mahmúd Gáwán. That discriminating statesman, charmed with his ability, address, and other good qualities, adopted him as his son, raised him to the position of Commander-in-chief of the Bahmaní forces, and conferred the province of Bijapur on him as a jágir. On the death of Gáwán, Yúsuf retired to Bijapur, and in a short time made himself king of that place. He married the sister of a Hindu feudatory, Mukund Ráo, and thus initiated that policy of contracting matrimonial alliances with Hindu chiefs which the Mughal emperors afterwards followed, so much to their advantage. The lady whom he married is known in history as Bubují Khánum. Yúsuf tolerated all religions. Hindus he not only tolerated, but raised to high offices in the State. He adopted Marathí as the language of the court; but his long residence in Persia made him partial to the Shiyás, and he adopted the

Yúsuf Adil Sháh.

Bubují Khánum.

Shiyá as the State religion of Bijapur. The Sunnis of India took umbrage at this and formed various plots to ruin the interests of his family. But Yúsuf's son and successor, Ismail, though a minor when he ascended the throne, soon exhibited signs of extraordinary physical and intellectual powers, and Bubují Khánum was a lady of remarkable ablities The Deccani Musalmans, who were disloyal to the Adil Sháhí dynasty, were gradually removed from their offices and their places filled with foreigners. The restless Amir Bárid was always plotting against Ismail; but, when an opportunity presented itself, the latter led a powerful expedition against Bidar, captured the city, and made Amir Bárid prisoner. From that time the Bárids ceased to have an independent political existence, though Amir Bárid was generously restored to his kingdom. Burhán Nizám Sháh of Ahmadnagar married the sister of Ismail; but this connection did not prevent the two States from engaging in hostilities, during the course of which Ismail signally defeated his brother-in law. Shortly afterwards, the relatives came to an understanding that one should conquer Berar and the other Golkonda. But, in the vicinity of Golkonda, Ismail caught malarious fever, of which he died in 1534. Ismail abolished the Shiyá religion in Bijapur. He strengthened the fortifications of his capital and beautified it with magnificent buildings, which still excite admiration.

Ismail Sháh.

On the death of Ismail, Bubují Khánum raised Ibráhim Adil Sháh to the throne. Ibráhim, who had constantly to fight against the kings of Ahmadnagar and Vijaynagar, died in 1557. His son, Ali Adil Sháh, in alliance with Rám Rájá of Vijaynagar, invaded Ahmadnagar, in 1558. In this war the Hindus are said to have so insulted and ill-treated their Muhammadan enemies that a feeling of intense indignation was aroused among Muhammadans of all classes, and the five kingdoms of the Deccan made common cause against them. They led an immense army into Vijaynagar, and,

Battle of Tálikot.

in 1565, defeated Rám Rájá in the sanguinary and decisive battle of Tálikot, in which he was slain and the Hindu capital sacked and destroyed. Ali Adil Sháh was assassinated in 1579.

Chánd Bibi.

On his death, his wife, Chánd Sultáná, became Regent on behalf of his minor son, Ibráhim, but she experienced great difficulty in governing the kingdom. The foreign and Deccani parties in the State often fought with each other and enlisted the help of the neighbouring States in their conflicts. Disgusted with this state of things, Chánd Sultáná retired to her paternal kingdom, Ahmadnagar, her heroic struggles against difficulties at which place have already been narrated.

Bijapur annexed.

Ibráhim Adil Sháh governed Bijapur with a strong hand; but the Nizám Sháhís were always a thorn in his side; and he therefore contracted an alliance with Akbar, whereupon that monarch resolved upon the conquest of Ahmadnagar. Three kings reigned in Bijapur after Ibráhim. The Márháttás became powerful during their rule, and Sivájí established the kingdom of Satára. Bijapur was merged in the Mughal empire in 1686.

CHAPTER XIV.

STATE OF INDIA UNDER THE PATHÁNS.

The government of the Patháns.

THE Pathán empire of Delhi began to decline from the time of Muhammad Tughlak, and in fifty years was completely destroyed. Out of its ruins arose a number of independent Muhammadan kingdoms. The Pathán emperors held India by something like military occupation. They occupied the great cities, established colonies, either of Afghán tribes or of foreign mercenaries, and left the rest of the country to govern itself. They collected taxes from the tracts of country held immediately under them, and tribute from Hindu Rájás who acknowledged their supremacy; but they seldom interfered in social, religious, or municipal matters, which the Hindus were allowed to manage in their own way. The Patháns checked risings of the Hindus and protected the country from foreign invasion, but passed the rest of their time in the pursuit of pleasure.

The policy of the small kingdoms.

But with the establishment of the small kingdoms a change took place. The Musalman rulers were compelled by the necessities of the times to mix with the Hindus and to entrust them with offices of responsibility in the State. Where the influence of the Molláhs was strong, as in Guzerat, the Hindus were often persecuted, their temples destroyed, and pilgrimages prohibited. It is said that the various places of pilgrimage in northern India, except Benares and Purí, disappeared under the Muhammadan rule. Kurukshetra, Prabhás, Vrindávan, and Ayodhyá had to be re-established in the sixteenth century as places of pilgrimage. Persecutions of the Hindus, however, did not result in their wholesale conversion.

Conversion to Muhammadanism.

The aboriginal races and the followers of Buddhist monks often embraced Muhammadanism in large numbers. The Telis and Joláhás of the North-Western Provinces, and the Nikáris, Pájáris, Patuás, and other castes in Bengal were converted about this time. They, however, received their Muhammadanism, not from the Molláhs, or orthodox Musalman theologians, but from Pírs (saints), Fakirs (mendicants), and other holy men, who never found much favour with the orthodox classes of Musalmans.

How the Bráhmans governed the Hindus.

The majority of the Hindus remained what they were, in spite of the persecution of the Molláhs and the persuasion of the Pírs and Fakirs. The Hindus had no kings in the plains; but these were the cradle of Hindu civilisation, and so the Bráhmans, in the absence of sovereign power to protect their religion, had recourse to strict social and domestic regulations. It is a remarkable fact that all their *Smriti* compilations were made after the Muhammadans had obtained a footing in India.

Mádhavácháryya, Viśveśvar Bhatta, Chandeśvar, Váchaspati Miśra, Ácháryya Chúrámani, Pratáprudra, Raghunandan, and Kamalákar all flourished during this period, and fixed Hindu manners and customs in different parts of India.

During the Pathán period, Hindu society underwent another great revolution. The Musalmans are strict monotheists, and their contact produced amongst the Hindus a number of reformers who preached somewhat monotheistic doctrines. These reformers were not much opposed to Hindu social, domestic, and other regulations; they simply availed themselves of the liberty of conscience which Hindu society grants in spiritual matters, and preached theistic doctrines. As in the fifth and sixth centuries before the Christian era, so in the fifteenth and sixteenth centuries after it, the reformers persuaded men to renounce the world. Thus the Hindu community was again divided into two classes of teachers, the Bráhmans and the mendicants. The latter, in the fifth century before Christ, were not monotheists, while in the fifteenth century they were so. Like the Buddhists and Jains, the later reformers made the several vernaculars the medium of communication with the people and raised many of the dialects to the dignity of literary languages. The followers of Chaitanya improved Bengali; those of Nának, Punjabí; those of Kavíra, Hindí; and those of Tukárám, Marathí.

Monotheistic reformers.

BOOK V

SMALL HINDU KINGDOMS.

CHAPTER I.

THE KINGDOM OF VIJAYNAGAR (1336-1565).

THE dismemberment of the Patháṇ empire gave rise to many Muhammadan kingdoms within its boundaries. But it is a remarkable fact that, beyond these boundaries, many Hindu States rose to opulence and power about the same time. The principal of these were Vijaynagar in southern Mewar and Bághelkhund in central, and Orissa in eastern, India. These States had to engage in constant wars with their Muhammadan neighbours to maintain their independence.

Hindu kingdoms of the period.

Of these Hindu States the kingdom of Vijaynagar was the chief. Shortly after the overthrow of the Hoyśála Ballály of Dvárasamudra by Málik Káfur, the general oi Aláuddín Khiliji, the Muhammadans overran the whole of Southern India, from Rámeśvara to Malabar; and this part of the country remained for a time in a state of utter confusion and anarchy. The Delhi emperors were not in a position to control these distant dependencies directly. But they sent out governors; and these governors, as well as representatives of old royal families and ambitious soldiers of fortune, tried to establish their own supremacy, or at least to appropriate a share of the immense territory thus suddenly thrown into confusion. The kings of Vijaynagar established their supremacy about this period.

Anarchy in Southern India.

The founder of the family was Bukka. His son, Sangama, and his grandsons, Harihar and Víra Bukka, ruled Southern India from 1336 to 1379. In the extensive empire thus created out of the ruins of the old dynasties, they completely re-orgnised Vedic Hinduism. The prime minister of Harihar and Víra Bukka, was the great Mádhavácháryya, the commentator of the Vedas and the compiler of a vast number of treatises on all conceivable subjects connected with their study. He was the leader of the revival of the Vedic religion, and was not only a great scholar, but a great general also; for he expelled the Musalmans from Goa. The Bahmanis invaded Vijaynagar during the reign of Harihar II., the son of Víra Bukka, and hostilities between the two powerful kingdoms, professing two different religions, were of constant occurrence.

The Bukka family of Vijaynagar.

Revival of Vedic religion

Abdur Razzak, the ambassador of the king of Samarkand, was struck with admiration at the magnificence of the city of Vijaynagar in 1444. He also speaks highly of the manners of the court. Deva Ráv II., the great-grandson of Harihar II., appears to have been the last king of the Bukka family. A period of anarchy followed his death, during which each of the ministers tried to establish his supremacy. At last one of them, Narasinha, succeeded in destroying his competitors and ascending the throne; and his family rose to greater power and influence than that which had preceded it. Narasinha's son, Krishnadev Ráy, reigned from 1509 to 1530, and the whole of Southern India acknowledged his supremacy. His son, Achyuta Ráy, reigned from 1530 to 1542. His son, Sadásiva, reigned from 1542 to 1567. During these reigns the kingdom became very powerful and included the whole of Southern India within its boundaries. Sadàsiva being a man of a queit disposition, his ministers acted in his name just as they liked. Of these Ràm Rajá, the son-in-law of Krishnadev Ráy, was a great warrior. He joined the king of

The Narasinha family.

Bijapur in invading Ahmadnagar and acted with great barbarity towards his Muhammadan enemies. The Muhammadan powers resented his conduct by jointly leading an expedition against Vijaynagar and completely destroying the power of Rám Rajà, as already stated. The capital was so completely destroyed that on the death, without issue, of Sadàśiva, who survived its destruction for four years, Tirumalla, the brother of Rám Ràjá, who was recognised king, had to remove his capital to Pennákonda, where he reigned for a long time. Venkatapati, the son of Tiru Malla, removed the capital to Chandragiri. His viceroys governed Madurá, Tanjore, and other provinces.

The Battle of Tálikot.

The fall of the family.

From Venkatapati III., the English obtained the site of the present city of Madras in 1639. The pensioned chief of Annegundi is the representative of Vijaynagar family.

CHAPTER II.

The Kingdom of Rewa (1250-1895).

It has already been stated that the Bághelás became the rulers of Guzerat after the fall of their relatives, the Chálúkyas, and that they reigned there for more than a hundred and twenty years. A branch of this family migrated to what is modern Bághelkhund, and gradually established an extensive kingdom. Dalakeśvar and Malakeśvar of this family preserved the integrity of their possessions by defeating the emperor, Bulban, in battle. The family aggrandised themselves at the expense of the Gonds and other neighbouring tribes. During the decline of the Delhi kings, they annexed certain Muhammadan districts and converted Muhammadan musjids into temples, in one of which an Arabic inscription is still an object of worship to the Hindu population. The Bàghelás had to carry on a severe contest with the Sultàns of Jaunpur for the possession of Kálpi, which was at last wrested from them. Sikandar Lodí, Bábar, and Akbar treated

The Bághelás.

the Bághelàs with great respect. Miyàn Tánsen, the chief musician of Akbar's court, began his career as the musician of Rámchandradev, one of the Bághelá kings. Their original capital was Bandogarh; but it was afterwards removed to Rewa, whence the Bághelá kings still continue to rule over their ancient possessions.

CHAPTER III.

THE KINGDOM OF MEWAR (750-1895).

Padminí.

OF the Rájput principalities, Mewar never submitted to the Muhammadans. Its early history is lost in obscurity. The Ránás of Mewar claim descent from Rám, but some are of opinion that they are not of pure Hindu origin. The founder of the tribe was Guha. Báppá Ráol, who is said to have distinguished himself in the defence of Chitor against the Muhammadans under Muhammad bin Kásim, was the founder of the dynasty. Samara Sinha of their family is said to have married the sister of Prithví Ráy and died by his side at the battle of Tiráorí in 1193. Padminí, the consort of one of the princes of Mewar, was celebrated for her beauty, and the fame of it infatuated Aláuddín to such a degree that he demanded her of her husband. This led to a fierce conflict, in the course of which Aláuddín succeeded in destroying Chitor, the capital of Mewar; but he succeeded neither in gaining possession of the person of Padminí, who, at the last moment, saved her honour by plunging into fire, nor in subduing the stubborn spirit of the Rájput chief, who fled alone into the mountains. The Musalmans soon lost Chitor, as Hambíra, a scion of the old royal family, regained it. Of the descendants of Hambíra, Kumbha and Sangrám Sinha were the most famous.

Mahárání Kumbha.

Mahárání Kumbha had to fight against the united hosts of Málava and Guzerat, but he succeeded in expelling the combined armies, and preserving the integrity of his possessions. The Musalmans having about this time gained possession of Gavá, the kings of Mewar led a crusade against them. Ráná Sangrám Sinha was an enemy of the kings of Delhi; and he is said to have won sixteen battles against the Musalmans. He meditated for a long time the expulsion of the Musalmans from Madhyadeś, the holy land of the Hindus; and the disunion of the Muhammadan kings and the weakness of Ibráhim Lodí favoured his design. He, therefore, gladly aided Bábar against Ibráhim Lodí, never thinking that Bábar would try to establish a dynasty in India. But when, after the battle of Pánipat, Bábar gave unmistakable indications of his intention of founding an empire in India, the Mahárání lost no time in opposing him. He proclaimed war against him and made immense preparations, but was defeated with great slaughter in the battle of Sikri, near Agra, in 1527. Bábar, though greatly weakened by so fierce a contest, wisely determined to follow up his success by the capture of Chanderí, the stronghold of Mediní Ráy. The death of these two great generals, shortly after the battle of Sikri, ruined for ever the hope of Rájput supremacy in India.

Sangrám Sinha.

The story of Bahádur Sháh's seizure of Chitor has been already given in Book IV. Chap. V. After Humáyún's fall, however, Bahádur again invested Chitor and destroyed the city. Akbar twice besieged and destroyed it. It was for this reason that the later Ránás relinquished Chitor, and established their new capital at Udaypur, one of the most inaccessible points of the Aravallí range, into which the Mughals never succeeded in penetrating. The subsequent history of Mewar is intimately connected with that of the Mughal empire, and will be given in Book VI.

Foundation of Udaypur.

CHAPTER IV.

THE KINGDOM OF ORISSA (1050-1565).

THERE was for a long time a small principality in the southern Márhátá country, ruled over by a family named Kangu, which in Sanskrit would be Ganga. Their possessions were small, and they had often to submit to powerful neighbouring sovereigns. In the eighth century of the Christian era, a branch of this family established itself in Kalinga and extended its power and influence. Rájarája of this dynasty married the daughter of the great conqueror, Rájendra Chola. Chola Gangadev, the issue of this marriage, conquered, between 1081 and 1118, the kingdom of Utkala, and built the celebrated temple of Jagannáth at Purí to commemorate his conquest.

Ganga Conquest of Orissa.

The temple of Jagannáth.

The temple was beautified and the worship arranged by Ananga Bhìmdev, the fifth king of the dynasty. One of his descendants, Narasinhadev, invested the city of Gaur during the reign of Aláuddín Khilıjı and greatly harassed the Musalmans of Bengal. It is said that the Uriyás obtained possession of Bengal down to Triveni, the sacred *ghát* of which is popularly attributed to the Hindu kings of Orissa. Pratáprudradev of this dynasty was a great patron of literature. During his reign Chaitanyadev lived at Purí and preached his celebrated doctrine of *Bhakti* (devotion). Pratáprudra became a disciple of Chaitanya and introduced his religion into Orissa. Shortly after the death of Pratáprudra, there was a revolution in Orissa, which placed Mukundadev, an inhabitant of Telingána, on the throne. The change of dynasty was followed by national weakness, taking advantage of which, Kálápáhár, the general of Sulaimán, invaded Orissa and annexed it to the kingdom of Bengal in 1565.

Conquest of the country.

CHAPTER V.

The Portuguese in India.

European commerce in India.

All the races that had, from a period of remote antiquity, entered India, had come by land. But, by the end of the fifteenth century, the people of Western Europe had begun to come by sea. Their first object was trade, and their second conquest. The Portuguese, who were known in India by the term Firingí, came first. After them came the people of Holland, known as the Olandáz. Then came the English, and last of all the French, who are known as the Farásis. From the time of Alexander the Great, the people of Eastern Europe had held commercial relations with India. During the ascendency of the Khalifas the Arabs appropriated the trade of India and that of the Indian Archipelago. They used to sell, at a very high profit Indian products, snch as silk and cotton piece-goods and spices, to the merchants of Venice and Genoa, who carried them to western and northern Europe, where they made an immense profit, the trade being almost a monopoly of these two republics. The English, French, Portuguese, and other nations were anxious to do away with this monopoly; but the only way to India, hitherto known, lay through the Mediterranean and the Red Sea. Venice and Genoa were masters of the Mediterranean and the Arabs were supreme in the Red Sea; and thus the only resource left to the people of Western Europe was the discovery of a new route. Some thought that they would reach India by crossing the sea westwards. The expeditions that were sent out in search of the western route, however, did not discover India, but a far larger continent. The discoverer, Columbus, believed it to be India, and so it was named New India, or the West Indies, and the copper-coloured aborigines were named the West Indians. Others thought that they would reach India by a north-western route, and many expeditions were fitted out for its discovery, but without

The Western route.

much result. Some, again, thought of reaching India by doubling the southern extremity of Africa. These at last succeeded. Vasco da Gama, a celebrated navigator of Portugal, doubled the Cape of Good Hope in 1498, and succeeded in reaching India. He landed at Calicut, then governed by a petty chief with the title of Zamorin, who was very much afraid of his powerful neighbour, the king of Vijaynagar. The Arab merchants, naturally jealous of the Portuguese, induced the Zamorin to set his face against them; but the kings of Cochin, Kananar, and Quilan favoured the Portuguese, and their trade began to flourish. The Portuguese, however, came to the conclusion that, unless they ruined the Arabs, they would never profit by their Indian trade; and, acting under this impression, they sent a powerful fleet to India. In 1507 the kings of Bijapur, Guzerat, and even of Egypt sent powerful fleets to oppose the Portuguese, who, however, succeeded in gaining a decisive victory. Within three years of this, they occupied Goa, belonging to the kingdom of Bijapur, but they were afterwards expelled. They returned, however, in the course of a few years, re-occupied that place, and made it the capital of the Portuguese possessions in the Indian Seas. The two great Portuguese viceroys were Almeida and Albuquerque. After this event the Portuguese directed their attention to the extension of their commercial and political influence in the eastern Peninsula and in the eastern Islands.

Route round the Cape of Good Hope.

Goa becomes the Portuguese capital in India.

BOOK VI.

THE MUGHAL EMPIRE

CHAPTER I.

Bábar (1526-1530).

Bábar was descended on his father's side from Timúr, and on his mother's from Changìz Khán. He lost his father at the age of twelve and succeeded him as king of Farghána. Even at that early age he twice seized Samarkand, then the capital of the Turkish empire. The Uzbeks were at this time becoming very powerful in Central Asia. They expelled him first from Samarkand and then from Farghána. Bábar fled to Balkh, whence the people expelled his cousin and made him king, but the Uzbeks drove him even from this place, and he determined to flee to Kábul. He suffered much while crossing the Hindukuś in the depth of an unusually severe winter; but at last he succeeded in reaching Kábul, almost alone, his followers having perished in the snow. The Kabulis expelled his uncle's son and made him king. The Uzbeks were at that time involved in a serious war with the kings of Persia, and thus were not in a position to give him trouble at Kábul, where he reigned in peace for some time. Though he had suffered much and undergone many changes of fortune, yet he was only twenty-three years old when he became the ruler of Kabul, in 1504. He reigned for twenty-two years in Kabul before he invaded India.

Bábar's early life.

Daulat Khán Lodí, the governor of the Punjab, disgusted with the slights and insults heaped upon the Pathán nobles by Ibráhim Lodí, invited Bábar to invade India, which he did, as has already been described. The battle of Pánipat made him master of an extensive territory, from the western limits of Bengal to the eastern boundary of Persia. The Pathàns attempted to set up a new kingdom at Jaunpur under the leadership of Daryá Khán Loháni On hearing of this, Bábar set out for Jaunpur and defeated him In this expedition he obtained possession of Benares and Patna while his son, Humáyún, tranquillised and settled Oudh

Destruction of the Pathán power.

Káná Sangrám Sinha, jealous of the power which had thus suddenly sprung up on the ruins of the Lodi dominions, espoused the cause of a Pathán Sardár and invaded the kingdom of Bábar. Bábar knew the Rána's power, and was not a little dismayed at the immense preparations that were being made against him The battle of Sikiri (1527), which followed, has been already described in Book V Chap III Bábar died in 1530 A D.

And of the Ráj-put power.

In northern Hindusthán, the Rájputs and the Patháns had contended for supremacy for many generations Bábar destroyed the Pathán power at the battle of Pànipat, and the Rájput power at the battle of Sikri.

CHAPTER II

Humáyún (1530-1540)

Bábar had four sons The eldest, Humàyún, ascended the throne of Delhi, the second, Kámrán, became the ruler of Kabul and Kandahár, and to these territories Humáyún added the Punjab. This was an impolitic step, as it cut off Hindusthán from those mountainous regions from which the Musalman emperors drew their supply of soldiers. Humáyún conferred on his other two brothers the governments of different provinces of India.

Humáyún and his brother.

Humáyún's brother-in-law plotted against his life; but the plot was discovered, and he fled to Bahádur Sháh in Guzerat. A Lodí chief also took refuge with that monarch. Ráni Karnávatí of Mewar, about this time, sought the protection of Humáyún against him. All these circumstances combined to induce Humáyún to lead an expedition against Bahádur (*See* Book IV. Chap. V.).

Sher Khán.

In the eastern provinces of the empire of Delhi, Sher Khán, a Pathán chief, had become very powerful. He belonged, like Muhammad Ghori, to the Sur tribe. Sher Khán's father had obtained a jágir from one of the kings of Jaunpur, at Sasseram, in Behar. In early youth, Sher studied Persian History and Persian poetry with distinguihed success at Jaunpur.

His early life

Then he became a soldier of fortune, serving any master who would pay him well, whether Mughal or Pathán. He entered the service of Mahmúd Lodí, the son of Sikandar Lodí, who made himself master of Behar in 1529. Bábar defeated Mahmúd Lodí and appointed Jalál, the grandson of Daryá Khán, to the government of Behar. Jalál being a minor, his mother, Dudu, was appointed Regent. Sher Khán was a great favourite of Dudu, and he soon made himself master of the entire province of Behar. He treacherously obtained possession of the two strong hill forts of Rhotás and Chunar.

Conquest of Behar and Bengal.

Thus secure in the possession of Behar, he invaded Bengal and took possession of it. Mahmúd, the king of Bengal, sought the protection of Humáyún, who, flushed with his recent successes in Guzerat, readily espoused his cause, declared war against Sher Khán, and invested the fort of Chunar. It took him several months to get possession of it; during which Sher Khán consolidated his power in Bengal. Humáyún then occupied Patna and Gaur without opposition, while Sher Khán concealed himself in the jungles. The rains now set in with great violence in Bengal; the whole country became inundated, and Humáyún's retreat was cut off. Sher Khàn then issued from his hiding-place, occupied Behar, Benares, and Chunar, and invaded Kanauj and Jaunpur. Humáyún was reduced to the greatest straits; and, as soon as the rainy season ended, he began his retreat from Gaur to Agra. He met Sher Khàn at Baxar (1539).

Battle of Baxar.

Both parties entrenched their camps and waited for an opportunity to engage. Sher Khán, leaving his camp pitched where it was, attacked Humáyún with his entire army from the rear. Humáyún's soldiers, thinking that they were attacked on both sides, were panic-stricken and fled. Humáyún plunged into the Ganges on horseback; the exhausted horse sank in the river; but a water-carrier saved Humáyún's life by giving him a little space on the inflated skin on which he was crossing the stream, and he at last succeeded in reaching Agra, where his brothers were busily engaged in concerting plots against him. His presence disconcerted them, and he began to make fresh preparations for war. Meanwhile Sher Khán took possession of Bengal and collected a large army to invade the Mughal dominions. The armies met in the vicinity of Kanauj, where Humáyún was defeated in a sanguinary battle and compelled to flee from India with his family. Kàmrán made peace with Sher Khán by making over the Punjab to him. Thus the Pathán empire was for a second time established in India, when Sher Khán ascended the throne of Delhi, under the title of Sher Sháh, in 1540 A. D.

Conquest of Hindusthán.

CHAPTER III.

SHER SHÁH (1540-1545).

ON obtaining possession of the Punjab, Sher Sháh erected a strong fort at Rhotás, on the Jhelum, in order to prevent an invasion of Hindusthán from Kabul. In the following year he conquered Màlava and invested the strong hill fort of Ráysin. The garrison sur-

Siege of Ráysin.

rendered, on condition that their lives and properties should be spared; but, in violation of the terms of capitulation, he put the whole of them to the sword. The next year he invaded Márwar, and, in order to sow dissensions in the enemy's camp, sent a number of forged letters to the Rájá, throwing suspicion on one of the most powerful of the Márwar chiefs. The chief collected his tribesmen, 12,000 in number, and attacked Sher Sháh so furiously that his camp was thrown into disorder and his life endangered. He succeeded, however, in repelling the attack and declared that he had nearly lost the empire of India for a handful of *jowar* (millet, the only crop that then grew in Márwar). The following year he invested the fort of Kálanjara. The last Chandel king of the place, Kírtti Sinha, defended it obstinately. Sher Sháh offered him terms of capitulation; but his character for treachery was now well-known, and Kírtti Sinha placed no confidence in his overtures, but kept up an incessant fire from the ramparts. A cannon ball struck his magazine and caused a terrible explosion, and Sher Sháh, who was near, was so severely scorched that he died a few hours afterwards. Sher Sháh's son, Salím, took Kálanjara and put an end to the Chandel dynasty.

War against Márwar.

Siege of Kálanjara.

Sher Sháh was the son of a petty Jágirdár. By dint of extraordinary perseverance and force of character, he made himself master of the whole of Hindusthán. He was an able ruler. He constructed a highway from Gaur to Rhotás, in the Punjab, planted it on both sides with trees, excavated wells and constructed *serais* at convenient distances. He fixed the land revenue at a fourth of the produce and introduced a system of post horses.

Sher Sháh's character.

CHAPTER IV.

SUCCESSORS OF SHER SHÁH (1545-1556).

Salím.

THE eldest son of Sher Sháh being a man of weak intellect, the Pathán nobles raised his second son, Salím, to the throne. Salím ruled wisely for nine years. On his death, his brother, Muhammad, put his son to death, and ascended the throne. Muhammad was a man of licentious character and fond of low company. He was popularly known as Adili.

Adili.

Himu.

Himu was a poor Hindu who kept a shop at Delhi. He was very ugly and deformed; but he became a great favourite of Adili, who placed him in charge of all the affairs of the State, and he managed them with success. A rebellion having broken out in Chunar, Adili and Himu proceeded to that place and quelled it. But in the meantime Ibráhim Sur, a near relation of Adili, took possession of Agra and Delhi, and Sikandar Sur, of the Punjab. Ibráhim, on gaining possession of Delhi, proceeded eastwards to oppose Himu; but was defeated and put to flight. Muhammad Sur, the governor of Bengal, rebelled at this time; but Himu suppressed the rebellion and made excellent arrangements for the good government of the province.

Humáyún re-conquers Delhi.

While Himu was engaged in the east, Humáyún emboldened by the weakness of the Sur dynasty, and taking advantage of the dissensions that prevailed in Hindusthán, invaded the Punjab, expelled the governor of Sikandar Sur, and entered Sirhind. There he defeated Sikandar and took possession of Agra and Delhi without opposition in 1555 A. D.

Humáyún's death.

But Humáyún was not destined to enjoy his new kingdom long. Within six months of his occupation of Delhi, he slipped on the polished marble steps of his library, and falling to the ground, sustained a shock from which he died in the course of a few days.

Himu was already approaching Delhi with 30,000 disciplined troops, when he heard the news of Humáyún's death, which he took to be a good omen. He obtained possession of Agra without difficulty; expelled Humáyún's garrison from Delhi, and assumed the title of Mahàrájádhirája Vikramáditya. Without losing much time, Himu advanced towards the Punjab, where Humáyún's famous son, Akbar, then only fourteen years of age, was watching the progress of affairs in Hindusthán. On hearing of the advance of Himu, he convened a council of war, in which every one advised him to retrace his steps to Kabul. But Akbar, though young, did not relish this advice, and voted with his guardian, Bairám Khán, for an advance. Himu's army far outnumbered that of Akbar; yet the latter boldly resolved on attacking him at Pánipat. Himu displayed consummate generalship; but he was defeated, owing to the rashness and turbulence of his Pathán soldiers, and was taken prisoner (1556). When he was led into the presence of Akbar, Bairàm placed an unsheathed sword before the young Prince and asked him to cut off the head of the infidel and assume the title of Ghází. Akbar touched the forehead of Himu with the sharp edge of the sword and withdrew it; but Bairám severed the head from the body at one stroke. Thus perished Himu, who was a genius in both military and civil affairs. At the time of his death his master, Adili, was residing at Chunar. He died in a war against his rebellious governor of Bengal.

Second battle of Pánipat.

CHAPTER V.

Akbar's Minority (1556-1560).

When defeated at the battle of Kanauj and forced to flee from his kingdom, Humáyún made an attempt, with the wreck of his army, to conquer Sindh, then ruled by the Arghún family, which nominally acknowledged the suzerainty of Delhi. In the course of two years, his slender resources were exhausted, and he

Humáyún's flight through the desert.

gave up all hope of conquering Sindh. Without money and without resources, the ex-Emperor of Delhi resolved to place himself and his family under the protection of Máladev, the Rájá of Jodhpur. His sufferings in the desert, from Sindh to Jodhpur, were terrible. He had only a few followers, and even some of these deserted him. After undergoing indescribable hardships, the small cavalcade reached Jodhpur; but the Rájá refused to afford Humáyún protection, and he had to recross the desert and throw himself on the mercy of Rána Prasád of Amarkot. He was greatly harassed, on his return journey, by Máladev's men on a suspicion of his having been guilty of the killing of kine, and, though he obtained an asylum at Amarkot, he was in a short time obliged to leave that place also.

During the residence of Humáyún at Amarkot, his queen, Hámidá, a native of Khorásán, gave birth to a male child, on

Birth of Akbar.

the 14th of October, 1542. The child was the famous Akbar. Humáyún was away at the time on a military enterprise, and was encamped at a distance of a day's march from Amarkot. When the news of the birth of a son reached him, he had nothing to present to his friends but a pod of musk. This he broke open, and, distributing its contents among them, expressed a hope that his son's fame might be diffused over the world like the odour of that perfume Shortly after this, a growing coldness on the part of Rána Prasád compelled Humáyún to flee to Persia, and, on his way, he placed Akbar and his mother under the protection of Hindál, one of his younger brothers, then governor of Herat under Kámrán. For four years Akbar lived under the protection of his uncle; but, on Humáyún's conquest

His early life.

of Kandahár, with the assistance of the king of Persia, Akbar was sent to him. During the war between Humáyún and Kámrán for the possession of Kabul, Akbar twice fell into the power of the latter, and narrowly escaped being put to death. Humáyún put out Kámrán's eyes in 1553 and firmly established his power at

Kabul. From this time Humáyún began to associate Akbar with himself in the business of the State, and at the storming of Ghazní the youth greatly helped his father, by whose side he fought with distinguished bravery

After the battle of Pánipat, Akbar took possession of Agra and Delhi. Bairám Khán was his guardian, on whom he depended entirely both in peace and in war.

Bairam Khán

The Mughal empire was at this stage beset with dangers, and it was Bairám's exertions that preserved it. But Bairám was a man of a choleric disposition and suspected everybody. When Himu invested Delhi, Tardi Beg Khán commanded the garrison. He surrendered the city to Himu, and for this Bairám beheaded him without trial. In a similar manner he made away with many distinguished noblemen, and Akbar resolved upon freeing himself from the tutelage of so cruel a guardian. Akbar left the camp of Bairám Khán and repaired to Delhi, on a pretext of seeing his mother, who was reported to be seriously ill, and there he assumed charge of the State independently of a guardian, in 1560. Bairám obtained Akbar's permission to retire to Mecca; but he was assassinated on the way, in Guzerat, by a Pathán soldier, whose father he had killed with his own hand.

CHAPTER VI.

Akbar (*Continued*).

The Conquest of Hindusthán (1560-1592).

Though Akbar's empire nominally extended far and wide, his real power was confined to Kabul, the Punjab, and Delhi; and even in these provinces peace had not been fully established.

The Pathán emperors were Afgháns, and the Afgháns therefore assisted them in time of need. The dynasty founded by Bábar was new to Afghánisthán, and it could not depend upon its Afghán subjects. In Hindusthán, too, the Afgháns

Weakness of Akbar's position.

were very powerful, and when Akbar assumed the government of the empire, he was, in a manner, absolutely helpless. His army consisted of a number of adventurers from Tartary and Turkisthán, who cared more for personal gain than for the permanence of the Mughal empire. But, though so helpless in the beginning, Akbar succeeded, by dint of ability, perseverance, earnestness, and political foresight, and, above all, by the strength and force of his character, not only in bringing the whole of Hindusthán under his rule, but in annexing a considerable portion of the Deccan also.

The period from 1560 to 1567 was spent by him in subduing the rebellious among his own followers. The Patháns attacked Jaunpur under the leadership of Sher Sháh II., and Akbar deputed his general, Khán Zamán, to check their advance. Khán Zamán checked the Patháns, but attempted to make himself independent. Báz Bahádur, the son of Sher Sháh's governor of Málava, having established himself as an independent sovereign, Akbar despatched Adam Khán against him. He, too, tried to become independent. Akbar guessed his purpose, and by rapid marches unexpectedly presented himself before him. Adam Khán, disconcerted, confessed his error and was transferred to a distant province. The task of subduing Báz Bahádur then devolved upon Abdul Khán Uzbek, and at last Báz Bahádur accepted service under Akbar. Asaf Khán, a general of Akbar, obtained immense booty by the conquest of Garamandal from Rání Durgávatí, the daughter of Kírtti Sinha of Kálanjara; and, on Akbar's demanding the money, he raised the standard of rebellion. But these rebellions of his friends did not alarm Akbar, who quelled them one after another. He sometimes travelled a hundred and sixty miles in one day on horseback, and, in the absence of ferry-boats, swam across broad rivers. He never allowed his enemies to mature their plans.

Pacification of Jaunpur,

Of Málava,

and of Garamandal.

At the age of twenty-five, Akbar had not only succeeded

in establishing peace in his extensive dominions, but begun to lay his plans for the conquest of foreign states. Rájá Vihári Mall and his son, Bhagavándás of Amber, were his intimate friends. He married the daughter of Vihári Mall, and appointed both his father-in-law and his brother-in-law to high offices in the State. The Rája of Márwar, after some fighting, made peace with him. Uday Sinha, the Rána of Mewar, evacuated Chitor, on its invasion by Akbar, and it fell into his hands in 1568. Nine years after this event Uday's son, Pratáp Sinha, founded the present capital, Udaypur, in the depths of the Aravallí range, and regained much of his ancestral dominions. The Ránás of Udaypur never submitted to the emperors of Delhi or entered into matrimonial relations with them. Kálanjara and Ranastambhapur fell into the hands of Akbar in 1570.

The Rájputs.

War with Mewar.

The kingdom of Guzerat was about this time torn by factions, and party dissensions ran very high. Itimád Khán, a Hindu slave converted to Muhammadanism, became supreme in the State and governed the country in the name of Muzaffar III. His sudden rise created a host of enemies. Akbar expelled a number of Mirzás, or descendants of Timúr, from his dominions for their turbulence, and they retired to Guzerat, where, joining the malcontents, they created great disturbances. Itimád Khán, unable to cope with them, invited Akbar to take possession of the country, an invitation which he gladly accepted. In the course of a few months, he annexed Guzerat to his dominions, and, appointing Muzaffar Sháh a member of his court, granted him extensive jágirs for his support.

Annexation of Guzerat,

The turbulent Pathán nobles, gradually driven from Hindusthán, retired to Bengal, where they made the position of Dáud Khán, the last of the Kiráni kings, so irksome that he consented to hold the country as a dependent of Akbar. But soon after this he attempted to evade the terms of the treaty, and Akbar sent an

and of Bengal.

army to Bengal and occupied it Dáud fled to Orissa, and the Patháns followed him there The Mughals, on the other hand, seized the jágirs of the Patháns in Bengal, and showed no disposition to obey the Imperial mandates Seeing both the Mughals and the Patháns assume so defiant an attitude, Akbar appointed Hindus as Viceroys of Bengal, and thus succeeded in establishing a firm Government there Mán Sinha and Todar Mall, both Hindus, governed Bengal for a long time The Patháns though humbled and subdued remained powerful in Orissa, where Akbar granted them extensive jágirs Hákim Mirzá brother of Akbar, headed several rebellions against him, and he had on several occasions to proceed in person to quell them. He appointed Rájá Bhagavándás Viceroy of the Punjab in 1582.

Annexation of Kásmír,

From ancient times Hindu Rájás had reigned in Kásmír. But, during the middle of the fourteenth century, the last Hindu Rájá of that country was deposed and killed by his Muhammadan minister, who ascended the throne under the title of Shamsuddín. About the year 1540, the Tibetans invaded Kásmir, and a period of anarchy ensued, to the great suffering of the inhabitants Akbar put an end to this anarchy by his conquest of the country, granted the Rájá an extensive jágir in Behar, and fixed his residence at Delhi, where he became a member of Akbar's court

of Sindh,

The Arghúns were about this period expelled from Sindh and Multan by another race of military adventures But before the latter had had time to establish themselves in their new conquest, Akbar invaded the country and appointed its king a member of his own court

and of Kandahár.

Beyond the limits of Hindusthán, Kabul was always regarded as a Mughal province But after the rebellion of Hákim Mirzá it came completely into the hands of Akbar, who, in 1594, taking advantage of a protracted war between the Uzbeks and the Persians, succeeded in annexing Kandahár to his dominions

CHAPTER VII.

AKBAR (*Continued.*)

CONQUEST OF THE DECCAN (1592-1605.)

AFTER the conquest and annexation of Hindusthán, Kabul and Kandahár, Akbar found time to interfere in the politics of the Deccan. It has already been stated that the king of Ahmadnagar conquered Berar in 1572. But, after a few years, civil war broke out in Ahmadnagar, and one of the parties sought the assistance of Akbar. Being occupied with other affairs at the time, he was not in a position to render it. But in 1595, another party, which held the capital, Ahmadnagar, appealed to him for assistance, promising to make over the city to him. Akbar despatched an army in response, but before it reached Ahmadnagar, the celebrated Chánd Sultána had succeeded in occupying the place. She invited all the parties to unite for the defence of the capital; her call was responded to with alacrity, and the Mughals, though they invested Ahmadnagar, failed to capture it. But Chánd Sultána, in order to save Ahmadnagar, was compelled to cede Berar. Shortly after the conclusion of peace with the Mughals, the inhabitants of the city murdered Chánd Bibí and afforded the Mughals an opportunity of re-investing it. After a short struggle they captured the city and removed the king to the fort of Gwalior. But the kingdom of Ahmadnagar did not come to an end with the loss of its capital. The dynasty lingered on for some time, and the Nizám Sháhís figured again in the history of subsequent reigns.

War against Ahmadnagar.

The king of Khándeś lived in constant dread of the Nizám Sháhí kings. He, therefore from the very beginning, sought the protection of Akbar, which he obtained. But, after the capture of the city of Ahmadnagar, Akbar annexed the kingdom of Khándeś also. On the annexation of Khándeś, Berar, and a portion of Ahmadnagar, Akbar appointed his son, Dániyàl, to the vice-

Annexation of Khándeś.

royalty of his possessions in the Deccan. The kings of Golkonda and Bijapur sought the friendship of Akbar by sending ambassadors to his court.

Prince Salím.

Salím, the eldest son of Akbar, became very turbulent about this time; and Akbar, to conciliate him, issued a proclamation appointing him his successor. Salím was also appointed to the Subadárship of Ajmir, with the entire charge of the military operations against the Rána of Udaypur. But while his father was engaged in the Deccan war, he raised the standard of rebellion, assumed the title of king, and occupied Behar, Allahabad, and Oudh. Akbar wrote kind letters to him and appointed him Subadár of Bengal and Orissa; and, after a short time, Salím came to Agra and was received affectionately by his father.

Salím's health was seriously impaired by his excesses, and Akbar was compelled to fix his residence at Allahabad. There, too, he misbehaved himself to such an extent that Akbar had to place him under the treatment of two of the most celebrated medical men of his time, with orders to maintain a strict control over him. Akbar's second son, Dániyál, died in 1604; the shock proved too much for him, and he was taken seriously ill in the following October. His illness in extreme old age convulsed Delhi society with speculations as to the succession. Salím was his only child, and according to law he should have succeeded. But his rebellion against his father and his disobedience to his will made him extremely unpopular. Salím's eldest son, Khusru, was the son of Rájá Mán Sinha's sister and the son-in-law of Kháni Azim; hence many were in favour of his succession. Salím ceased to frequent the palace. But Salím's third son, Khurram, took a solemn vow not to leave his grandfather's bedside as long as he was alive. Akbar, aware of these events, invited Salím to his bedside, declared him his heir, and exerted his influence to reconcile the *umaráhs* (noblemen) to him. Akbar died in the year 1605.

Akbar's death.

CHAPTER VIII

AKBAR (*Concluded*)

AKBAR'S CHARACTER AND ADMINISTRATION

His character

AKBAR was a man of wonderful genius Humáyún wished at his birth that his fame might be diffused over the whole world like the odour of musk, and never was a father's wish so fully realised No monarch is so famous in the annals of India He was very tender to human suffering and was never severe to any one without cause He was extremely averse to the destruction of human life His unwillingness to take Himu's life was a notable instance of this Though he had to engage in numerous wars, he was no lover of war, but, on the contrary was fond of peaceful occupations When war became inevitable, he made all the dispositions for its conduct and often encouraged his generals and soldiers by his presence in the battlefield He remained no longer at the scene of war, however, than was absolutely necessary, but left its conduct to his generals and returned to his capital, where he devoted himself to the cultivation of the arts of peace His power of endurance was great, and he never shrank from making long and rapid journeys

His attitude towards the Hindus

The welfare of his subjects was always next to his heart He abolished the tax called *jizya* (poll tax), which the Muhammadan sovereigns imposed upon their Hindu subjects, and which served to keep up the invidious distinction between the conqueror and the conquered He abolished many Hindu rites which appeared cruel to him He discouraged the self-immolation of Hindu widows on the funeral pyres of their husbands He looked upon all systems of religion with equal veneration, and held that people could obtain salvation by following any religion Every evening it was his habit to hear disputations among the professors of various religions in support of their own particular doctrines To these evening assemblies, Hindus and

Jains, Christians and Musalmans, of various denominations, had equal access. A brother of Saint Xavier, the celebrated Missionary, who laboured hard for the conversion of the natives of India and Japan, was often present at these meetings and enjoyed a share of the emperor's respect. Akbar promulgated a new faith, which is known as the Iláhí religion, and is a sort of Sun-worship. He was himself a strict monotheist. But he considered the Sun to be the most glorious image of the Almighty Being in this world.

The Iláhí religion.

He abolished the taxes on Hindu pilgrims, from which Musalman sovereigns had previously derived a considerable portion of their revenue. He discouraged the study of the Arabic language, and induced the Musalmans to adopt Persian, instead of Arabic, names. The study of Sanskrit, on the other hand, received great encouragement from him. A Musalman historian says that no one who could not translate Sanskrit works into Persian, had any chance of obtaining office under the State.

Cultivation of Sanskrit.

The Rámáyana, Mahábhárata, Kathá-sarit-ságara, and numerous other Sanskrit works were translated into Persian during his reign. Urdu and Hindí poets received every encouragement from him. He was fond of music, and invited Miyán Tánsen from the court of Bághelkhund, and conferred high honours on him. From early childhood, Akbar was occupied with war and politics, and thus had few opportunities of studying science and literature. Two brothers, Faizi and Abul Fazl, were his great authorities in matters relating to letters and erudition. Faizi was the first Musalman to study Sanskrit Philosophy. Both the brothers were great scholars. They were men of irreproachable character; but they had no faith in any religion, and the Musalmans denounced them as atheists. Prince Salím hated Abul Fazl so much that he induced the king of a mountainous territory, by rich presents, to assassinate him. Akbar was so deeply affected by the news of his assassination that he touched no food or drink for three

Faizi and Abul Fazl.

days together. Akbar was a great lover of wit and raillery. Vírbal, a Bhàt Bráhman, was the great wit of his court. Vírbal was sent with a large army against the Yúsafzais and other wild tribes inhabiting the Sulaimán range, and lost his life there. His death also moved Akbar greatly.

His revenue administration.

Akbar divided his empire into fifteen *Subas* (provinces), each of which was presided over by a Subadár (governor of a province), who maintained the peace of the Suba under his charge. There was also a Diván (revenue officer) in each Suba. The collection of revenue was the principal function of the Diváns; but they also tried civil suits. Sher Sháh and Mahmúd Gáwán had made excellent revenue arrangements for Bengal and the Deccan. Sher Sháh had fixed the revenue at a fourth of the produce, but Akbar fixed it at a third. He caused a survey of the whole of Hindusthán to be made; classified lands according to their productive power, and introduced the system of payment in money instead of in kind. Rájá Todar Mall was Akbar's chief financier.

His army.

Akbar introduced the system of paying his troops at a fixed monthly rate. He was averse to the granting of jágirs to the soldiers. The generals, however, received jágirs for the maintenance of a fixed number of men. The umaráhs (noblemen) received commands of one to five thousand men; and no one received a higher command unless he was a man of proved and exceptional abilities. Commands of 12,000 were reserved for princes of the royal blood only.

CHAPTER IX.

JAHÁNGÍR (1605-1627).

ON the death of Akbar, his son, Salím, ascended the throne and assumed the title of Jahángir, or "Conqueror of the World." There was nothing to disturb the peace of Hindusthán at that time except hostilities with the Ránás of Udaypur. But Jahángír's eldest son, Khusru, annoyed at the accession of his father, raised the standard of rebellion in the Punjab and occupied the city of Lahore with his adherents. Jahángìr, however, lost no time in proceeding to Lahore and suppressing the rebellion, and seven hundred of Khusru's followers were impaled. Many of these belonged to the new sect of the Sikhs. Khusru himself was confined in the fort of Kabul, where he passed the remainder of his life.

Jahángír.

It has been already stated that, though Ahmadnagar was captured by the Mughals, yet the kingdom of the Nizám Sháhìs did not come to an end with that event. Málik Ambar, an Abyssinian officer of the State, removed the capital to Khirki, the modern Aurangabad, and made excellent arrangements for the good government of the country. Jahángìr sent three distinct armies, from Guzerat, Málava, and the Deccan, to suppress him. But Málik Ambar defeated them all and regained possession of Ahmadnagar (1610). The Deccani Musalmans, however, jealous of his power, deserted him, and he had no other alternative than to submit to the Mughals and surrender Ahmadnagar to them. Málik Ambar again seized Ahmadnagar and invaded Málava. But Khurram, Jahángìr's favourite son, compelled him to retire.

Málik Ambar.

Jahángìr had married a beautiful widow named Meherun Nisá and given her the title of Núr Jahán, "Light of the World." She gained such influence over him that he allowed her name to be associated with his own on his coins. She had a daughter by her

Núr Jahán.

former husband, whom she married to Jahángìr's fourth son, Shehriyár, for whom she tried to secure the succession. The ascendency of Núr Jahán gave umbrage to some of the great nobles; and Mahábat Khán, a general in his service, confided Jahángír in his own camp and tried to destroy her influence. But Núr Jahán was more than a match for the wily Mahábat and succeeded in rescuing her husband from his power. As long as Jahángìr lived, Núr Jahán's power remained supreme in the State. She was clever, intelligent, and energetic. She raised her father and her brother to high offices and governed both the emperor and the empire through them. Her partiality for Shehriyár alienated the feelings of Khurram and led him to head a rebellion against his father in Bengal. He was, however, pacified and remained content with the governments assigned to him.

Mahábat Khán.

Though Jahángìr was himself fond of wine and opium, yet he issued several edicts against the use of both. During his reign the Portuguese merchants introduced tobacco (so called from the island of Tabago in America) into India; but Jahángìr prohibited its use throughout his dominions. Sir Thomas Roe, the Ambassador of James I., king of England, came to India and had several interviews with the emperor on the subject of English trade with India. He succeeded in securing many valuable concessions for his nation. Much interesting information about the state of the country may be gathered from his letters. Jahángír died in 1627.

Sir Thomas Roe.

CHAPTER X.

Sháh Jahán (1627-1658).

Khusru and Párwez having died during the lifetime of their father, Jahángír's third son, Kurram, proclaimed himself emperor, under the title of Sháh Jahán, 'Lord of the World.' Núr Jahán made

Sháh Jahán.

an attempt to raise Shehriyar to the throne; but he was put to death, and Nur Jahán's influence came to an end. The first event of Sháh Jahán's reign was the rebellion of one of his generals, Khán Jahán Lodí, who made common cause with the king of Ahmadnagar and attempted to check the progress of the Mughal arms in the Deccan. After continual fighting for ten years, the rebellion was put down, and Ahmadnagar included within the boundaries of the empire of Delhi, in 1636 A.D. A Márháttá general tried his best to support the tottering fortunes of the Nizám Sháhí kingdom. But, unable to cope single-handed with the Mughals, he surrendered the kingdom to them and entered the service of the Bijapur State. This was Sháhjí, the father of Śivají, the founder of Márháttá greatness.

Annexes Ahmadnagar.

Sháh Jahán attempted to regain possession of a portion of the empire of Timúr. He conquered Badakshán, with the help of an army sent from Kabul, but he was unable to retain his influence in Turkisthán.

On the fall of the Ahmadnagar State, the kings of Bijapur and Golkonda were greatly alarmed. They tried conciliatory measures, but in vain. Sháh Jahán sent his third son, Aurangzeb as Viceroy of the Subas in the Deccan, with instructions to annex Bijapur and Golkonda to the Mughal empire. The history of Mir Jumlà in this connection has already been given in book IV., Chapter XII. These two kingdoms would certainly have disappeared if Sháh Jahán had not fallen seriously ill and his condition been declared hopeless, in 1658. On receiving the news of his father's illness, Aurangzeb hastily entered into treaties with the kings of Bijapur and Golkonda, and proceeded to Hindusthán to try his chance for the succession.

Mir Jumlá.

Sháh Jahán had four sons, of whom the eldest, Dárá, resembled Akbar in many things. He was a follower of the Iláhí religion and had translated several of the Upanishads into Persian. Learned men from many countries flocked to his court. Sháh Jahán loved him

Sháh Jahán's sons.

greatly, and he always remained with his father and assisted him in conducting the affairs of the State. The second was Sháh Shujá. He was an able general, but excesses had undermined his mental and physical constitution. He was Subadár of Bengal, Behar, and Orissa. The third was Aurangzeb, who was able and crafty. He was Subadár of the Deccan. The fourth, Murád, young and thoughtless, was Subadár of Guzerat.

Dárá's character.

The Musalmans had never approved of the innovations introduced by Akbar, and they consequently disliked Dárá, who followed his policy. Aurangzeb, therefore, to gain an advantage over Dárá, proclaimed himself a staunch Musalman and began to incite orthodox Musalmans against him. He wrote an artful letter to Murád, in which he declared that he was his well-wisher, and that his only object in taking up arms was to prevent the succession of Dárá, because if that atheist became emperor, the Musalman religion was likely to disappear from India At the same time he gave Murád to understand that earthly prosperity had no attraction for him, and that he would retire to Mecca, after destroying the arch-enemy of the Muhammadan religion. The unsuspecting Murád believed in these professions of his brother and joined him with the entire resources of the Suba of Guzerat (March, 1658). Yaśovanta Sinha, the Subadár of Málava, opposed the united army near Ujjayiní, in the interests of Dárá, but he was defeated and compelled to flee to his own country (April, 1658). The Rájputs were staunch supporters of Dárá, and with their help he defeated Sháh Shujá at Benares and returned to Agra, flushed with success.

Aurangzeb's victories

Sháh Jahán, however, gradually recovered his health and tried his best to put a stop to the civil war that was raging among his sons, but in vain. Dárá and Aurangzeb met in the vicinity of Agra, and Dárá was defeated in a sanguinary battle and compelled to flee to Delhi, in June, 1658. Aurangzeb took possession of Agra and sent a messenger to his father; but

Sháh Jahán would not consent to abandon the cause of Dárá. Aurangzeb, therefore, surrounded the palace with his trusty veterans; sent Murád a prisoner to the fort of Gwalior, and assumed the conduct of affairs under the title of Alamgír, "Conqueror of the World." Dárá in the west and Shujá in the east, however, were preparing for war. Aurangzeb, therefore, lost no time in sending his great friend, Mír Jumlá, against Sháh Shujá, and followed him with a large army. The brothers met at Kajoá, half-way between Allahabad and Etawa, in January, 1659 and, after a severe conflict, Shujá was compelled to retreat. Mír Jumlá pursued him to Bengal, and he fled to Arakan. The Buddhist king of the country afforded him an asylum for some time, but nothing is known of his ultimate fate. Dárá, on the other hand, finding Delhi untenable, fled to Lahore; from Lahore to Multan; from Multan to Bakkar, and from Bakkar to Guzerat, which declared for him and enabled him to collect an army. But Aurangzeb shortly afterwards met him near Jaypur, defeated him and compelled him to flee. The Jám of Jun, in Sindh, betrayed him into the hands of Aurangzeb, July 26, 1659; and he was tried by the Molláhs for atheism and infidelity and sentenced to death.

The character of Sháh Jahán.

The Indian empire was never so prosperous as during the reign of Sháh Jahán. He was a man of a mild disposition and never injured any one without cause. He always tried to do justice and was exceedingly popular. Following the excellent policy of his grandfather, he made no distinction between the Hindus and Muhammadans. He was fond of pomp and display. The Peacock Throne on which he used to sit cost him six crores of rupees. He built the Táj Mahál, at immense cost, over the grave of his favourite queen, Mumtáj Mahál, and he was himself buried there. This exquisite mausoleum is still regarded as one of the noblest buildings in the world.

CHAPTER XI.

AURANGZEB (1658-1683).

AURANGZEB became ruler of the empire in 1658; but he did not ascend the throne, or assume the title of emperor, before the year 1659. Secure on the throne, he found that Mir Jumlá had become very powerful, and, to keep him at a distance, he appointed him Subadár of Bengal. Two years after his appointment, Mir Jumlá led an immense army into Assam and easily occupied the capital. But shortly afterwards the rains set in, and an epidemic of cholera broke out in his camp and almost annihilated his army. He was compelled to retreat, and Jayadhvaja Sinha, the king of Assam, issuing from his hiding-place began to harass his rear. Defeated, insulted, and heart-broken, Mir Jumlá reached Dacca with a few followers and died shortly afterwards. Aurangzeb was greatly afraid of Mir Jumlá's power and ambition, and was unable to conceal his delight at his death.

Aurangzeb ascends the throne.

Death of Mir Jumlá

In 1666, Aurangzeb entered into a treaty with Śivají, the founder of the Márháttá empire, by which he undertook to pay him the *chauth*, or a fourth of the revenue of certain Subas, and to give his son a command of five thousand. Relying on this treaty Śivájí went to Delhi to seek an interview with Aurangzeb. Aurangzeb, however, gave him a seat with the umaráhs (nobles) of the third class; and, feeling insulted at this, Śivájí left the durbar. Aurangzeb kept him under guard and laid several plots for his assassination. But Śivájí was more than a match for the imperial hypocrite. On the occasion of a full moon he sent out large baskets of sweetmeats for distribution to the Bráhmans; and, when the unsuspecting Mughal sentinels were off their guard, he entered one of these baskets and left Delhi in it. Coming to a place of safety, he assumed the garb of a Sannyásí, and, in the course of a year, reached his capital, Ráygarh. The treacherous

Śiváji comes to Delhi.

conduct of Aurangzeb confirmed his hatred of the Mughals, and he resolved upon destroying their empire. The history of the Márhátta wars will be given in Book VII.

Re.imposition of the Jizya.

Aurangzeb re-imposed the invidious tax called *jizya* on his Hindu subjects in 1671. The Hindus had lived very happily since the abolition of the tax by Akbar; and its re-imposition created great discontent. The Hindu inhabitants of Delhi petitioned the emperor against it, but in vain. The Rájput generals next besought him to take off the obnoxious tax. But their prayer was disregarded, and they rebelled. It was with great difficulty that Aurangzeb succeeded in suppressing the rebellion, and it paved the way for the downfall of the Mughal empire. The majority of the Musalman umaráhs were foreigners, who came to India simply to try their fortunes. Every one was ambitious of founding an independent kingdom for himself. Aurangzeb's predecessors had succeeded in keeping them in check with the assistance of the Rájputs. But

Rájput revolt.

Aurangzeb's policy having alienated the feelings of the Rájputs, the emperor had to depend solely on the Muhammadan umaráhs, with the result that, shortly after his death, many of them established independent kingdoms, and thus hastened the ruin of the empire. In the wars with the Mughals, the leader of the Rájputs was Ráj Sinha, theRáná of Udaypur, whose extraordinary heroism and patriotism have elicited the admiration of European historians. Aurangzeb was unable to subdue him, and, after an arduous and protracted struggle, had to grant him favourable terms.

State of the Deccan in 1683.

While Aurangzeb, as Subadár of the Deccan, was engaged in the wars against the kingdoms of Bijapur and Golkonda, he had formed the ambitious design of extending the Mughal empire to cape Comorin by destroying these two Muhammadan kingdoms. The rebellion of the Rájputs for a long time prevented him from accomplishing his object; but now, relieved of the Rájput war, he set out in person, in 1683, for the Deccan with an immense army and selected first Burhánpur as the place for his encampment, and then Aurangabad. The twenty-five years which had elapsed since his march to the north to secure his succession to the throne, had, however, greatly changed the political aspect of the Deccan. Besides Golkonda and Bijapur, a powerful Hindu kingdom had been established by Śivájí. It was two hundred miles in length and one hundred in breadth, and was full of inaccessible mountains and impregnable hill forts. Śivájí was, indeed, already dead, but the spirit with which he had inspired the Márháttás survived.

CHAPTER XII.

AURANGZEB—*(Concluded)*.

WARS IN SOUTHERN INDIA (1683-1707).

The Mughals in the Konkan.

ŚAMBHUJÍ was the leader of the Márháttás when Aurangzeb marched to the south. Two or three of the principal commanders of Aurangzeb and his eldest son, Sháh Álam, were engaged in constant efforts for the destruction of Śambhují's kingdom. On Sháh Álam's approaching the Konkan, the Márháttás dispersed; and he took fort after fort, till the whole country submitted. But in the inaccessible mountains all his horses, camels, and oxen perished, and there was a scarcity of food in his camp. Śambhují seized the opportunity to harass him, and Sháh Álam had to take to flight. Aurangzeb removed his encampment from Aurangabad to Ahmadnagar and despatched a large force for the conquest of Bijapur. The Márháttás began to plunder the country behind him and set fire to the villages. The Mughal generals proving unsuccessful, Aurangzeb came down to Sholapur in person. The Márháttás entered Guzerat, plundered the city of Baroach, and made a treaty with the king of Golkonda to oppose the Mughals. Abul Hasan, the last king of Golkonda, had placed the entire responsibility of government in the hands of his Bráhman minister, Madan Panth. Madan Panth conducted the administration of the country with great ability, but that did not save him from the jealousy of Muhammadan nobles, especially of Ibráhim Khán, the commander-in-chief; and when the Mughals invaded the country Ibráhim Khán joined the invaders, and the Musalman inhabitants of the city rose against the Hindus and murdered the minister. Sháh Álam entered the capital and gave it up to plunder for three days. The king took refuge in the fort of Golkonda, and Aurangzeb made peace with him on very favourable terms, in 1686.

War against Golkonda.

Immediately after this Aurangzeb laid siege to Bijapur. A breach was made in the immense city wall, and through this Aurangzeb, who superintended the siege operations in person, entered the city, took the king captive, and declared the Bijapur kingdom at an end. The fall of Golkonda followed, after a brief interval, in 1688. After the fall of these two Muhammadan kingdoms, Aurangzeb sent his generals to conquer the small Hindu kingdoms in the south. The Márháttás took refuge behind the walls of their hill forts. Fortune was very favourable to Aurangzeb on this occasion. One of his generals, receiving information that Śambhují was passing his days in pleasure at Sangameśvar in the Konkan, suddenly attacked him and made him captive. He was brought before Aurangzeb, who asked him to embrace Muhammadanism. On this, Śambhují used such harsh and insulting language that Aurangzeb, immediately ordered his death, after having his tongue cut out and his eyes put out (1689). An account of Aurangzeb's further operations against the Márháttás is given in Book VII., Chapter II.

Fall of Bijapur.

Capture of Śambhují.

The resources of the Mughal empire were completely exhausted by the long wars with Bijapur, Golkonda, and the Márháttás, and there was no prospect of the last of these wars

Mughal and Marhátta armies contrasted.

coming to a close. The emperor began personally to superintend the siege operations against the Márháttá hill forts. and worked day and night like a common soldier. The Mughals had to incur immense expenditure in sending even a handful of men anywhere. They were compelled to make arrangements for supplies at every stage. For every hundred fighting men they had to employ two hundred camp followers. The Márháttá army, on the other hand, was differently constituted. Their horsemen even dispensed with saddles for their horses. A few *seers* of *chholá* (gram), tied at the end of their *dhutis*, was all the commissariat they needed. They required no tents at night; but slept under the spreading arms of big trees. It was difficult for Mughal armies to cope with such soldiers. The Márháttás never engaged in pitched battles. They plundered the enemy's commissariat; they ravaged the country in his rear and increased the difficulty of collecting supplies; they stole horses and camels from the enemy's camp. The Mughal troopers required special training and it was difficult to replace a soldier when he died or became incapable of active service. But every Márháttá was a horseman, and he required no special training to become a soldier. As the Mughal army diminished, the Márháttá army increased in number. The Márháttás had already exhausted the Subas of the Deccan by their ravages, and they now fell upon Málava and Guzerat. The Mughal empire could no longer bear the expenses of the war. The Márháttás re-conquered the hill forts, and Aurangzeb, in despair, fell back upon Ahmadnagar. There he died, on the

Death of Aurangzeb.

21st of February, 1707, completely exhausted in both mind and body, at the advanced age of eighty-nine, after a long reign of more than fifty years.

His character.

Aurangzeb sowed the seeds of the destruction which his posterity had to reap. The empire, the foundations of which were laid in the good understanding between Hindus and Muhammadans, was overthrown through their mutual strife. Aurangzeb tried to make himself popular with the Musalmans by oppressing the Hindus, and thus he made the once loyal Rájputs, the Sikhs, and the Játs his enemies. The Márháttás were from the beginning the enemies of the Musalmans. Aurangzeb never placed confidence in any one. During the earlier years of his reign, he always, took the precaution of sending two generals with an army, one, a Hindu and the other, a Musalman. But after the Márháttá and Rájput wars he rarely employed the Hindus, but sent one Mughal or Pathán general and one of his sons in joint command of the army. He never trusted his sons; but was always afraid lest they should some day reduce him to the condition to which he had reduced his father, Sháh Jahán. If a prince was sent against the Hindus, they artfully wrote letters to him, promising to support him if he attempted to ascend the throne; and they took care to have these letters intercepted by Aurangzeb. Prince Akbar, having roused his father's suspicions in this way, had to flee from the Mughal to the Rájput camp, from the Rájput to the Márháttá camp, and from the Márháttá camp to Persia, where he died.

CHAPTER XIII.

BAHÁDUR SHÁH (1707-1712 .

Bahadur Sháh.

PRINCE Sháh Álam having held a correspondence with Abul Hasan, the last king of Golkonda, a short time before the final overthrow of that monarchy, Aurangzeb's suspicions were roused against him. He was kept a prisoner at large in the camp of his father, and then sent to Kabul as Subadár. On his father's death, he assumed the title of emperor, changed his name to Bahádur Sháh, and lost no time in proceeding to Agra at the head of a large army. Aurangzeb's second son, prince Azim, was in his father's camp when he died. He proclaimed himself emperor and marched to Agra with the wreck of the Deccan army. In the civil war which ensued, Azim was killed, with all his family. Aurangzeb's third son, prince Kám Bakhsh, was at Hyderabad, and did not acknowledge Bahádur Sháh as emperor. Bahádur proceeded to the Deccan, and in the war that ensued, Kám Bakhsh lost his life. Zulfikar Khán was appointed Subadár of the Deccan, with the privilege of remaining at court and governing his Subas through his deputy, Dáud Khán. Dáud entered into a treaty with Rájá Sáhu, or Śivájí II. Bahádur Sháh brought the Rájput war to an end by virtually declaring Udaypur, Jodhpur, and Jaypur independent. But the Sikhs began to be very troublesome about this time. At the end of the fifteenth century, Bábá Nának preached a new religion and declared that God accepts the worship of any one, whether Hindu or Musalman, if it is conducted in a spirit devotion. The disciples of Nának were known as the Sikhs. They remained quiet for a long time at Lahore and in its vicinity, but the orthodox Musalmans were very hostile to them. Their *Guru* (preceptor) was implicated in Khusru's revolt in 1606, and many of the Sikhs were impaled alive. After the suppression of that rebellion, they expelled from Lahore and compelled to take shelter in the mountainous regions between the Jumna and the Sutlej. About the year 1675, the tenth Guru, Govinda, trained them in the art of war, so as to enable them to retaliate their wrongs on the Musalmans. But the Musalmans attacked their forts and captured them, killed every of Guru Govinda's family, and treated the Sikhs with great barbarity. Guru Govinda was sent to the Deccan, where he was killed by one of his personal enemies. The Sikhs now attacked the eastern portions of the Punjab, under the leadership of Bándá, destroyed the Masjids, killed the Mollábs, and put village after village to the sword. The Suba of Sirhind suffered most at their hands and they advanced as far as Saharanpur. But as soon as the Mughals put their army in motion, they fled to their hill forts. Bahádur marched in person against them and shut up Bándá in a hill fort. The fort fell into his hands, but Bándá escaped.

The Sikhs.

Bahádur Sháh died at Lahore, in February 1712; and, after a short struggle, his eldest son became emperor under the title of Jahándár Sháh He reigned for six months only He was a man of very licentious character, and the umaráhs soon became disgusted with him Azim Osháh the second son of Bahádur, was Subadár of Bengal, with liberty to remain at court and govern his province through a deputy In this case, the deputy was Azim Osháns son, Farukhsiyár Azim Osháh was killed in the war of succession, and Farukhsiyár, reduced to helplessness, had to throw himself upon the protection of Saiyyad Husain Ali, governor of Behar Husain Ali and his brother, Abdullá, the governor of Allahabad, collected a large army and marched towards Delhi In the war that ensued, Jahándár was killed and Zulfikar Khán beheaded as a traitor

Jahándár Sháh.

CHAPTER XIV

FARUKHSIYAR (1712-1719)

FARUKHSIYAR, on ascending the throne made Abdullá his vizier (prime minister) and Husain Ali his commander in-chief The two Saiyyads became in fact the rulers of the empire, and although Farukhsiyár often endeavoured to act for himself and to destroy their influence, he always failed He sent Husain Ali against the Rajá of Marwar and secretly instigated the Rájá to prolong the war Husain Ali was conscious that his long absence from Delhi would be ruinous to the interests of his family and he speedily brought the war to a close by entering into a treaty with the Rájá on condition of his giving his daughter in marriage to Farukhsiyár Husain Ali was sent to the Deccan as Subadár, while Farukh secretly instigated Dáud Khán, the Subadár of Guzerat, to oppose his progress The armies met, and Dáud was killed in the battle Farukhsiyár then incited the Márháttás to do their best to keep Husain Ali occupied as long as possible They needed no such instigation They troubled and harassed Husain Ali just as

The Saiyyad brothers

they had done Aurangzeb. But Hussain Ali, anxious to return to Delhi, made peace with the Márháttás (1717). The terms were that Rájá Sáhu should get back all the places included in the kingdom of Śivájí, and receive the *chauth* and *sardesmukhi*, that is the fourth and tenth of the revenue of all the Subas in the Deccan, and that he should pay a tribute of ten lakhs of rupees a year and keep a contingent of 15,000 horse always in readiness for the imperial service. Immediately after the peace had been concluded, Husain Ali left for Delhi, accompanied by 10,000 Márháttá horse.

Treaty with the Márháttás.

About this time Farukhsiyár was engaged in a conspiracy with a number of umaráhs for the ruin of the Saiyyad brothers; but his cowardice and vacillation so disgusted them, that they joined Abdullá. Husain Ali reached Delhi when the conspiracy had already fallen through, and had no difficulty in gaining possession of the palace and putting an end to Farukhsiyár's life (1719). Within six months of this event, the Saiyyads raised two scions of Bahádur's family to the throne in succession but both of them died of consumption. The brothers then made Muhammad Sháh, a grandson of Bahádur Sháh, emperor, in September 1719, and carried on the government in his name. Saiyyad Abdullá was indolent and fond of pleasure, and he had no liking for the work of vizier, which he entrusted to Ratan Chánd, an Ágarwálá Baniá, who managed matters in the interes his master with fidelity. The Musalman umaráhs were jealous of the power of this Hindu and headed several rebellions. There were, in fact, rebellions in every direction, to which the Saiyyads put an end by giving the rebels what they wanted. But at last Chin Kalich Khán, their mortal enemy, rebelled.

Death of Farukhsiyár.

Chin Kalich Khán was the son of Aurangzeb's favourite general, Ghází Khán, and was engaged in the wars in the Deccan. As he had many friends in that country, the Saiyyads recalled him and compelled him to take up the governorship of

The Nizam becomes independent.

Moradabad. This filled him with discontent, and he was the first to join Farukhsiyár in his conspiracy against the Saiyyads; but he was also the first to desert him, in renewed expectation of high rewards from the Saiyyads, and was enraged when they gave him the Subadárship of Málava, instead of that of the Deccan. He stormed the fort of Asirgarh and collected his adherents there. The Saiyyads sent an army from the north and another from the south. But he defeated both of them and assumed the Subadárship of the Deccan (1721). This was, in fact, the first independent kingdom that was established on the ruins of the Mughal empire. The kingdom is still in existence, and Chin Kalich Khán's descendants are still known as the Nizams of Hyderabad; he having received from the emperor of Delhi the title of Nizamul Mulk (Deputy of the Empire).

The Saiyyads were greatly alarmed at the assumption of so much power by the Nizam, in defiance of their authority, and Husain Ali resolved to proceed in person to the Deccan. Muhammad Sháh was about this time engaged in a conspiracy with a Turkish nobleman, Muhammad Amin, and a Persian merchant, Sádat Ali. This was not unknown to Husain Ali, and he resolved upon carrying the emperor with him to the Deccan; but after he had proceeded a few stages from Delhi, a fierce Kálmuk, stabbed him to death. After the death of Husain Ali, there was little difficulty in destroying his brother, Abdullá.

The Saiyyad brothers overthrown.

CHAPTER XV.

MUHAMMAD SHÁH (1719-1739).

THE emperor now gained freedom of action, with Muhammad Amin as vizier; on his death, the emperor sent for the Nizam and made him his vizier. The Nizam saw at once that the Delhi empire was doomed. Soon coming to distrust his minister the emperor tried to get him assassinated, but without success, and he left for his Suba in the Deccan. The emperor then made Kamáluddín his vizier, and Sádat Ali Subadár of Allahabad and Oudh. This was the origin of the Oudh family.

The Oudh family.

The Márháttas, not content with plundering the Deccan, now extended their operations to Málava and Guzerat. The emperor appointed Abhay Sinha, the Rájá of Márwar, Subadár of Guzerat, and Giridhar Sinha, Subadár of Málava; but the Márháttás conquered both countries, killed Giridhar Sinha with his whole family, and drove away Abhay Sinha. Another Subadár, Rájá Jay Sinha II, of Jaypur, made over Málava to the Márháttás and concluded peace with them. The whole country between the Narmadá and the Chambal was finally ceded to the Márháttas in 1738. In the following year, India was visited by one of those calamities which had so often overtaken her (1730).

The Márháttás in Málava and Guzerat.

In the beginning of the eighteenth century, Persia underwent a series of revolutions, at the end of which, Nádir, a soldier of fortune, belonging to the tribe of the Kazars, near the Caspian, took possession of Ispahán, the capital, and assumed the title of Sháh. Russia, Turkey, and Afghánishán felt the force of his arms. Emboldened by repeated victories over these powers, Nádir Sháh invaded India in the year 1739, with the sole object of plunder. Sádat Ali and the Nizam opposed his advance about a hundred miles to the west of Delhi, but without avail. Nádir encamped outside the walls of Delhi, and Muhmmad Sháh came to pay him a visit. In his crown he wore famous diamond, the Kohinúr. Nádir, seized with a desire to possess himself of it, gave him to understand that an exchange of turbans was regarded in Persia as a token of friendship. Thereupon Muhmmad, with his own hand, placed the crown containing the Kohinúr on Nádir's head and received Nádir's turbans in its place. While at Delhi,

Invasion of Nádir Sháh.

Nádir lived in the imperial palace, and a few days passed in peace. But the inhabitants of Delhi insulted the Persian soldiers, and often pelted Nádir Sháh himself with stones and even fired at him Enraged at this, he ordered a wholesale massacre. From early morning to 3 o'clock in the afternoon the city was a scene of rapine and slaughter, and numbers of house were set on fire Filled with pity for his subjects, Muhammad begged Nádir to put a stop to the massacre, whereupon Nádir issued an order to stop it, and such was the discipline of his army that the order was immediately obeyed Nádir plundered the treasury and seized all that it contained—money, jewels, and even the Peacok Throne—pillaged the houses of the wealthy, collected revenue from every Suba, and then, re-seating Muhammad Sháh on the throne, and calling on the Indian umarahs to obey his orders on pain of incurring his severe displeasure, retraced his steps to Persia.

Sack of Delhi

CHAPTER XVI

MUHAMMAD SHAH—*Concluded* (1739-1748).

On the departure of Nádir Sháh, it was found that the Nizam and the Márháttás had already possessed themselves of the whole of the Deccan. Málava and Guzerat had separated from the empire. The Sikhs were very powerful in Sirhind and the Punjab. Bengal still paid the revenue punctually, but the Emperors had no hold on the eastern provinces Sádat Ali had made himself master of the provinces between Agra and Bengal. The Rohillas were virtually independent, even in the Subas of Agra and Delhi. The Játs had already occupied a portion of the Suba of Agra. Kabul, Kandahár, and the districts to the west of Sindh had been annexed to Persia. In short, the Emperor was emperor of India only in name. He had a small army, but it was dispirited and disorganised, and his authority was nowhere obeyed beyond his palace. Raghuji Bhonslá, the Márháttá Rájá of Nagpur, invaded Bengal in

1742. The Subadár, Ali Vardi Khán, appeared for help to the emperor, who ordered the Peshwa to proceed to Bengal.

The Márháttá invasion of Bengal.

The Peshwa promptly obeyed the order and expelled Raghují, but himself plundered the country. Ali Vardi Khán discontinued the payment of revenue and became virtually independent. About this time the Rohilla Afgháns began to interfere in the affairs of Delhi, and one of the greatest enemies of India appeared in Afghánisthán. This was Ahmad Sháh Abdáli. He was a favourite general of Nádir Sháh, and, on the dismemberment of his empire, had made himself master of Afghánisthán and gradually conquered Kandahár, Balkh, Kásmir and Sindh. Lahore soon fell into his hands, and he appeared on the western bank of the

Ahmad Sháh Abdáli.

Sutlej, with the intention of crossing over to Hindusthán, in 1748. But prince Ahmad, Muhammad Sháh s eldest son, opposed him there with a large army and compelled him to retire. The vizier, Kamáluddín, was killed in this battle; and the emperor, Muhammad Sháh, died a month afterwards. The Nizam and Rájá Sáhu also died in the same year. Thus all the leading men who had swayed the destinies of India since the death of Aurangzeb, died about the same time.

CHAPTER XVII.

SUCCESSORS OF MUHAMMAD SHAH (1748-1762).

ON ascending the throne, prince Ahmad appointed Sáfdar Jang, the nephew and heir of Sádat Khán, to the viziership, which had fallen vacant through the death of Kamáluddín. The

His second invasion.

vizier tried his best to put down the Rohillas, for the safety both of Delhi and of Oudh (1750). But they defeated the united armies of the emperor and the vizier (1751). The vizier, in despair, invited the assistance of the Márháttás, who greatly harassed the Rohillas. Ahmad Sháh Abdáli returned to India a second time (1751). Lahore fell into his hands, and he threatened to attack Delhi. This greatly terrified the inhabitants, who had the atrocities of Nádir's invasion still fresh in their memory. The emperor formally made over the Punjab to the invader, and thus averted the danger.

Affairs at Delhi.

The vizier, however, was much opposed to the cession, and this created a breach between him and the emperor, who thereupon took the advice of Gházíuddín, the grandson of the Nizam, and, with the assistance of the Márháttás, drove the vizier out of Delhi. Shortly afterwards, Gházíuddín murdered Ahmad Sháh and raised a son of Jahándár Sháh to the throne, under the title of Álamgír II. in 1754

The Abdálí sacks Delhi.

Ahmad Sháh Abdálí entered India for the third time in 1756 and presented himself before the gates of Delhi. The city was plundered and sacked, and Álamgír threw himself on the conqueror's mercy. Ahmad Sháh married a Mughal princess and caused another princess to be married to his son, and, in order to save the emperor's life from the machinations of Gházíuddín, appointed Najimuddaulá, a Rohilla chief, commander-in-chief of the Imperial forces. Gházíuddín, therefore, invited the assistance of the Márháttás. Rághava, the Peshwa's brother, took possession of Delhi, and Prince Ali Gauhar and Najimuddaulá saved themselves only by flight. Adína Beg, Ahmad Sháh's inveterate enemy, invited Rághava to the Punjab; and he soon

The Márháttás conquer Lahore.

overran the province and appointed a Márháttá its Subadár in 1758. The Afgháns thereupon fled precipitately to their country. The Márháttás began to talk of establishing a Hindu empire; and there was, in fact, no power in India that could successfully cope with them. But it was not long before two foreign powers appeared at the opposite extremities of Hindusthán and put an end to all their hopes. These were the English in the east and the Afgháns in the west.

At the time of the Márháttá invasion of the Punjab, Ahmad Sháh was engaged in the north-eastern portion of his dominions. On his return to the capital, he felt it to be absolutely necessary to put down the Márháttás, and, re-entering India in the beginning of September 1759, found, the Punjab an easy conquest, and advanced to Shaharanpur. Thereupon Gháziuddín put the emperor to death (1759); but the emperor's son, who was then in Behar, assumed the title of Sháh Álam II., and proclaimed himself emperor there. Ahmad Sháh met and defeated a detachment of the Márháttás, but they pushed forward a large army against him, under the command of Sadáśiva Ráo Bháo. Sadáśiva rashly resolved to risk a pitched battle, contrary to the custom of the Márháttás and against the advice of the experienced Márháttá chiefs, especially of old Malhar Ráo Holkar. In response to Ahmad Sháh's appeal to the Indian Musalmans, the Subadár of Oudh and the Rohillas joined him.. Both parties prepared for a decisive action, but neither ventured to begin. Both entrenched their camps. Ahmad Sháh paid for his supplies, and he had an abundance of them; the Márháttás, on the other hand, collected their supplies by plunder, and there was such scarcity of food in their camp that Sadáśiva Ráo sued for peace. But the Muhammadans, at the instance of Najimud-daulá, who pointed out the danger to the Indian Musalmans if the Márháttás remained in power, refused to grant it. Sadáśiva had no alternative now but to risk a battle, and on the 6th January, 1761, he advanced towards the Muhammadan camp under a well-sustained cannonade. His Muhammadan general, Ibráhim Khán Gárdí, attacked the Rohillas with such impetuosity that they were compelled to abandon the field. The Márháttás were on the point of gaining the victory, when Ahmad Sháh advanced with his Afgháns, having sent another body of soldiers to attack the Hindus in the rear. In a moment, as if by a spell, the whole scene was changed. The Márháttás fled precipitately from the field, hotly pursued by Ahmad Sháh. Sadáśiva Ráo and Viśvás Ráo were killed in the action,

Fourth invasion of Ahmad Sháh.

Third battle of Pánipat.

and Ibráhim Khán Gárdí was placed in confinement for accepting service under the Hindus. Thus, in the course of a day, the political future of India was entirely changed.

The fall of the Mughal empire.

The history of the Mughal empire may now be brought to a close. The emperors had become absolutely powerless, and were dependent either on the Márháttás or on the Afgháns even for their personal safety. Though the Mughal empire had already ceased to exist, it may not be uninteresting to give here a short account of the Imperial family.

The subsequent history of the Imperial family

In 1765 Sháh Álam II. granted the Diváni of the provinces of Bengal and Behar to the East India Company, who agreed to pay him twenty-six laks of rupees a year, and made over to him the provinces of Korá and Allahabad on condition of his remaining under British protection. For some years Sháh Álam II. held his court at Allahabad and enjoyed peace. But in an evil hour the emperor listened to the advice of the Márháttás and repaired to Delhi to gratify the empty vanity of sitting on his ancestral throne. The English thereupon discontinued his pension and sold Korá and Allahabad to the Nawáb of Oudh (1772). The Márháttás were at best lukewarm friends to him, and at last the ruffian, Rohilla Ghulám Kádir, blinded and imprisoned him (1787. The English gained possession of Delhi, freed him from confinement, and granted him a pension in 1803. On his death in 1806, his son, Akbar II., was acknowledged as the titular emperor and heir to the pension. On Akbar's death in 1837, the same privileges were also accorded to his son, Bahádur Sháh II. But Bahádur joined the Sepoy Mutiny in 1857, and for this crime he was banished to Rangoon, where he died in 1862. The title of Emperor of Delhi was abolished after the Mutiny.

BOOK VII.

REVIVAL OF THE HINDUS.

Introduction

THE Patháan emperors held the greater part of northern and nearly a third of southern India in military occupation. Colonies of Afgháns, or Muhammadan mercenaries from Central Asia, held the great centres of Hindu power and influence in check. The rest of the country was left almost to itself, and was rarely interfered with, if the Hindu Rájás owned a nominal allegiance and paid a nominal tribute. Defiance always led to hostilities, and wars were carried on with great brutality But still there were out-of-the-way places all over India, where, protected by mountains, forests, or rivers, the Hindu Rájás defied the power of the Muhammadans and developed types of civilisation on the ancient Hindu model, but greatly modified by the surrounding Muhammadan influence

Condition of India under the Pathán emperors.

The dismemberment of the Pathán empire had simply the effect of decentralising Muhammadan power, and, instead of one, there were nearly a dozen Muhammadan capitals. Immigration of sturdy and powerful races from Central Asia still continued unabated, and these, being distributed over a dozen capitals, kept the whole country in a perpetual tumult; for it was to these small Muhammadan kingdoms that the Hindus owed the loss of their mountain fastnesses. During the fifteenth and sixteenth centuries, the principalities of Tipárá, Kamatpur, Bir-

Under the small kingdoms

bhúm, Orangal, Champánagar, Orissa, and others succumbed to the influence of these Muhammadan kingdoms. But, during these very centuries, friendly intercourse seems to have sprung up between the Hindus and their conquerors. The fierce spirit of proselytism, which characterised the Muhammadans during the imperial Pathán period, the spirit to which we owe the conversion of nearly a third of Bengal, half the Rájput races, the greater part of Káśmír, and vast tracts in Málava, Guzerat, and the Deccan had, to a great extent, abated. Intermarriage with the Hindus, their employment in the higher offices of the State and as military leaders, and the adoption of various Hindu customs by numerous Muhammadan families, made the beginning of an amalgamation of the races, or, at least, of mutual toleration.

Mutual toleration.

Akbar, with a profound insight into human character, adopted a policy which simply emphasized this spirit of toleration that had already sprung up between the races in the course of the previous centuries. Friendly intercourse increased, the Muhammadans began to respect and reverence learned Bráhmans and Sannyásís, while the Hindus also had recourse for spiritual instruction to Muhammadan Pirs and Fakirs. The thrifty Hindus began to grow in wealth and power, and became an element of strength in the Mughal empire. The small Hindu principalities, which still retained their independence, shared in the general prosperity of their co-religionists in the Mughal empire, and it often happened that these independent chiefs accepted military service under it. If the policy adopted by Akbar had continued to be the accepted policy of the Mughal emperors, the destiny of India would have been very different. But circumstances forced Aurangzeb to adopt a pronounced Muhammadan policy, which estranged the feelings, not only of his Hindu subjects, but also of the friendly Hindu chiefs. The Rájputs revolted; the Játs created disturbances in the immediate vicinity of the capital; the Sikhs, unable to bear a most inhuman perse-

Akbar's policy of conciliation.

Intolerance of Aurangzeb.

cution, took a religious vow to be avenged of their wrongs; the wild tribes everywhere made common cause with the Hindus; and the Márháttás determined, not only to establish an independent kingdom in the Muhammadan territories themselves, but to sap the very foundations of the Mughal empire by carrying violence and rapine from one end of it to the other.

Hostile attitude of the Hindus.

Beyond the limits of the Mughal empire, that is, in the extreme north and south of India, as well as in the forests of Central India, the activity of the Hindus was very great. In the Himálayan provinces it led to the foundation of the Gurkhá kingdom, and in the south to the consolidation of the power of the Maisúr State. Central India, never conquered by the Muhammadans, fell, to a great extent, into the hands of the Márháttás. The latter part of the seventeenth and the whole of the eighteenth century form a period of the revival of Hindu influence in the politics of India. It is proposed here to give a history of this revival with its consequences. It will be necessary, therefore, so far as the limited space at my command permits, to give the history of the Márháttás, Sikhs, and Gurkhás. Of these, again, the Márháttás were the most powerful, and, their history will therefore, occupy a much greater space than that of the other races put together.

Their political power.

CHAPTER I.

Sivájí.

Though the Márháttá country was annexed to the Muhammadan empire, yet there were many small independent Hindu kings who reigned in the Sahyádri and in the Konkan. After a severe struggle, extending over nearly two centuries, the Muhamamadans at last succeeded in subjugating these inaccessible strongholds of Hindu independence, under the

The Márháttá country under the Musalmans.

leadership of that estimable statesman, Mahmúd Gáwán. Though the country was subdued, yet the collection of revenues remained entirely in the hands of the Hindus, as in the other provinces of the Bahmaní kingdom. Every village was under the charge of a revenue officer named *Grámádhikári*, and every district under a *Deśádhikári*, *Deśamukhya*, and *Deśapándya*, who received a tenth of the revenue as sardeśmuhki, or the dues of a deśamukhya. After the fall of the Bahmaní dynasty, the Hindu deśamukhyas in Maháráshtra became subordinate to either the Nizám Sháhí or the Adil Sháhí dynasties. They used to collect revenue, garrison hill forts, and, in time of war, to fight under the standard of some Muhammadan general. Many of the deśamukhyas obtained extensive jágirs for distinguished services. Of these, seven large Márháttá jágirdárs served the Bijapur and two great families the Ahmadnagar State. Of the former, the Sawants of Wari still continue to rule a small sea-coast territory as feudatories of the British Empire. Of the latter the more powerful were the Yádavas of Sindhkeir, believed to have been descended from the Yádavas of Devagiri. This family was allied by marriage to that of the Bhonslás; and as both the families served under the Ahmadnagar State, a friendly feeling always subsisted between them. Sháhjí Bhonslá was married to the daughter of Lukhjí Yádava Ráy, and Śiváji, the founder of the Márháttá power, one of the children of this marriage, was born in 1627.

The great Márháttá families.

Málik Ambar, the Abyssinian chief, has already been mentioned in connexion with the history of Ahmadnagar. Sháhjí, his right-hand man, was a powerful military genius, and had considerable talents for civil administration. On the fall of Málik Ambar's party, Sháhjí set up a scion of the Nizám Sháhí dynasty and tried to revive the Ahmadnagar State; but failing in this, he left the Ahmadnagar territory, which was annexed to the Mughal empire, and accepted service under the Bijapur State. He was employed in subjugating the Carnatic on behalf of Bijapur, and

Sháhjí.

succeeded in establishing a small principality in Southern India, with its capital at Tanjore. It was at first dependent on Bijapur, but its independence was acknowledged in 1679. Poona formed the nucleus of his hereditary jágir in the Márháttá country, and he retained possession of it through all the varying fortunes of the kingdoms of Bijapur and Ahmadnagar.

Śiváji's minority.

When leaving the Márháttá country for the Carnatic, he placed Poona under the charge of an experienced officer, Dádájí Kondeo, who was also appointed to the guardianship of his youthful son, Śivájí. Śivájí soon became an excellent horseman. He was trained in a thoroughly orthodox Hindu fashion. The stories of the Rámáyana and the Mahábhárata inspired him with respcet for everything that was good in Hinduism, and he made a vow "to protect the Bráhmans and kine e[illegible] the Marha[illegible]sk of life." In the valleys adjoining Poona, there [illegible]ved the wild tribe of the Máwális. Dádájí tried to reclaim them; but Śivájí converted them into soldiers.

On the death of Dádáji, Śivájí assumed the management,

Śivájí as a jágirdár.

not only of Poona, but also of all the possessions of his father in the Márháttá country. He employed the entire resources of the jágir in increasing his army and in furnishing it with arms and accoutrements. As the jágir contained no hill fort, he, in 1646, took possession of Torna belonging to the king of Bijapur, whose anger at this act he succeeded in appeasing. In quick succession, Śivájí built Ráygarh, obtained possession of Sinhagarh by bribing the Muhammadan governor,

Capture of hill forts.

and usurped Purandar under the pretext of settling a quarrel between its varions claimants. All these were strong hill forts, and their possession emboldened Śivájí to such a degree that he ventured to plunder

Quarrels with Bijapur.

a convoy of treasure belonging to the Bijapur State. On this, the king sent for Sháhjí from the Carantic, cast him into prison and threatened to wall up its door unless Śivájí submitted. In vain did Sháhjí represent that Śivájí was not only a rebellious vassal of the king but also a rebellious son to himself. At this juncture, Śivájí wrote a humble letter to Sháh Jahán, offering to transfer his allegiance to that monarch. Frightened at this bold stroke of policy, the king of Bijapur released Sháhjí from prison, and, in a short time, at the intercession of his Hindu minister, Murári Panth, allowed him to proceed to the Carnatic.

Plunder of Mughal territories.

On the release of his father, Śivájí for the first time plundered the Mughal territory and secured a treasure, of three lakhs of rupees and three hundred horses These formed the nucleus of the famous *Bargir* (Márháttá horsemen), the terror of all India for over a hundred and fifty years. He admitted the Muhammadans into his army, and, with their help, conquered the whole of the Konkan, with the exception of Bombay, Goa, and Jinjira, belonging to the English, the Portuguese, and the Abyssinians respectively

Afzal Khán sent against him.

The king of Bijapur, enraged at the loss of the Konkan, Afzal Khán, a haughty Pathán general, to put down Śivájí Afzal Khán was offended at being sent against so insignificant an enemy, and Śivájí, on his part, gave out that he was very much afraid of Afzal Khán's power He, however, bribed a Bráhman officer of Afzal and through him arranged a private interview in which he treacherously killed Afzal with a deadly weapon called *Bághnakh* tiger's claw), which he carried concealed in his hand.

Takes revenge on Bájí Ghorpure.

On the death of the general and the dispersion of his army in 1659, the king himself took the field against Śivájí. But a fresh disturbance in the Carnatic compelled him to leave the war in the Konkan in the hands of Bájí Ghorpure, who, some years before, had treacherously arrested Sháhjí and brought him a prisoner from Tanjore to Bijapur. Śivájí suddenly attacked Ghorpure's capital, sacked it, and put him to death with his whole family. Shortly after this, Śivájí removed his capital to the impregnable fort of Ráygarh.

The famous general, Sháyista Khán, was sent against Śivájí by the Mughal emperor in 1661. Sháyista Khán captured several hill forts and fixed his residence at Sháhjí's house at Poona. But Śivájí suddenly attacked the house at night and killed his son; and Sháyista Khán narrowly escaped with his life. After this Śivájí plundered Surat, led a piratical expedition against Barsilor, one of the rich seaports of the Bijapur kingdom, and returned to his capital, laden with booty. He assumed the title of Rájá and began to coin money in his own name in 1664. Incensed at these reverses, Aurangzeb sent Dilir Khán and Rájá Jay Sinha to the Deccan. They began vigorous operations against Śivájí who, greatly alarmed, listened to Jay Sinha's advice and proceeded to Delhi. How he was received there, has already been narrated. To conciliate him, Aurangzeb conferred on him the title of Rájá and returned him the territories conquered by the Mughals; while the kings of Golkonda and Bijapur granted him the fourth and the tenth of the revenues of their kingdoms. Thus secure in his own kingdom, Śivájí directed his attention to its civil and military administration.

War with the Mughals.

Śivájí goes to Delhi.

Śivájí used to pay his soldiers monthly salaries from his treasury, and never allowed their pay to fall into arrears; but they had no claims to the plunder, which was credited to the State. He collected revenue according to the old Hindu custom and never allowed arrears to accumulate. He prohibited the collection of extra cesses. If a high officer or a Bráhman became his prisoner of war, he would release him without ransom. His council consisted of eight *Pradháns*, or chief ministers, with the Peshwa for their head, or *Mukhya-Prádhan*. The *Senápati*, or commander-in-chief, was also one of the Pradháns. A learned Pandit thoroughly versed in the various Śástras was another of them, with the title of *Nyáyadriś* or "overseer of justice." These and other civil arrangements occupied

His system of administration.

Śiváji for two years, at the end of which time he again undertook military operations against the Mughals. Aurangzeb had issued orders to his son, prince Sháh Álam, to arrest Śiváji.

War with the Mughals

On hearing this, Śiváji lost no time in taking the hill fort of Sinhagarh and occupying Kalyán. He also plundered Surat for the second time in 1670. Aurangzeb made several changes in the command of the Deccan, which gave the Márháttás only fresh opportunities for extending their plundering expeditions.

Śiváji in Karnát.

Śháhji died in 1671. Three years afterwards, Śiváji ascended the throne at Ráygarh with great pomp and assumed the title of Mahárájá. In 1677, Śiváji proceeded to his father's kingdom of Tanjore now ruled by his step-brother, took possession of his share of the paternal kingdom, and conquered several places belonging to the Muhammadans. In 1679, the Mughals laid siege to Bijapur, the king of which applied to Śiváji for assistance; and Śiváji plundered the Mughal provinces behind the besieging army so effectually that they had to raise the siege. The king of Bijapur, grateful for the services so promptly rendered, acknowledged him as the independent Rájá of Tanjore and the neighbouring districts. Śiváji died in 1680, at the age of fifty-three.

His character.

Śiváji was the son of a common jágirdár. But by his energy, tact, intelligence, and military skill he not only founded a new Hindu kingdom, but inspired the Márháttás with a spirit of resolute perseverance and indomitable courage, and turned a race of peaceful cultivators into a warlike nation. The majority of the great jágirdárs amongst the Márháttás remained loyal to the Musalmans, and only a small minority joined his ranks. But every Hindu wished well to Śiváji and rendered him assistance, direct or indirect. Beyond the limits of the Márháttá country also, the Hindus had acquired great influence. Murári Panth at Bijapur and Madan Panth at Golkonda were right-hand men to the Sultans; and the Musalman kings often relied on their Hindu generals. But none of the influential Hindus ever attempted to assert their independence. It was Sháhjí and Śivájí who resolved upon throwing off the Muhammadan yoke, in this Sháhjí failed, but Śivájí succeeded. The kingdom founded by Śivájí may be said to have been annihilated shortly after his death; but the national spirit which he had infused into the hearts of the people of the Márhattá country, created a great revolution throughout India and ultimately destroyed the Muhammadan supremacy and the Mughal empire.

CHAPTER II.

SUCCESSORS OF ŚIVÁJÍ (1680-1720).

Śambhují.

ŚIVÁJÍ's eldest son, Śambhují, a young man of a turbulent and licentious character, had been imprisoned in the fort of Pánálá by his father for misconduct. The Márhattá chiefs were not well disposed towards him, and efforts were made to keep the news of Śivájí's death secret. Śambhují, however, succeeded in obtaining the news, took possession of the fort of Pánálá, collected his adherents, presented himself at Raygrah, ascended his father's throne, and imprisoned and killed many who had plotted against him. Instead of carrying on the war with the Mughals vigorously, Śambhují employed the first few years of his reign in fruitless attempts to conquer Goa and Jinjira, which had defied the power even of his father. Aurangzeb destroyed the kingdoms of Golkonda and Bijapur, Śambhují looking on as an indifferent spectator. The affairs of the Márhattá State now fell into disorder. Remittances of revenue from the Carnatic ceased; the proceeds of plunder no longer reached the treasury and the hoarded treasure of Śivájí became exhausted. Śambhují enhanced the rents of the cultivators; but this merely spread discontent among the Márhattás. How, in this state of things, Aurangzeb attacked Śambhují, has already been described in Book VI. Ch. XII.

On Śambhují's death, in 1689, his minor son, Śivájí II., was raised the to throne, and his brother, Rájá Rám, became regent.

Aurangzeb now entrusted the conduct of the war to Zulfikár Khán. A Márháttá chief betrayed the capital, Ráygarh, into the hands of the Mughal general, and young Śivájí II. and his mother were taken prisoners. Aurangzeb kept them in confinement in his own seraglio. He used to call Śivájí and Śambhují thieves; so he gave the minor Śivájí the name of Sáhu, or honest man, by which name Śivájí II. is known in history. Aurangzeb liked Sáhu, got him married twice in his own camp, and granted him extensive jágirs. But he never relaxed his efforts for the destruction of his kingdom. One by one, he captured almost all the hill forts in the Konkan. Rájá Rám, in despair, fled to the Carnatic, and established his head quarters at Ginji. He created a new appointment, namely, the *Pratinidhi* (or substitute to represent the king in his absence). As soon as the Konkan was completely subjugated, Zulfikár Khán was directed to invest Ginji. Up to this time, the Márháttás had been satisfied with collecting the chauth and sardeśmukhí the fourth and tenth of the revenue respectively, from the Mughal territories. The sardeśmukhí belonged to the king and the chauth was credited to the State. But Rájá Rám invested a new impost called *Ghásdáná* (forage money) to encourage the plundering chiefs. Rám Chander Panth was deputed to the Konkan to re-conquer the Márháttá forts and this he did with considerable success. The Márháttás began to plunder the supplies of the besiegnig army at Ginji with such effect that Zulfikàr Khán was at last compelled to beg Rájá Rám to allow him to remove his camp to Wandewash. When Aurangzeb heard of this proposal, he pushed his camp on to Bijapur and sent a strong reinforcement to Ginji. The siege operations were carried on with vigour, and Ginji fell into the hands of the Mughals in 1698, but Rájà Rám escaped to the Konkan.

Rájá Rám Regent.

Rájá Rám king.

Siege of Ginji.

At the suggestion of Rám Chander Panth, Satára was made the capital of the Márháttá kingdom. But Rájá Rám never stayed anywhere long. He sent Kunde Ráo Dhábári to Guzerat and Párśvají Bhonslá to Berar to collect the Márháttá dues, and thus laid the foundations of the Márháttá kingdoms of Baroda and Nagpur. Aurangzeb now split up his army into two divisions, and, assuming the command of one of them, laid siege to the Márháttá forts. The command of the other was entrusted to Zulfikár Khán, with instructions to engage the Márháttás in the open field and to prevent their ravaging the country. Aurangzeb took Satára and many other hill forts and on one occasion Zulfikár pursued Rájá Rám so closely that he reached the fort of Sinhagarh, simply to die of exhaustion, in 1700.

War in the Konkan.

Rájá Rám's death.

Rájá Rám's eldest son became king, under the title of Śivájí III., and his mother, Tárá Bái, regent. Tárà Bái travelled constantly with her minor son from one hill fort to another. She convened a meeting of her *Sardárs* (chiefs), explained to them the dangers to which they and their country were exposed, and exhorted them to do their best to save their country from its enemies. They responded enthusiastically to her call and succeeded in re-conquering a large number of hill forts before the death of Aurangzeb, in 1707. But the Mughals set Sáhu at liberty, in order to sow dissensions amongst the Márháttás, and in this they succeeded. Many of the Màrháttá Sardárs took up the cause of Sáhu, when he ascended the throne at Satárain 1708. But Tárá Bái also had her adherents and determined to support the cause of her son. This gave rise to a civil war; and the Mughals tried to weaken both parties by supporting their claims alternately. In 1712, Tárá Bái's son died, and her adherents raised Śambhují II., the second son of Rájá Rám, to the throne and continued the civil war. In 1717 Saiyyad Husain Ali ackowledged Sáhu as the king of the

Śivájí the Third.

Rájá Sáhu.

Civil War.

Márháttás and made a treaty with him (see Book VI. Ch. XIV). This event gave Sáhu a preponderating influence in the Márháttá country. But Śambhují occupied the greater portion of the Sahyádri and established his capital at Kolhápur, and the civil war continued.

The subsequent history of Śivjál's family.

Bálájí Biśvanáth Bhatta, a Konkan Bráhaman, having greatly distinguished himself about this period by his ability in the work of collecting revenue, Rájá Sáhu appointed him *Peshwa*, (*lit.*, one who places papers before the king, that is, the Chief Minister) and succeeded, with his assistance, in obtaining favourable terms from the Mughals. Bálájí accompanied Husain Ali with 10,000 horse to Delhi and obtained from the emperor a ratification of the treaty made by that officer. On his return to Satára, Bálájí greatly improved the arrangements for the collection of the various kinds of revenue. He died in 1720, and was succeeded in the office of Peshwa by his son, Bájí Ráo. Sáhu recognised Kolhápur as an independent kingdom in 1730, and thus brought the civil war to an end. Rájá Sáhu died in 1748. The whole power of the Márháttá State had already passed into the hands of the Peshwá, who, on his death, raised Rám Rájá, a grandson of Rájá Rám, to the throne and governed the Márháttá empire in his name. The new Rájá possessed no power. Even the fort of Satára was garrisoned by the Peshwa's soldiers. The English annexed the Peshwa's territories and granted the Rájá of Satára independence in 1818. The last king died without issue (1848), and Satára became a British district; but the descendants of Śivájí are still reigning at Kolhápur.

CHAPTER III.

BÁJÍ RÁO PESHWA (1720-1740).

Bájí Ráo Peshwa.

BÁLÁJÍ BIŚVANÁTH BHATTA was the founder of the Peshwa family. But the man who made the Peshwa the real head of the Márháttás and the Márháttás the greatest power in India, was Bájí Ráo the eldest son of Biśvanáth Bhatta. He was handsome, modest and exceedingly popular, and acquired great aptitude for both civil and military pursuits at an early age. He was resolved to destroy the Mughal empire and to establish a Hindu empire in its place. He was the first Márháttá to penetrate into Hindusthán with a view to establish Márháttá ascendency there. Senápáti Dhábári and Pratinidhi Śrípati Ráo were his great rivals. TheSenápati had established himself in Guzerat, and the Pratinidhi had his head quarters at Satára. The Nizam was also an enemy of Bájí Ráo. He endeavoured to help both the Senápati and the Pratinidhi as against Bájí Ráo; but in both these attempts he failed. The Senápati lost his life in battle, and Bájí Ráo got the upper hand in Guzerat, where he appointed Dhábárí's minor son as Senápati, and Pilají Gaekwar, the founder of the Gaekwar family of Baroda, as his assistant. The Pratinidhi lost his credit with Rájá Sáhu, who made Báji Ráo Subadár of the Konkan and all in all at Satára. The Nizam had to pay heavily for helping the Senápati and the Pratinidhi. After discharging all the Márháttá dues, he paid a visit to Báji Ráo's camp and induced Báji to invade Hindusthán. The Subadár of Málava invaded Bundelkhund, the Rájá of which invited Bájí Ráo to come to his assistance. Bájí Ráo, who was then in Málava, promptly complied with his request and drove the invader out of Bundelkhund; and the Rájá gratefully made over to him the province of Jhansi in full sovereignty.

Jhansi acquired.

Kunhaji Bhonslá of Berar, showing signs of disaffection, was confined in the fort of Satára, and Raghují Bhonslá, the founder of the Nagpur family, favourite of Rájá Sáhu was sent to watch the Márháttá interests in Berar. Bájí Ráo having thus succeeded in consolidating his power over all the Márháttá chiefs, now turned his attention elsewhere. At the head of a large army, he next marched nto Málava, whence he wrote to Muhammad Sháh, urging him tofo rmally grant him the powers he had assumed in

Raghují Bhonslá

Guzerat and Málava, and followed up his letter by plundering Hindusthán up to the gates of Delhi Khán Daurán, the vizier, from Delhi, and Sádat Ali from Oudh, proceeded to oppose the Márháttás and though their united armies succeeded in cheking Báji s progress for a time, but he came in again and again and plundered the suburbs of Delhi in order to show the Mughals that they were powerless against him

Crosses over to Hindusthán

These events convinced the emperor of the helplessness of his position and he wrote pressing letters to the Nizam, earnestly soliciting him to accept the viziership He was appointed to the Subadárship of Malava and Guzerat in addition to that of the Deccan and all the tributary princes were ordered to join his army The Nizam encamped at Bhupal Bájí Rao completely surrounded the encampment with 80 000 horse The supplies were cut off and the transport animals carried away. The Nizam expected a reinforcement from the Deccan, but Bájí Ráo s brother advanced with the Rájá s body guard to oppose their crossing the Tápti The sufferings in the invested camp became intolerable It was indeed protected by artillery, but Bájí Ráo discreetly kept out of its range The Nizam at last, agreed to give Báji Rao the Subadárship of Malava, to cede to him all the territories between the Narmadá and the Chambal, and to pay him fifty lakhs of rupees from the treasury of Delhi (1738

The Nizam becomes vizier of Delhi.

Cession of Málava to Bají Ráo

In the following year, while Nadir Sháh was engaged in plundering Delhi, Báji Ráo and his brother wrested the islands of Salsette and Bassein from the Portuguese The Nizam, according to his promise, made over Málava and the other provinces to Bájí Ráo, who divided the country between his generals, Ranaji Sindhia and Malhar Ráo Holkar This is the origin of these two great families, who still rule Málava as feudatories of the British Empire About this time, Bájí Ráo resolved to punish Raghují for disobedience to the Rájá's

The Houses of Holkar and Sindhia

orders to proceed to Bhupal and for plundering Allahabad without permission. Raghují, however, saw the gathering storm and bent before it. At an interview with Bájí Ráo it was resolved that Raghují should invade the Carnatic and plunder it, while Bájí Ráo conquered the Deccan. But before these proposals were carried into effect, Bájí Ráo died, in 1740.

Bájí Ráo's character.

The early death of Bájí Ráo was one of the greatest calamities that befell the Márháttá empire. Both at home and abroad, he had numerous enemies; but none of them were successful in their opposition to him. The king was not always favourably disposed towards him, and he had often to undertake expeditions at his own risk. Owing to this cause, during the last years of his life, he became greatly involved in debt. His creditors often sat *dharná* at his door (*i. e.*, they declared that unless the debt were paid off they would take neither food nor drink; and in accordance with the rules of hospitality, the debtor also had to fast). A bold military leader and a successful civil administrator, he was in the habit of rewarding merit wherever found. Many of his followers became great rulers. He was ambitious beyond measure. In one of his speeches in the council of Rájá Sáhu, he boldly bade his Márháttá compeers strike at the withered trunk, and the branches would fall off of themselves. The eloquence and earnestness with which he pressed his advice, on another occasion, to carry the Márháttá standard beyond the Narmadá, moved the Rájá so strongly that he exclaimed; "You are the worthy son of a worthy father, you will plant it on the Himálayas."

CHAPTER IV.

BÁLÁJÍ BÁJÍ RÁO (1740-1761).

RAGHUJÍ's expedition to the Carnatic was eminently successful. Rájá Sáhu appointed Bálájí Bájí Ráo, the able son of Bájí Ráo, as Peshwa in August 1740, in spite of Raghují's opposition. The new Peshwa was exceedingly popular. In 1742, the Peshwa obtained from Rájá Sáhu the exclusive privilege of collecting the Márhátta dues from all the countries to the north of the Narmadá. The Sudadárship of Málava was his d ue after the death of his father, but the emperor granted it to another. Shortly after this, Bháskar Pandit, the Diván of Raghují Bhonslá, invaded Bengal by way of Rámgarh, defeated Ali Vardi Khán, the Subadár, and obtained two crores and a half of rupees by plundering the house of the banker, Jagat Set. The emperor begged Bálájí Bájí Ráo to save Bengal, which he did promptly and effectually. In return he granted him the Subadárship which he so much coveted.

Bálájí Bájí Ráo Peshwa.

Bháskar Pandit in Bengal.

Foiled in his enterprise in Bengal. Raghují proceeded to Satára, whither Damají Gaekwar, who, on the extinction of the Senápati's line, had become the real ruler of Guzerat, also repaired. Bálájí also presented himself at the capital and prevailed upon Rájá Sáhu to arbitrate the differences between himself and Damají, and Raghují. Rájá Sáhu made the following settlement. In return for the privilege granted in 1742, he now asked the Peshwa to part with Oudh, Behar, and Bengal, the prilege of collecting Márhátiá dues from which provinces was granted to Raghují; and Damají was required to submit an account to the Peshwa of all the booty obtained in Guzerat. After this settlement, Raghují proceeded to plunder Bengal, and Damají the territories in Guzerat that still remained to the Mughals.

Raghují and the Peshwa.

On the death of Rájá Sáhu in 1748 and the accession of Rám Rájá, the Peshwa made every arrangement for the maintenance of the royal household, and himself removed to Poona, which from this time became virtually the capital of the Márháttá empire. Rám Rájá agreed to accept everything done by the Peshwa as his own act. The arrangements with the various Márháttá chiefs were confirmed; and they were satisfactory to all the chiefs with the single exception of Damají Gaekwar, who was, however, compelled to make peace with the Peshwa on condition of dividing the present and future possessions of the Márháttás in Guzerat equally with him. In accordance with this treaty Damají and Rágnava, the brother and general of the Peshwa, led their combined armies against the defenceless Mughal territories in Guzerat; and Ahmadabad, the Mughal capital, soon fell into their hands (1755).

Events on the death of Rájá Sáhu.

Bálájí and Damají Gaekwar

The Nizam died in 1748. His eldest son, Gháziuddín, was the commander-in-chief at Delhi, and his second son, Násir Jang, assumed the Subadárship of the Deccan. The Carnatic was convulsed with internal dissensions at this time and Násir Jang had to go there in person. The victory of Ambar put an end to the commotions; but one of the Pathán Nawábs of the Carnatic stabbed Násir Jang to death, and his sister's son, Muzaffar, was also assassinated a short time afterwards in 1751. On the death of Muzaffar, Salábat Jang, the third son of the Nizam, assumed the Subadárship. Dupleix, the French governor of Pondicherry, greatly assisted him. He sent a number of French troops to Hyderabad under the French general, Bussy, and obtained a grant of the revenue of the Northern Circars for their maintenance. Bálájí Bájí Ráo thought he saw a good opportunity for appropriating a portion of the Nizam's territories, by supporting the cause of Gháziuddín against that of Salábat Jang, who, acting

Násir Jang and Muzaffar Jang.

Gháziuddín.

under the advice of Bussy, led an army against Poona. Sadáśiva Ráo, a grandson of the founder of the Peshwa family and Diván to the Peshwa, was sent against him, and he so effectually harassed the invading army by cutting off their supplies and stealing their transport cattle that they were obliged to fall back upon Ahmadnagar. Raghují, too, took this opportunity to get possession of the forts of Gwailgarh, Nárnála, and Mánik Durg belonging to Salábat. Gháziuddín came to Aurangabad about this time, and was joined by the Peshwa and a large number of the Deccan soldiers. Everything had been settled for his assumption of the Subadárship, when in an evil hour he accepted an invitation from his step-mother, and was poisoned by her. Gháziuddín's death made the position of Salábat Jang secure. But the Peshwa did not give up the districts in Berar assigned to him by Gháziuddín for the assistance rendered to him.

Ahmadnagar betrayed to Sadáśiva.

One of the officers of the Nizam made over the fort of Ahmadnagar to Sadáśiva Ráo for a handsome bribe in 1759, This led to a war between Salábat Jang and the Peshwa. But Salábat was not prepared for the war, and was obliged to sue for peace, which was granted by the Márháttás on condition of his ceding to them the districts of Daulatabad, Bijapur, and Asirgrah, yielding a revenue of sixty-two lakhs of rupees.

It was about this time that Rághava led a Márháttá army through Hindusthán to the Punjab and appointed a Márháttá Subadár at Lahore, the furthest point in the north which the Márháttá power had yet reached. But family dissensions proved the ruin of their cause.

Rághava in the Punjab.

Rághava returned from Attock, covered with glory, but without plunder. On the contrary, he brought home a debt of eighty lakhs of rupees, and so he was taunted his cousin, Sadáśiva. This taunt led Báláji into appointing Rághava Diván and sending Sadáśiva against Ahmad Sháh Abdáli as commander.

Events after the battle of Pánipat.

A description of the battle of Pánipat has already been given. Bálájí was on his way with a large reinforcement to assist Sadáśiva, and had already crossed the Narmadá when the news of the battle reached him. The Peshwa returned to Poona, to die of a broken heart in the course of six months. The Peshwas were at the zenith of their glory during the reign of Bálájí, and the Márhattá country attained great prosperity. This prosperity was due to the genius of Sadáśiva and Rághava, but the empire was lost through the wrongheadedness of both.

CHAPTER V.

MÁDHAVA RÁO (1761-1771).

The minority of Mádhava Ráo.

MÁDHAVA RÁO, the eldest son of Bálájí Bájí Ráo, succeeded to the Peshwaship in September 1761. He was then only seventeen, and Rághava, his guardian, conducted the affairs of the State. But in a short time the uncle and the nephew disagreed, and both Raghují and the Nizam fomented the quarrel. Mádhava Ráo, though a minor, saw that family dissensions threatened to prove the ruin of the only Hindu kingdom in India, and, presenting himself alone at his uncle's camp, voluntarily became his prisoner. Nizám Ali, the fourth son of the Nizam, had already supplanted his brother, Salábat Jang. He was dissatisfied with the conduct both of the uncle and of the nephew, and urged Janají Bhonsla, Raghují's successor, to assume the leadership of the Márhattás, promising him his entire support. The Nizam and Janají led their united armies to Poona, which they partially destroyed. Owing to the treachery of the latter, Rághava completely defeated Nizám Ali, who, however, came to the camp of the victor, and so flattered him that, contrary to the general usage of the Márháttás, he let him off with the cession of a very small district. Mádhava Ráo displayed so much courage in the war, that Rághava sent him against Hyder Ali in 1763. Mádhava Ráo obtained great advantages over Hyder, and now had time to punish Janají for his treacherous conduct in joining Nizám Ali and plundering Poona. He invaded his territory and appropriated a portion of it in 1766.

Rághava and Nizám Ali.

About this time, the English obtained possession of the Northern Circars from the Nizam, with whom they entered into an offensive and defensive alliance; Nizám Ali's object being to destroy the Márháttá power with their help. If Hyder Ali joined the confederacy, it would be formidable, and so Mádhava Ráo invaded Hyder's territories and compelled him to pay thirty-two lakhs of rupees as arrears of the Márháttá dues. Rághava attempted to divide the Márháttá possessions with his nephew in 1768, and was imprisoned and brought to Poona. After this event Mádhava Ráo took the administration into his own hands and lived for three years more; but during this period, he led several expeditions against Hyder and Janají, and extended the Peshwa's dominions at the expense of those two potentates. He sent his commander-in-chief, Biśvají Krishna, to Hindusthán; and the latter, being joined by Holkar and Sindhia, levied contributions from the Rájput princes and even from the Ját Rájá of Bharatpur, and plundered the whole of Rohilkhund in retaliation for the injury inflicted on the Márháttás by the Rohillas at the battle of Pánipat. Biśvaji induced Sháh Álam to renounce British protection and proceed to Delhi in 1771. While Biśvají was still at Delhi, young Mádhava Ráo died of consumption, and his wife burnt herself on his funeral pyre. Mádhava

Mádhava Ráo and Hyder Ali.

Biśvají Krishna in Hindusthán.

Ráo's younger brother, Náráyan Ráo, recalled Biśvají to the Deccan.

Character of Mádhava Ráo.

It is doubtful whether the Márháttás ever had a better administrator than Mádhava Ráo. He was able, bold, and discreet. He had many enemies both at home and abroad, but he kept them all in check and succeeded in extending the Márháttá dominions up to Delhi. His selection of officers was always judicious, and he employed some of the ablest men, such as Rám Śástrí and Náná Farnavis in the service of the State. Mádhava Ráo, though young, was absolutely fearless. On one occasion, Madají Sindhia delayed at Poona only four days after he was ordered to march: Mádhava Ráo sent for him, rebuked him publicly, and compelled him to leave Poona within twenty-four hours. Fearless himself, he delighted in finding moral courage in others. On one occasion, Mádhava Ráo had no time to attend to public business on account of some religious ceremonies. Rám Śástrí, annoyed at this, prepared to resign. But Mádhava Ráo justified his conduct by saying that he was a Bráhman, and he had done what a Bráhman should do. To this Rám Śástrí's bold reply was: "The performance of religious ceremonies is, indeed, the duty of Bráhmans, but not of those who rule empires. If you want to perform the duties of a Bráhman, descend from the *Masnad*." This sharp rebuke had the desired effect. Thenceforth Mádhava Ráo never again neglected public business for the sake of religious ceremonies. Every chief in those days was in the habit of exacting forced labour from his tenants. Mádhava Ráo abolished this system altogether. During his administration, bribery in civil courts became almost unknown under the careful supervision of Rám Śástrí. The only fault in Mádhava Ráo's character was that he often lost his temper.

CHAPTER VI.

MÁDHAVA RÁO, NÁRÁYAN (1771-1782 .

MÁDHAVA RÁO, on his death-bed, sent for his uncle, and, placing his younger brother, Náráyan Ráo, in his hands, exhorted him not to ruin the Márháttá empire by family dissensions. But in the course of a few months, Rághava, acting under the advice of his wife, Ánandí Bái, assassinated Náráyan Ráo, and, in order to divert the attention of the Márháttás from this atrocious deed, made extensive preparations for a war against Nizám Ali. But Rám Śástrí, convinced of his guilt, came to him and called upon him to take his trial at his court. On his refusal, he said: "The crime you have committed can be expiated only with life. Your family shall never prosper. I will not enter Poona so long as you rule, and I will never accept public service under you." So saying, he left Poona and retired into private life.

Murder of Náráyan Ráo.

Rám Śástrí's curse on Rághava.

Though Rám Śástrí resigned his appointment as Pandit Ráo, others continued at their posts. Rághava was very successful in his operations against Nizám Ali. The cunning Nizám Ali, however, adopting an attitude of humility, visited him in his camp, and placing the subadár's seal, in his hand, asked him to take any portion of his territories he chose; and Rághava, in a fit of generosity, returned the seal, saying he would take nothing. Nizám Ali returned to his capital, well pleased, but the Márháttás were greatly discontented. Sukha Rám Bápu, Náná Farnavis, and other old servants returned to Poona, and raising the posthumous child of Náráyan Ráo to the throne, governed the Márháttá State in his name. This child was Mádhava Ráo Náráyan. All the old servants of the State joined his party, and Sindhia supported him.

Mádhava Ráo Náráyan.

Rághava's partisans began, one by one, to desert him, and he was obliged to throw himself on the mercy of the Government of Bombay, and enter into a treaty at Surat, in 1775, with the English, who assisted him with men and money. He obtained several victories over the ministers; but the Supreme Government disapproved of the action of the Government of Bombay, and the English withdrew. The Governor-General sent an ambassador from Calcutta to enter into a fresh treaty with the ministers, by which the English agreed not to assist Rághava. This is known as the treaty of Purandar (1776)

The first Márhá-ttá war.

The treaty of Purandar.

After the treaty of Purandar, two parties were [illegible]med at Poona, headed by Náná and his uncle, Morábá, respectively. The rising fortune of Náná made his uncle extremely jealous of him, and he resolved to make Rághava Peshwa again. Holkar declared for his party, and Morábá invited the Bombay Government to help him with men and money. The Supreme Government took up the cause of Morábá and sent a strong contingent from Bengal to Poona. The Bombay Government engaged in the war with alacrity, and arranged with Rághava that he should be the guardian of the minor Peshwa. The English crossed the Western Gháts, and on January 9th, 1776, their army reached Tulligram, only eighteen miles from Poona. Náná Farnavis had previously destroyed that place, and he now threatened to destroy all the villages between it and Poona, and even to set fire to the capital itself. Under the circumstances the English resolved to retreat, the Márháttás pursuing them closely. They were at last obliged to enter into a convention at Wargáon, in 1779, the conditions of which, being very unfavourable, were rejected by the Governor-General.

The second Márháttá war.

Convention of Wargáon.

The Government of Bombay made great preparations for the war and, on hearing that Captain Goddard had reached Central India from Bengal, requested him to come to Bombay. The Governor-General sent another expedition through Central India. The fort of Gwalior fell into the hands of the English, and they stormed the fort of Ahmadabad in Guzerat, and conquered the greater part of that province and the Konkan. The fort of Bassein, after an arduous siege, opened its gates to them. But, at this juncture, information was received at Calcutta that all the Márháttás (except the Geakwar), the Nizam, and Hyder Ali had formed a coalition to expel the English from India. Captain Goddard pushed on to Kolhápur, but, found further progress impossible. Dissatisfied with the way in which operations were being carried on in the Western Presidency, the Supreme Government, with a view to intimidating Sindhia, the principal supporter of the ministers, sent an army from Hindusthán to invade his territories. The army fell suddenly upon Sindhia's camp, and inflicted great loss on him. Sindhia was now compelled to treat, and obtained favourable terms in 1781. The following year (1782), through his good offices, the treaty of Salbái was concluded between the English and the ministers at Poona, by which the English agreed to restore all their conquests since the treaty of Purandar, with the exception of Salsette, Elephanta, and two other small islands, which were retained by them. It was also agreed that Hyder should be compelled to restore to the English all the territories that he had conquered from them. The infant, Mádhava Ráo Náráyan, was recognised as Peshwa, and Rághava received a pension of three lakhs of rupees a year.

Treaty of Salbái.

CHAPTER VII

MÁDHAVA RÁO NARAYAN (1782-1795)

AFTER the recall of Bisvají Krishna from Hindusthán (1773), the Márháttás lost all their influence in that country The Nawáb of Oudh, the Rohillas, and other Muhammadans were engaged in constant warfare with one another. Sháh Alam succeeded in regaining the whole of the provinces of Agra and Delhi with the help of his able minister, Najaf Khán. Najaf Khán died in 1782, and his son, Afrásiáb Khán, unable to maintain his position, sought the protection of Sindhia who joined him near Agra. Afrásiáb Khán was assassinated shortly afterwards, and Madají Sindhia easily made himself master of Delhi The emperor, at his instance, granted the title of Vakili Mutálak (Representative of the Empire to the Peshwa, and Sindhia remained at Delhi as the Peshwa's deputy, and was appointed Amiral Umaráh and Subadár of Agra and Delhi

Sindhia at Delhi.

In 1790 the English, the Nizam, and the Márháttás formed a triple alliance against Tipu Sultan, the king of Maisúr The details of the war are given in Book VIII Chapter V This war immensely increased the influence of Náná Farnavis in the Márháttá country

About this time Madaji Sindhia came to Poona His ostensible purpose was the investiture of the Peshwa with the title of Vakili Mutálak, granted by the emperor, but his real object was the destruction of the influence of Náná and the Bráhmans The ceremony of investiture was performed with the greatest pomp Sindhia ingratiated himself with the minor Peshwa, who was not well pleased with Náná Farnavis, a strict guardian Náná begged him not to listen to Sindhia's persuasions, but his influence with the Peshwa was nearly gone. Sindhia's general in Hindusthán obtained a victory over Holkar about this time, and this increased Sindhia's influence at Poona. But Náná

Sindhia at Poona

was soon relieved from his awkward position by the death of Madají Sindhia in 1794 He was succeeded by his nephew, Daulat Ráo Sindhia

Náná Farnavis now became supreme in the Márháttá country, and took this opportunity to accomplish one of the cherished objects of his life, namely the settlement of accounts with the Nizam Everything was favourable to his designs The army of Sindhia was present at Poona Holkar and the Rájá of Nagpur came with all their troops The Gaekwar sent a strong contingent Náná was not a man to lose such a favourable opportunity He wrote to Nizám Ali to pay up the arrears of the Márhatta dues The Nizam's minister requested Nána to come in person failing which he would be forced to come So there was no alternative but war

Battle of Kardlá.

The armies met at Kurdlá in 1795 The sound of the cannonade terrified the Nizam s Begums, who were in the field, and he retired to the fort of Kurdla As soon as he had left the battle-field his own troops plundered his camp, and the Marhattas obtained an easy victory The Nizam surrendered his minister, consented to pay three crores of rupees as arrears of the Marháttá dues, and ceded all the districts from the Tápti to Purindá Náná Farnavis now became the most powerful man in India, but his humiliation was at hand

The education, which Nana gave the young Peshwa, was of a very strict order He had always to remain in the Durbar, surrounded by old Bráhmans of Nana s party, and had scarcely time to breathe freely Raghava s eldest son, Bájì Ráo, was of the same age as the Peshwa

Báji Ráo

Bájí Ráo possessed a handsome person, a mild and docile disposition, and great conversational powers He was a good horseman and a good scholar, and the Peshwa was always anxious to cultivate his society But Náná set his face against this, and rebuked the Peshwa very harshly Humiliated and disgusted with life, Mádhava Ráo Náráyan committed

Suicide of Mádhava Ráo Náráyan

suicide, by throwing himself from the terrace of his palace, on the 25th October, 1795.

The event completely stupefied Náná, for, after Mádhava Ráo Náráyan, the succession devolved on Bájí Ráo.

CHAPTER VIII.

Bájí Ráo and the Overthrow of the Márháttá Power. (1795-1818).

Bájí Ráo II. made Peshwa.

NÁNÁ Farnavis resolved, after some hesitation, to support the cause of Bájí Ráo II. while his opponents set up Chimnájí Appá. But the influence of Náná in the Deccan was great, and he succeeded in raising Bájí Ráo to the Peshwaship.

Subsidiary Alliance.

In 1799 the Marquis of Wellesley inaugurated a new policy, in order to increase the influence of the East India Company. As the Márháttás used to say: "Let us have *chauth* and *sardeśmukhí*, and we will not molest you, or let others molest you;" so the English now began to say:—"We will undertake to protect your country from foreign invasion; we will keep a Resident at your capital and a body of soldiers; let us have either money or territory to meet the cost of maintaining the soldiers; if you wish to discipline your troops we will do that for you, but no European should be allowed to enter your service without our permission." This is known in history as the system of *subsidiary alliance*. After the Battle of Kurdlá, Nizám Ali entered into a subsidiary alliance with the English and lost his independence; and, because he did so, he was able to leave property worth four crores of rupees a year to his descendants. The English invited the Peshwa to enter into a subsidiary treaty, but Náná advised him to reject the offer.

Subsidiary Treaty with the Nizam

The fall of Tipu in 1799, as subsequently described, greatly alarmed the Márháttás, and they began secretly to perpare for war against the English. At this juncture, Náná Farnavis, the greatest of the Márháttá statesmen, died (1800). The ability with which he ruled the Márháttá empire for thirty years, during a period of confusion, disorder, and anarchy is wonderful. He could read a man's character as if by intuition. He had no liking for Bájí Ráo, and used to say that, if Bájí became Peshwa, the Márháttá empire would be destroyed; and, therefore, he was opposed to him. He was a great friend of Madají Sindhia; but, when that chief tried to make himself independent in Hindusthán and train his armies after the European fashion, under men like Perron and De Boigne, he cut off his connexion with him. He used to say that to fight Europeans with European weapons was simply to court defeat.

Náná; his death and character.

On the death of Náná Farnavis, Sindhia and the Peshwa fell out on the subject of the division of his property. Sindhia got the upper hand, and Bájí Ráo became a prisoner in all but name. But Sindhia had at this time to contend with a powerful enemy in Hindusthán. This was Yaśovanta Ráo Holkar, a natural son of Tukají Holkar. He had driven out his brother, Káśi Ráo, Sindhia's protégé. The regiments of Holkar, trained by Dudrenec, declared for Yaśovanta Ráo, and plundered Sindhia's territories. Sindhia hastily left Poona; but before he reached Ujjayiní, his capital, Holkar had already plundered it, and Sindhia, in retaliation, attacked and plundered Indore. On reaching Hindusthán, Sindhia found that Holkar had already gone to the Deccan, where he shortly afterwards defeated Sindhia's army in a pitched battle, and became master of the situation. After Sindhia's departure from the Deccan, the Peshwa had put to death many of the Jágirdárs, who were opposed to the interests of his father and of himself, and confiscated the property of others. Among those whom he had killed was Vittají, the

Sindhia and Bájí Ráo.

Holkar and Sindhia.

brother of Yaśovanta Ráo The sudden success of Yaśovanta's arms, therefore, filled him with alarm, and he fled from Poona, and, throwing himself on the protection of the English, entered into a subsidiary alliance with them This is known as the treaty of Bassein (1802) On the other hand, Yaśovanta Ráo raised Amrita Ráo, an adopted son of Rághava, to the Peshwaship, and began to plunder the country But, on the advance of the English with Bájí Ráo, Holkar fled to his own possessions, and Amrita Ráo consented to retire to Benares on a pension of eight lakhs of rupees

Treaty of Bassein.

Though Bájí Ráo had entered into a subsidiary alliance with the English, yet he sent his emissaries in secret to Sindhia and Raghují Bhonslá, and urged them to come to his rescue He excused his action on the grounds of the pressure of untoward circumstances, of the presence of the hostile army of Holkar at Poona, and of the absence of all friendly powers Sindhia and Bhonslá at his instigation, made war against the English, the results of which will be related in Book VIII

Its consequences.

During the whole course of this war, Sindhia and Bhonslá repeatedly urged Holkar to join them, but he held aloof Yaśovanta Ráo followed the Márhattá system of predatory warfare, and, his attitude becoming threatening, Lord Lake sent him several letters to ascertain his intentions, but in reply Holkar simply rose in his demands, and war became inevitable The results of this war, too, will be related in Book VIII

Immense sums of money were due to the Peshwa from the Nizam and the Gaekwar on account of arrears of Márháttá dues The English, who had now taken all of them under their protection, called upon Bájí Ráo to have these accounts settled. This demand he evaded under various pretexts On one occasion, the Gaekwar sent his minister, Gangádhar Śástrí, to Poona under a safe conduct from the English. But Gangá-

Bájí Ráo and the English

dhar was murdered. The English, greatly dissatisfied with Bájí Ráo, came to learn that Tryambakjí, the minister of the Peshwa, was implicated in this murder Bájí Ráo handed over Tryambakjí to them; but he escaped, and raised the standard of rebellion, in which he was secretly helped with money by the Peshwa Bájí Ráo also raised new levies But his new minister, Bápu Gokla, advising him to take measures publicly, Bájí Ráo placed him in entire charge of the preparations

New treaty with Bájí Ráo

The English, displeased with the conduct of Bájí Ráo, compelled him, in 1817, to enter into a treaty with them by which his powers were considerably curtailed He was prohibited from sending ambassadors beyond his own territories, or entertaining foreign ambassadors at his court, in other words, he was forbidden any longer to consider himself as the head of the Márháttá confederacy This treaty touched him to the quick, and hastened his preparation for war.

The Pindáris

About this time, the Pindáris became very troublesome in Central India They were accustomed to follow the Márháttá camps and subsist by plunder, but when the Márháttá powers gave up plundering, and began to train regular soldiers, the presence of the Pindáris became unwelcome in their camps After the Márháttá wars of 1803-5, they exhausted all the Native States of Central India, and then fell upon British territory The Pindáris made no distinction of caste or creed, whoever entered their camp was welcome to join them

Their suppression.

The English now engaged in a war of extirpation against the Pindáris Three army corps from the north, south, and west converged upon them, and in a short time they were defeated and dispersed The remnant joined the standard of Bájí Ráo.

Bájí Ráo thought of outwitting the English by cunning He incited the Márháttá chiefs to make an effort to regain their independence, and all consented to fight under the leadership of the Peshwa. But the English sent a strong force to watch Sindhia's camp, and completely neutralised him. Holkar's army, in which the Patháns had the upper hand, however, marched to the Deccan, but was defeated at Mehidpur by Sir Thomas Hislop and Sir John Malcolm, on December 20, 1817 They consequently lost much of their prestige and power, and were not in a position to afford any further help to Bájí Ráo Appá Sáheb, the guardian of the minor Rájá of Nagpur, was the only person who was able to render him effectual help; and this he did Both Bájí Ráo and Appá Sáheb attacked the Residencies in their respective dominions almost at the same time. But, after six months of fighting, the Rájá of Nagpur submitted, and Appá Sáheb, the leader of the war party, fled to Lahore to seek the protection of the Sikhs. The English carried on the administration of Nagpur in the name of the minor Rájá

The battle of Mehidpur.

Nagpur Submits to the English.

The Governor-General was positive in his orders to the Bombay Government not to treat with Bájí Ráo. Consequently, after the death of Bápu Gokla, Bájí Ráo had to surrender at discretion The English took possession of his territories, reserving only a small district for the Rájá of Satára, Pratáp Śiva the son of Rám Rájá's adopted son He also was prohibited from holding any political relations beyond his own State

The surrender of Bájí Ráo.

Bájí Ráo, in surrendering made only one stipulation, *viz*., that his pension should not be less than that of his brother, Amrita Ráo, and so, with a pension of eight lakhs of rupees, he was made to retire to Bithur, a sacred spot on the Ganges near Cawnpur, which is said to have been the hermitage of Válmikí. Bájí Ráo's adopted son, Náná Sáheb, was the author of the massacre of the Europeans at Cawnpur during the Sepoy Mutiny. The Rájá of Nagpur dying without issue, his State was annexed to the British dominions in 1855. The Gaekwar had entered

Bájí Ráo at Bithur

into a subsidiary alliance even before Báji Ráo, and his State still continues to exist After the battle of Mehidpur, Holkar entered into a subsidiary alliance, and was compelled to part with Tonk Rámpur, which was given to his general Amír Khán, who also entered into a subsidiary alliance His family is still in possession of Tunk Rámpur Sindhia did not enter into a subsidiary alliance till 1843

The condition of the other Márháttá States

Thus the power of the Márháttás, who, in 1759, had formed the project of bringing the whole of India under one rule, and had succeeded in establishing their control over the emperor of Delhi in 1785, and humbling the greatest Muhammadan power in India in 1795, was completely and irretrievably broken The few Márháttá chiefs, who retained their authority after the year 1818, lost their prestige, and were reduced to the position of feudatories of the great power which, in the course of a century, brought not only all India but many countries beyond it under its sway

CHAPTER IX

The Rise of the Siks (1712 1809)

The history of the rise of the Sikhs has already been given in Book VII Chapter XIII After the death of Bahádur Sháh, Bandá again became powerful between the rivers Sutlej and Jamuná But he was at last made captive and brought to Delhi, where he and his followers were put to death with great barbarity The Musalmans made an attempt at this time o extirpate the Sikhs but were unsuccessful The Sikhs formed themselves into small bands called *Misls*, which plundered different parts of the Punjab There were altogether eleven of these Misls known in history The leaders of the Misls constructed forts, where they concealed the treasure gained by plunder, and whither they fled when pursued by the Musalmans The chiefs of these Misls were generally Játs professing the Sikh religion Each Misl could boast of five

The Musalmans and the Sikhs.

or six distinguished warriors, and contained from ten to twelve thousand fiighting men. The Misls were constantly engaged in warfare against the Musalmans, and often against one another. Adína Beg, the sworn enemy of Ahmad Sháh Abdáli, tried several times to take one of them into his pay in order to suppress the rest. But he was not successful. Of the eleven, the Fulkiá Misl established its sway to the east of the Sutlej. The ancestors of the Mahárájá of Patiálá, and of the Rájás of Jhind and Nábhá belonged to it. Alá Sinha of Patiálá, having rendered great assistance to Ahmad Sháh Abdálí, received from him the title of Rájá. The ancestor of the present Mahárájá of Kapurthalá was the leader of the Ahluválá Misl. Chhatter Sinha, the grandfather of Ranajit Sinha, was the chief of the Sukarchakiá Misl. The other Misls were all destroyed by Ranajit Sinha.

The Sikh Misls.

After the signal victory gained by him at Pánipat, Ahmad Sháh Abdáli returned to Afghánisthán, and the Sikhs issued from their mountain fastnesses and took possession of the whole of the Punjab. They constructed numerous forts to secure their new possessions, and practised great barbarities on the Musalmans. This induced Ahmad Sháh Abdálí to send his comander-in-chief to the Punjab in 1762. But the Sikhs put him to flight, drove away the Subadár appointed by the Abdálí king at Lahore and took possession of the city. Ahmad Sháh twice returned to the Punjab to punish them; but, as soon as he appeared on the scene, the Sikhs retired to their forts; and when he withdrew, they took possession of the country. During the reign of Aurangzeb, two of the minor sons of Guru Govinda had been buried alive at Sirhind. The Sikhs in 1763 invested the city in great force, killed all its Musalman inhabitants, and razed it to the ground. When Ahmad Sháh came to the Punjab for the last time in 1768, the Misls were the real masters of the country. In 1792, Ranajit Sinha succeeded to the small principality established by his grandfather, Chhatter

The Sikh conquest of the Punjab.

Sinha, and his father, Mahá Sinha. The history of the Sikhs from 1763 to 1792 is a history of the attempts of the various Misls to aggrandise themselves at one another's expense. It was during this period that Jamu was conquered by them, and the Musalmans lost their last hold on the Punjab.

Ranajit Sinha.

On succeeding his father in the leadership of the Sukarchakiá Misl, the first endeavour of Ranajit Sinha was to destroy the Misls to the west of the Sutlej He saved the country from an invasion by the Afgháns. He conquered Lahore from the three Sikh chiefs who had held different parts of it from the time of the expulsion of Abdálí's Subadár, and established his capital there In 1801 he assumed the title of Mahárájá and began to coin money in his own name. The Musalmans rose against him several times, but he put them down with a strong hand In quick succession, he conquered Kášmír, Jamu, Multan, Bannu, Derá Ghází Khán, Derá Ismail Khán, and other places. The Sikh Misls on the east of the Sutlej now excited his cupidity, but in 1809, they placed themselves under the protection of the English. Ranajit's kingdom has been destroyed, but the Sikh principalities on the east of the Sutlej are still in existence as the last remains of the past glory of the great Sikh nation.

Cis-Sutlej States under British protection.

CHAPTER X.

Nepal (1750-1814).

Nepal is a small valley in the Himálayan regions in the north of India The Musalmans never attempted to conquer it. The Hindus conquered it twice during the Muhammadan period; but the majority of the inhabitants were Buddhists. There were many small principalities in Nepal of which Khátmándu, Bhátgáon, and Lalitpattan were the chief. In the beginning of the eighteenth century, the Gurkhás made themselves masters of one of the succession of valleys which form the lower strata of the Himálayan regions known

The Buddhist kings of Nepal

as the Gurkhá valley. These Gurkhás claimed descent from the Ránás of Udaypur, and belonged to the Śaiva sect of the Hindus. Nawáb Mir Kásim of Bengal interfered in the politics of Nepal, but without success. In 1768, the Gurkhá Rájá, Prithví Náráyan, conquered the valley of Nepal and united the principalities of Bhátgáon and Lalitpattan with Khátmándu, where he established his capital. The Buddhist kingdoms, though not a part of the Chinese empire, claimed Chinese protection and used to send periodical presents to keep the Pekin Government in good humour. On the establishment of a Hindu kingdom in Nepal, the Chinese invaded the country in 1792. But Ran Bahádur, the Gurkhá Rájá, agreed to send rich presents to China every fifth year, and so saved himself from the hands of the Chinese. Firmly established in Nepal, the Gurkhás rapidly conquered Kumáun, Garhwal, Náhan, and all the mountainous regions from Sikkim to Kángra.

The Gurkhá conquests.

CHAPTER XI.

STATE OF INDIA IN THE EIGHTEENTH CENTURY.

Hindu activity.

DURING the eighteenth century, the Hindus made great progress in every department of life. The Mughal empire was overthrown by the military power of the Márháttás; the Sikhs destroyed the influence of the Afgháns in the Punjab; two kingdoms only remained to the Muhammadans, namely, those of Oudh and Hyderabad; and these were saved simply because they were under the protection of the English. But even in these the Hindus often held high positions; and in Kabul itself there was a Hindu finance minister, named Thákur Dás. In the English Presidenices the Hindus greatly assisted their new master; and Rájá Nava Krishna and Kánta Babu acquired great wealth and high honours by their faithful services to the English. During this century, Sanskrit learning flourished greatly in India. Jagannáth Tarkapanchánan prepared a code of Hindu laws in Sanskrit at the request of Warren Hastings. The name of Rám Śástrí, a great Márháttá scholar, has already been mentioned. Mahárájá Jaya Sinha II., of Jaypur, was a great mathematician. Appay Dikshita, a Bráhman of Karnát, wrote commentaries on the various standard works on philosophy and smriti, besides many original treatises of great value. The celebrated Professors of Nyáya, Jagadiś Tarkálankár and Gadádhar Bhattácháryya, flourished during this period. The Vernaculars were cultivated with enthusiasm, and many excellant poems written in almost every one of these languages. Many excellent histories in Persian were also written by the Hindus. In commerce, too, the Hindus were prominent; and there were many rich commercial houses both in Bengal and in the Márháttá countries. In works of public utility and religious architecture the names of two ladies stand pre-eminent, namely those of Ahalyá Bái and Rání Bhavání Ahalyá Bái was the widow of Malhar Ráo Holkar's son, Kundají, and ruled Holkar's territories for thirty years with great ability. She renewed the temples of Viśveśvara at Benares and Vishnupada at Gayá, and constructed many roads. Rání Bhavání's name is well known in Bengal for her numerous religious and charitable work in various parts of the country, especially at Nátore in Rajshahi and at Benares.

Musalman activity.

The Musalmans, though they lost their political supremacy, yet cultivated science and literature with great assiduity. Numerous histories of India were written in Persian by the Indian Muhammadans during this century. Of the historical works, the most important were the *Akbarnámá*, giving a history of Akbar's reign, and the *Aini Akbari*, containing a constitutional history of the Mughal empire. Both these works were compiled in Akbar's time by Abul Fazl. *Khafi Khán's* history and the *Siyarul Mutakkherin* are excellent works written in the eighteenth century. The entire foreign trade of India with the exception of what fell into the hands of the European nations, especially the English, was in the hands of Musalman merchants.

BOOK VIII.

BRITISH PERIOD (1599-).

CHAPTER I

BRITISH COMMERCE IN INDIA 1599-1755).

ON the 31st December, 1599, the celebrated Queen Elizabeth of England granted a charter to a body of English merchants for the purpose of trading with India and the neighbouring countries. This body of merchants is known as the East India Company In a short time the Company established factories at Bantam, in Sumatra, and at Surat in India The Portuguese opposed the establishment of these factories; and hostilities ensued in which they were worsted Sir Thomas Roe was deputed to the court of Jahángir by James I, king of England, and he obtained valuable privileges for the East India Company from that emperor in 1615 A. D. The English established their factories at Masalipatam in 1628, and shortly afterwards at Hariharpur in Orissa They began to trade at Balasore in 1633 and at Hughli 1650. They obtained the site of the present city of Madras from the Rájá of Chandragiri in 1639 and built there a fort, which was named Fort St. George. In 1661 Charles II.,

Early settlements of the Company.

king of England, married the Infanta of Portugal, and obtained the island of Bombay as her dowry Unable to govern it himself, he made it over, in the year 1668, to the East India Company, who built a fort there Śiváji, while engaged in plundering Surat, attempted, in 1664 and in 1670, to seize the property of the English also, but they protected it with so much courage and resolution on both occasions as to inspire Śiváji and the Márháttás with a lasting dread of their power The Musalman governors, about this period, frequently ill treated the Company's servants and exacted money from them Annoyed at these exactions, the English, in 1686, cannonaded and partly burnt the town of Hughli, and captured several pilgrim ships on their way from Surat to Mecca Incensed at their proceedings, the emperor ordered their expulsion from the Mughal territories, and their trade was stopped accordingly, but he was soon induced to restore all their privileges About this period, the French established factories at Chandernagore and Pondicherry, the Dutch, at Chinsurah, and the Danes, first at Dinemárdángá, and then at Serampur, and their rivalry, to a certain extent, affected the trade of the East India Company But that trade was much more seriously affected by the operations of a rival East India Company which was formed in Scotland The two Companies were, however amalgamated, in 1702 The English purchased the villages of Calcutta, Sutánuti, and Govindapur in 1692, and erected a fort at Calcutta, which was named Fort William, after the reigning king, William III of England Having thus obtained possession of Calcutta, Madras, and Bombay, they made these places the head quarters of their commercial operations, and called them Presidencies Each Presidency had a Governor with a Council, who governed the English according to English law and the natives according to Indian law, and superintended the commercial operations of the different factories within their jurisdiction.

The English traded in peace in India up to the year 1744. But, in that year, war having been declared between the

French and the English in Europe, the former sent a large squadron to Pondicherry, under the command of Labourdonnais, one of their admirals, and Madras fell into their hands

The English and the French in the Carnatic.

The Nawab of the Carnatic offering his services as arbitrator between the two nations in Southern India, Dupleix attacked and defeated him and compelled him to give up the English cause. Major Lawrence, however, arriving about this time with an English squadron, the English soon regained their prestige and besieged Pondicherry On the establishment of peace in Europe in 1748, all fighting ceased in India, and the English recovered Madras.

The Successes of Dupleix

During the course of these wars, Dupleix saw that a handful of European soldiers were able to cope successfully with ten times their number of natives He accordingly began to interfere in the quarrels of the native princes with the view of establishing French influence in Southern India, and in this he succeeded. The Nizam died in 1748, and his second son, Násir Jang, became Subadár But Muzaffar, the son of the Nizam's daughter, tried to displace his uncle and make himself Subadár Anwaruddín, the Nawab of Arkot, died in the same year; and his son, Muhammad Ali, and Chánd Sáheb, the son-in-law of the previous Nawab, were rival claimants for the vacant office. The English took up the cause of Násir Jang and Muhammad Ali, while the French espoused that of Muzaffar Jang and Chánd Sáheb After some months of fighting, Muzaffar Jang became Subadár and Chánd Sáheb, Nawab Thus the French had everything their own way. and Dupleix was appointed governor of all the districts to the south of the Krishná. Muzaffar, however, shortly after his elevation, died by the hand of an assassin, and the French at once raised Salábat Jang, the third son of the Nizam, to the Subadárship.

Clive at Arkot

Muhammad Ali, driven out of his father's province, threw himself into the fort of Trichinopoly, which Chánd Sáheb invested. Muhammad Ali sought the aid of the English, and Clive, who had come to India as a clerk and thrown up his appointment to join the army, advised the President to create a diversion in Muhammad Ali's favour by investing Arkot, the capital of Chánd Sáheb. The President accepted his advice and entrusted him with the conduct of the operations. With a handful of English and native soldiers Clive easily captured the place. Chánd Sáheb sent a large portion of the besieging army to Arkot to retake it, but with no success. The English, on the other hand, succeeded in sending a large force to Trichinopoly under the command of Lawrence and Clive, and Chánd Sáheb was defeated, tried for treason, and executed. The French thus lost their influence, and Dupleix was recalled. Bussy remained at Hyderabad, with a French contingent, in the service of Salábat Jang; and Clive returned to England. In a short time, however, on the eve of a great war in Europe, in which England and France were involved as allies of the contending parties, the East India Company sent Clive back to India to thwart the designs of the French. Clive was appointed commander of the Madras Army, and Admiral Watson, of the fleet. On reaching the coast of Bombay, they were requested by the President of the Bombay Council to suppress, in conjunction with the Peshwa, a Márháttà pirate, named Angriá,

Piracy suppressed.

who held the strong fort of Gheria, on the coast of the Konkan, and plundered ships of all nations. He was descended from Śivájí's admiral, and never acknowledged the Peshwa's authority. Admiral Watson destroyed the ships of Angriá, and Clive took his fort by land. After achieving this signal success on the way, Clive reached Madras just in time to learn that the English settlement at Calcutta had been seized by Siréjuddaulá, the Subadár of Bengal, and the English expelled from that province; and he and admiral Watson were sent from Madras for the recovery of Calcutta.

CHAPTER II.

Affairs in Bengal (1704-1772.)

Murshid Kuli Khán.

The eastern provinces of the Mughal Empire, comprising Bengal, Behar, and Orissa, enjoyed peace and prosperity in the earlier years of the eighteenth century, under the wise rule of Murshid Kuli Khán, who, in 1704, removed his head quarters to Mukśudabád, which from that time began to be called Murshidabád, after his name. He ruled the province for many years, first as Diván, then as Naib Názim, and finally as Subadár. He revised the land settlement of Akbar and considerably increased the revenue, which he used to remit punctually, and was consequently in great favour with the Imperial court at Delhi. On his death, which took place in 1725, his son-in-law, Shujáuddín, was nominated his successor, and he also governed Bengal with great ability for fourteen years. He was succeeded, on his death, by his son, Sarfráz Khán. This weak and indolent young man was soon deprived of his power by an old officer of the family named Ali Vardi Khán, who had great influence in the province. Ali Vardi Khán's

Bargir Hangámá.

reign was much disturbed by the predatory expeditions, known as *Bargir Hangámá*, of the Márháttás, under Raghují Bhonslá, Rájá of Nagpur, and his minister, Bháskar Pandit. Ali Vardi Khán implored the emperor to assist him, and the emperor requested Bálájí Bájí Ráo to relieve Bengal, as had been already related (*see* Book VII., Chapter IV).

Cession of Orissa to the Márháttás.

But, after the settlement of the matter in dispute between Bálájí and Raghují by Rájá Sáhu, Raghují again invaded Bengal and plundered the whole country to the west of the Hughli. Ali Vardi Khán, unable to resist him, procured the assassination of his general, Bháskar Pandit. This only enraged the Márháttás, whose depredations in Bengal increased; and after ten years of incessant warfare, Ali Vardi Khán was, at last, in 1752, obliged to pacify Raghují by the cession of the province of Orissa and by a promise to pay twelve lakhs of rupees a year, in lieu of the chauth of the provinces of Bengal and Behar

Ali Vardi Khán lived only four years after this pacification.

Sirájuddaulá.

He died in April 1756, and was succeeded by his daughter's son, Sirájuddaulá, who was only seventeen years old when he became Subadár Finding that the English, in order to prepare for war against the French, were strengthening the fortifications of Calcutta, he ordered them to desist and to dismantle the new works But, the English paying no heed to his orders, he marched against Calcutta with a large army and took possession of the city and the fort One of his generals confined a hundred and forty six English prisoners in a small room which admitted of no ventilation, and hundred and twenty-three of them died in the course of a single night This event is known in history as the Massacre of the Black Hole

The Battle of Plassey

The British authorities at Madras, on receiving the news of this terrible event, sent Clive and Watson to Bengal, and Calcutta easily fell into their hands The Hindu and Musalman grandees of Bengal, who were at this time conspiring against Sirájuddaulá, sought the alliance of the English, and Clive led an army to Murshidabád A battle was fought at Plassey on 23rd June, 1757, in which the English were victorious Sirájuddaulá fled, but was betrayed into the hands of Mir Jaffar and killed by his son The conspirators then raised Mir Jaffar to the Subadárship of Bengal, Behar, and Orissa The new Nawab reimbursed the English for all their losses and by his extravagance soon exhausted the treasury, which he tried to replenish by confiscations This led to rebellions in several of the provinces; and, had it not been for the English army and Clive, Mir Jaffar's government would have been overthrown. He had another serious danger to contend against, in the shape of an invasion of Bengal, headed by Ali Gauhar, the son of the emperor, who had received from his father the Subadárship of these provinces; but the promptitude of Clive and the courage of the British troops relieved him from this difficulty also.

Clive returned to England in 1760, and Mr. Vansittart, his successor, was induced by his Council to remove Mir Jaffar and to appoint his son-in-law, Mir Kásim, in his place. Mir Kásim engaged to pay large sums of money to the Company and to its servants, and, being unable to pay the whole, he made over the revenue of the rich districts of Burdwan, Chittagong, and Midnapur to the Company. This was the first territorial acquisition of the East India Company on a large scale. In a short time he increased the revenue of Bengal by nearly thirty per cent But he found that the English had really become masters of the country, and that, unless he succeeded in expelling them, he would remain a Subadar only in name. He accordingly removed his capital to Monghyr, where, beyond the observation of the English, he began to make preparations for war. But before these preparations were complete, a misunderstanding arose with the English on the subject of the transit duties. The Company enjoyed the privilege of trading duty-free, on condition of paying a small annual *peshkus*, or a consolidated sum. The Company's servants, about this time, not only asserted their claim to the same privilege, but allowed their native favourites to trade under its cover. Under the circumstances, Kásim abolished the transit duties altogether; and this led to hostilities. Mir Kásim's armies were twice defeated at Udvánálá and Gheriá (1763). Mir Kásim, thereupon, fled to Oudh, and on his way he put a number of English prisoners to death at Patna. The Subadár of Oudh and the emperor of Delhi espoused his cause and invaded Behar; but the allies were signally defeated by Major Munro at Baxar (1764). The Subadár of Oudh fled to his own country, while the emperor, without means or resources, loitered on the confines of Behar.

War with Mir Kásim.

The Battle of Baxar.

On receipt of the news of hostilities between the English and the Subadár of Bengal, the Court of Directors requested Clive to return to Bengal On his return, he found that the Council had already re-appointed Mir Jaffar to the Subadárship He at once proceeded to Murshidabád and made a treaty with the Nawab, by which the military defence of the country was made over to the English and the Nawab agreed to carry on the civil administration with fifty three lakhs of rupees a year This was the celebrated Double Government of Lord Clive, which was then regarded as a master stroke of policy After the settlement with the Nawab, he proceeded to Behar and obtained from the emperor the Diváni of Bengal, Behar, and Orissa; agreed to pay him twenty-six lakhs of rupees a year, and made over to him the provinces of Korá and Allahabad, which Nawab of Oudh was compelled to cede to the English Balavanta Sinha, the Rájá of Benares, who had supported the English, was confirmed in his possessions, and the emperor made a free gift of the Northern Circars to the English

Arrangement with Mir Jaffar.

The Company obtains the Diváni.

After settling foreign affairs in this way, Lord Clive returned to Calcutta and directed his attention to the better regulation of the government of the provinces The work of collecting revenue was entrusted to native officers, supervised by Englishmen The European troops of the Company mutinied, but Clive put down the mutiny with a strong hand The officers of the Company, who were ill-paid in those days, were in the habit of amassing money by private trade and by taking presents from the natives. To stop this Clive proposed to make over to them the profit arising from the monopoly of salt; but the authorities in England rejected this proposal.

Lord Clive's administration.

Warren Hastings came to Bengal as Governor in 1772 The debts of the Company then amounted to a crore and sixty lakhs of rupees, and the Directors were pressing for their payment. Before Warren Hastings arrived in India, the emperor, at the

Hastings as Governor.

instances of the Márháttás, had gone to Delhi, against the wishes of the English. They, therefore, stopped the payment of the tribute of twenty-six lakhs of rupees a year, and sold the provinces of Korá and Allahabad to the Nawab of Oudh for fifty lakhs of rupees. Both these sums went towards the payment of this debt.

The Rohilla war

The invasion of Rohilkhund by the Márháttás had reduced the Rohillas to great distress. The Nawab of Oudh was bent on appropriating Rohilkhund to himself, so that they were between two fires. They, however, paid forty lakhs of rupees to the Nawab, to enable him to purchase immunity for them from the hostility of the Márháttás. But the Márháttá army having been recalled to the Deccan, the Nawab had no occasion to pay them the amount. The Rohillas, therefore, asked him to refund it, which he refused to do. The Nawab, to avoid the risk of being involved in a war, single-handed, sought the alliance of the English, and, by paying them forty lakhs of rupees, obtained from them the services of an English contingent; and, with this help, he conquered Rohilkhund and annexed it to his extensive dominions (1774). Many people in England censured Hastings for hiring out soldiers on this occasion. But in defence of Hastings it is said that he was induced to help the Nawab, only because the loose confederacy of the Rohillas constituted a danger to Oudh and Bengal. Any Rohilla chief might any day bring in the Márháttás and disturb the peace of the English. By allowing a friendly power like the Nawab to absorb the Rohilla territories, Hastings simply ensured the peace of northern India.

Removal of offices to Calcutta.

Hastings removed all the offices from Murshidabad to Calcutta and took the Diváni into his own hands. He replaced the principal native civil officers by Europeans, and divided Bengal and Behar into several districts, presided over by Collectors, who were entrusted with the powers of civil Judges. The criminal administration remained in the hands of the Kázis, or Musalman Magistrates, as before.

CHAPTER III

Events in Madras (1756-1769).

Count Lally in Karnát

War was declared between England and France in 1756, and the French sent an army to Pondicherry under the command of Count Lally Shortly after his arrival, Lally took possession of Fort St David, on the Coromandal coast, which belonged to the English, and razed it to the ground. He then recalled Bussy from Hyderabad. This was a very impolitic step, for as soon as Bussy had left the Deccan, Salábat Jang lost his Subadárship and shortly afterwards his life also, and thus the French influence in the Deccan was completely destroyed in 1759. Lally now invested Madras; but, an English squadron arriving about this time on the coast, he was obliged to raise the siege

French influence destroyed.

Sir Eyre Coote defeated Lally at Wandewash, and, encouraged by the success, laid siege to Pondicherry, which fell into his hands in 1761 From this time the dream of a French empire in India vanished altogether The French have, indeed, recovered Pondicherry, but they have lost all their influence in India As in Bengal, so in Madras, the English from this time became supreme. Muhammad Ali, the Nawab of Arkot, was their protégé, and the native rulers, busy with their own quarrels, had no time to think about them.

The Northern Circars taken by the English

The English had long been anxious to obtain possession of the Northern Circars, the revenue of which Salábat Jang had assigned for the maintenance of Bussy's soldiers Clive induced the emperor to make a free gift of them to the English, but Nizám Ali, who succeeded Salábat Jang, refused to make them over. In their anxiety to get possession of the provinces, the English agreed to pay a tribute to Nizám Ali, and entered into an offensive and defensive alliance with him in 1766. This brought them into collision with Hyder Ali.

The Maisur State.

From the end of the fourteenth century, the Yádavas had reigned at Maisur as feudatories of the kings of Vijaynagar; but they had practically become independent after the fall of that kingdom. They grew more and more powerful, established their capital at Seringapatam, and extended the boundaries of their empire on all sides by annexing small Hindu kingdoms The old family of kings came to an end in 1733, and a period of anarchy and confusion followed, during which the Muhammadans selected Krishna Ráy, a scion of a distant branch of the royal family, and made him Rájá Krishna Ráj reigned nominally from 1734 to 1760 He was of an indolent disposition, and his minister, Nanda Ráj, was the real ruler of Maisur He appointed as one of his officers, a young adventurer named Hyder Ali, who soon rose to be commander in chief of the kingdoms Hyder next deposed the old king, made himself Sultán of Maisur

Hyder Ali

and conquered the whole country up to the Krishná in 1760 This brought him into collision with the Márháttás, the history of his war with whom has already been given in Book VII, Chapter V On Mádhava Ráo's return, Hyder defeated theRáná of Vednaur and obtained twelve crores of rupees by the plunder of his capital The possession of this immense treasure was the source of Hyder's power In this career of conquest, he reached the boundaries of the territories of the Nizam, who, thereupon, proclaimed war against him and applied to his English allies to assist him with soldiers But shortly afterwards he deserted the English and made peace with Hyder The English now became involved in direct hostilities with the latter, whose army invaded the Carnatic in 1769 and reached the immediate neighbourhood of Madras There was no Clive at that time in the Madras Council, and, alarmed at the presence of Hyder at their gates, they made a treaty the terms of which were very favourable to him It was, in fact, an offensive and defensive alliance on condition of mutual restitution of conquest

The first Maisur war

CHAPTER IV.

WARREN HASTINGS, GOVERNOR-GENERAL (1773-1785).

The Regulating Act.

THE East India Company, the main object of whose operations had hitherto been commerce, had now become rulers of extensive territories, in the government of which there were great irregularities and disorder. It often happened that the shareholders did not get their dividends, but their Indian servants, returned to England, after a short service, immensely rich. This drew the attention of Parliament to Indian affairs; and an Act, entitled the Regulating Act, was passed in the year 1772, by which it was enacted that the Governor of Bengal should be the Governor-General of the Indian possessions of the Company; that he should have four Councillors to advise him in the government of the country, and that a Supreme Court should be established in Calcutta for the trial of Europeans.

The first Governor-General.

Under this Act, Warren Hastings became the first Governor-General of India. Richard Barwell, Colonel Monson, General Clavering, and Sir Philip Francis, the last three of whom had never been to India, were the first four members of the Governor-General's Council. Sir Elijah Impey was the first Chief Justice of the Supreme Court.

The majority in the Council.

Shortly after the formation of the new Council a split occurred in it; Clavering, Monson, and Francis forming one party, and Hastings and Barwell the other. Questions were decided by a majority of votes, and Hastings lost all his power, the majority reversing everything he did. The three members came to the conclusion that Hastings was an oppressor and a tyrant. They resolved that the assistance afforded to the Nawab of Oudh in the Rohilla war was highly improper. They made a new arrangement with the Nawab of Oudh, by which the province of Benares was ceded to the Company, and Rájá Chait Sinha of Benares became their dependent. When the news of these dissensions in the Council got abroad, many persons came forward with complaints against Hastings. Mahárájá Nanda Kumár was one of them. By an Act of Parliament, the acceptance of presents from natives by an officer of the Company was declared to be a serious crime, and Nanda Kumár charged Hastings with having accepted presents from his son, Rájá Gurudás, on the occasion of the Rájá's appointment to a high office under the Nawab. The Councillors asked Hastings to credit the amount of the presents to the treasury. Hastings totally denied the charge and brought a suit against Nanda Kumár for conspiracy.

Mahárájá Nanda Kumár.

His execution.

While this suit was still pending, one Mohan Prasád preferred a charge of forgery against Nanda Kumár who was tried before Sir Elijah Impey, condemned, and executed (1775). The execution of Nanda Kumár is generally regarded as a great blot on the character both of Hastings and of Impey, but there is no evidence to show that Hastings had anything to do with Mohan Prasád's case. He had himself instituted a case and that was enough to crush his enemy. Even after the execution of Nanda Kumár, the dissensions in the Council ran high, but the death of Colonel Morson, in 1776, placed Hastings again in power by rendering his casting vote decisive.

Hastings in power

The history of the Márháttá war, undertaken at the instance of the Bombay Government, has already been given in Book VII, Chapter VI.

It has been related how the Madras Government was obliged to enter into an offensive and defensive alliance with Hyder Ali, in 1769. Shortly after this the Márháttás invaded his kingdom, and he applied to the Madras Government for aid, but in vain. This embittered his feelings against the English. On the French declaring war against the English in Europe in 1778, the latter possessed themselves, one by one, of all the French territories in India, till they came to Máhe, which was in Maisur territory. Hyder

Causes of the second Maisur war

requested them not to interfere with the French at Máhe, but they paid no heed to his request and captured the place. This led to hostilities with Hyder, who, with an immense army and a hundred pieces of cannon, marched towards Madras. Colonel Baillie opposed him, but had to surrender, whereupon Munro, who was marching against Hyder, had to fall back upon Madras Hastings now sent Sir Eyre Coote to take the command of the Madras Army Coote relieved Wandewash and signally defeated Hyder at Cuddalore (1781) The Dutch also declared war against the English about this time ; and the English took Negapatam from them Colonel Braithwaite, in command of an English force, was defeated by Hyder at Tanjore The French again sent a squadron to the Indian seas, which alarmed the English But, at this juncture, they were greatly relieved by the news of Hyder's death, in 1782 ; though, their veteran general, Sir Eyre Coote, dying about the same time, they were not in a position to reap all the advantages they expected from the event On the other hand the French general, Bussy, returned to India and entered the service of Tipu, the son of Hyder Ali Any apprehensions from Bussy, however, were of a short duration, as the pacification of 1782 brought the war with the French to a close, and Bussy was obliged to resign his command Shortly after his father's death Tipu proceeded to the Malabar coast to oppose an English contingent sent from Bombay Hastings was at this time straining every nerve to defeat Tipu Sultán , but the Council at Madras sent a messenger to him to sue for peace which Tipu granted, after some delay, on condition of mutual restitution of conquests This is known as the treaty of Mangalore (1783).

The second Maisur War

Hyder's death

The treaty of Mangalore

The Márháttá, Maisur, French, and Dutch wars cost the Government of India an immense sum of money, and the Governor General had recourse to extraordinary measures in order to meet this extraordinary demand for money, which gave handle to his enemies to raise an agitation against him in England.

It has already been said that the majority in the Council compelled the Nawab of Oudh to cede Benares to the Company, and that the Rájá of Benares became their dependent. Hastings now demanded from Chait Sinha, the Rájá, a payment of five lakhs of rupees towards the cost of the wars. The demand was just and reasonable, and sanctioned by the usage of the country; but the Rájá, though he was enormously rich, refused to comply with it and persistently pleaded poverty. Hastings proceeded to Benares to punish him

Chait Sinha.

This led to much fighting and great disturbances, during which Hastings's life was in danger. At last Rájá Chait Sinha, repeatedly defeated by the English, fled with the greater part of his wealth to Gwalior. In one of his forts was found a treasure of fifty lakhs of rupees. This fell to the soldiers as prize money, and the Government obtained nothing, but these proceedings increased Hastings's unpopularity

The Begums of Oudh.

Asafuddaulá, the Nawab of Oudh, owed the English about two crores of rupees, but he had no means of paying this enormous sum. His father, Shujáuddaulá, had given his step-mothers large sums of money and extensive jágirs, and the Nawab, since his accession, had been trying to get possession of this treasure, which, by law, belonged to the State But the majority in the Council granted the Begums a guarantee on the part of the Company. Now that Hastings pressed him for payment, he pleaded poverty and asked for assistance in seizing the treasure. Hastings thought this a good opportunity for punishing the Begums or aiding and abetting Chait Sinha, and sent an army to Fyzabad; but he got only seventy-five lakhs of rupees from them

Hastings's administration.

Hastings was an able administrator He made a settlement of revenue with the zemindars for five years, and this paved the way for its punctual realisation. The Supreme Court having attempted to extend its jurisdiction over the whole province,

Hastings delegated the appellate power of the Diván, now represented by the Governor-General in Council, to a new Appellate Court entitled the Sadar Diváni Adálat, and made Impey its Chief Judge Now Impey was Chief Justice of the Supreme Court, already established by royal charter, and was not subordinate to the Company But, having accepted this appointment under the Company, he was recalled, and the Court was abolished

His trial

Hastings was censured by the Directors for certain irregularities, in consequence of which he resigned his appointment in 1783 He left India in 1785 On his arrival in England he was very well received by the authorities, who would have granted him a patent of nobility but for his enemies, who impeached him in Parliament for high crimes and misdemeanours After a trial which lasted seven years, the House of Lords pronounced him 'not guilty' But the proceedings had reduced him to proverty, and the Directors of the East India Company, in consideration of his eminent services in India, granted him a handsome pension

CHAPTER V

Sir John Macpherson, Lord Cornwallis, and Sir John Shorf (1785-1789)

Sir John Macpherson was the senior member of the Supreme Council when Warren Hastings left India, and he became Governor Generel He governed the country for twenty months, and was succeeded in 1786 by Lord Cornwallis But

Lord Cornwallis

before his arrival, there was a great agitation in England on Indian affairs Mr Fox proposed that the Government of India should be transferred from the Company to the Crown and seven Commissioners appointed in England to superintend Indian affairs This proposal, however, did not meet with the approval of Parliament, and Fox resigned The new Prime Minister, Pitt the Younger, made a fresh proposal, which deprived the Company of all its powers, but not of its existence By his Bill, which became law on 13th August, 1784, he created a Board of Control for the purpose of supervising Indian affairs The powers of the general body of shareholders of the Company were reduced, and though the Court of Directors remained at the head of affairs, and, to all appearance, carried on the Government, they had to work under the supervision of the Board, which practically ruled India

The India Bills.

Lord Cornwallis introduced many reforms in the administration He increased the pay of the Company's servants so as to place them above the temptation of taking contracts or carrying on private trade. From this time forward bribery and corruption became almost unknown in British India He reduced the contributions levied from the Nawab of Oudh for military protection from seventy to fifty lakhs of rupees a year

Administrative reforms.

After the treaty of Mangalore, Tipu Sultán made many attempts to increase his power The Hindus in the western provinces of Maisur often resisted his authority, as a punishment, he forcibly converted a very large number of them to Muhammadanism and drove about two thousand Bráhmans to commit suicide to escape coversion This sent a thrill of horror through the Hindu world, and Náná Farnavis joined the Nizam in invading Tipu's territories Tipu, however, pacified them by the payment of a large sum of money and the cession of certain districts, and the war was brought to a close in 1787 In 1789 he invaded Travancore, which was under British protection, The English, therefore, were compelled to take up arms in defence of the Rájá But, before declaring war, Lord Cornwallis sought and obtained the co-

The third Maisur war.

operation of the Nizam and the Márháttás In the course of the war, which lasted for three years, Lord Cornwallis defeated Tipu in a general engagement at Ankerá, and took several hill forts by storm , and the Márháttás defeated his army at Simogá, with the assistance of a small English contingent (1791). In the third year of the war, his capital, Seringapatam, was attacked from different quarters, and he was forced to sue for peace He paid three crores of rupees as a war indemnity and ceded half his kingdom, which was equally divided by the allies (1792)

The Decennial Settlement

After the successful termination of the Maisur war, Lord Cornwallis returned to Calcutta and devoted himself to the good government of the Company's possessions Akbar had had the whole empire surveyed, the lands classified and the revenue fixed accordingly , and, though many changes had been made during the course of the next two centuries, the system in force was still mainly his The English made no innovations They were anxious simply to collect the revenue punctually, and made temporary settlements with the zemindars, sometimes for five years and sometimes for a year only In 1786 however the Court of Directors sent out instructions to make a settlement for ten years, holding out hopes that it would be made permanent if it worked well This was the Decennial Settlement

The Permanent Settlement.

Lord Cornwallis went further than this He granted the zemindars proprietary interest in the soil, and fixed the amount of revenue for ever. It was enacted for the protection of the tenants, that the zemindar should grant them leases as early as possible, and the Decennial Settlement was declared permanent on the 22nd March, 1793 The settlement has done much good to Bengal It has created a wealthy landed aristocracy bound by the strongest ties of interest to the British Government But, the provisions of the Act for granting leases to the tenants not having been enforced in the first instance, Government has been obliged, from time to time, to have recourse to further legislation for their protection.

Lord Cornwallis deprived the Collectors of their judicial powers, which he transferred to judges, appointed to take cognisance both of civil and criminal suits, an appeal lying from their decisions to the Governor-General in Council as Sadr Diváni Adálat These Courts had jurisdiction only over Natives of India, and the assistance of Pandits and Kázis was sought to explain the Hindu and Muhammadan laws to the judges.

Natives in the Public Service.

From this time the appointment of Natives to Government Service was restricted to Dárogáships of Police and Munsifships, the pay of a Dárogá being twenty-five rupees a month, and the Munsifs being paid by commission Lord Cornwallis sailed for England from Madras in October 1793, after having made the Company the greatest power in India, and in the same year the Company obtained a new Charter, by which their monopoly of Indian trade was partially abolished

Sir John Shore

Sir John Shore who had greatly assisted Lord Cornwallis in the settlement of the land revenue, was appointed Governor-General in his place. Sir John had resided in India for a long time and gained great experience in the work of administration During his Governor-Generalship the Márháttás defeated the Nizam at the battle of Kurdlá But the authorities in England being averse to the interference of their Indian officers in the affairs of Native States, he did not intervene Nawab Asafuddaulá of Oudh died in 1798, and a dispute arose about the succession. Sir John Shore went in person to Lucknow, and raising Sádat Ali to the Subadárship of Oudh, made a treaty with him by which Allahabad was ceded to the English and the cost of maintaining a British contingent was raised to seventy-four lakhs of rupees

At this time the Board of Control attempted to bring about an amalgamation of the Company's army with that of the British Crown This caused a mutiny of the Company's soldiers which Sir John had great difficulty in quelling, and, on his return from Lucknow, he laid down his office and left for England.

CHAPTER VI

Lord Wellesley (1798-1805)

Lord Wellesley.

Lord Mornington afterwards created Marquis of Wellesley, was appointed Governor-General in succession to Sir John Shore He was a member of the Board of Control and possessed some knowledge of Indian affairs Mr Kirkpatrick, who had long served as Resident in the Courts of Sindhia and the Nizam, came out in the same ship as the new Governor-General and gave him much information about the conduct and character of the native princes of India, from which his Lordship came to the conclusion that the policy of non-intervention, so much advocated in England, was unsuited to the country

On his arrival, he found that Tipu Sultán was engaged in an attempt to drive the English from India, that he had entered into a league with Nizám Ali, Náná Farnavis and the Afgháns, and that he had already concluded a treaty with the French Republic

State of India in 1799

The Nizam had a contingent of 15,000 men, trained by Raymond, a Frenchman belonging to the republican party Sindhia too, had regiments disciplined by Frenchmen. All this convinced Lord Wellesley that it was absolutely necessary to humble Tipu, and he ordered Lord Harris, the Commander-in-Chief at Madras, to march at once against his capital Lord Wellesley invited the Nizam to enter into a subsidiary alliance with the English , and the Nizam, having learnt from bitter experience that, unless protected by the English, his dominions would soon fall a prey to the Márháttás, readily consented (see Book VII Chap VIII)

The fourth Maisur war.

His anxiety to prosecute the war against Tipu with vigour, was greatly increased by a letter which he received, about this time, from Zemán Sháh, the Sultán of Kabul, informing him that he has arrived at Lahore with the intention of invading Hindusthán. Twenty-one thousand British soldiers and 10,000 troops of the Nizam's army marched from Vellore in the direction of Seringapatam in February, 1799 One of Tipu's armies was totally routed at Sedásir and the other, under Tipu himself, at Málavelli (1799 , whence he fell back, in hot haste, upon his capital Lord Harris, aware of the alarm which had taken possession of his mind lost no time in besieging the place, which is situated in the middle of the river Káverí Apprehending that the floods of the river might delay his operations in the rainy season, he made all expedition to bring the siege to a successful issue A breach having been effected in the walls of the city, the English advanced to the assault Tipu s soldiers fiercely opposed them at the breach, but in vain The capital was taken and Tipu s dead body was found lying near one of the gat s Lord Wellesley proclaimed the extinction of the kingdom of Tipu Sultán, and the ancient Maisur State was restored to the old royal famil of the Yádivas, who had been pining in captivity since the year 1760 All the members of the royal family were dead, except a child of five years of age, who was brought out of prison and made Rajá The English administered the country in his name, and Purníi, who had served Tipu in the same capacity, was made finance minister of the new state. Tipu's descendants were removed to Vellore, where they lived on pensions granted them by the English

The Hindu State restored.

What remained of Tipu s territories, after the restoration of the ancient State, was divided between the English and the Nizam The latter, however, made over his share to the English and entered into a fresh alliance with them, by which he agreed to maintain a larger number of British soldiers at Hyderabad than before Lord Wellesley offered the Peshwa a share of these territories on co ndition of his entering into a subsidiary alliance with the English But the Peshwa declined to accept the offer How Báji Ráo was compelled in the course of two years to reconsider this decision, has already been related.

Lord Wellesly pensioned the Rájá of Tanjore and the

Nawab of the Carnatic, and placed their territories under British officers; while as a countercheck to Zemán Sháh, he sent Captain Malcolm to represent the Government of India at the Persian Court.

Annexation of Rohilkhund.

The Nawabs of Oudh generally spent their time in pleasure and were never in a position to pay the stipulated amount of money for the maintenance of the British contingent at their capital. Lord Wellesley, therefore, induced Sádat Ali to commute the payment into the cession of Korá and Rohilkhund. The English gained two advantages by this transaction. They realised their dues punctually by administering the provinces through their own officers, and, the Nawab's territories being surrounded on all sides by British dominions, all anxiety on account of their protection ceased.

The authorities in England had always been opposed to territorial aggrandisement or interference in the affairs of Native States. The policy pursued by Lord Wellesley, which had nearly doubled their possessions in the course of four years, being disapproved by them, he resigned. But he agreed to stay for another year: and it was fortunate for India that he did so, for the Márháttás were about this time making great preparations for a war against the English.

Causes of the third Márháttá war.

The head of the Márháttá empire having entered into a subsidiary alliance with the English, Sindhia and the Rájá of Berar were filled with alarm. The English, in fact, now pressed their invitation on Sindhia to enter into a similar alliance; but he declined it, and joined the Rája of Berar in concerting plans for an invasion of British territories. Holkar was then at Poona and did not join the other Márháttá chiefs. The Governor-General sent armies from Maisur and Hyderabad to Poona and reinstated Bájí Ráo. Holkar had already left Poona before the arrival of the English.

While there was no doubt that Sindhia and the Rájá of Berar

were making preparations for war, they professed friendly intentions towards the English, and, in order to put an end to this ambiguous position, the Governor-General sent them an *ultimatum*, desiring them to withdraw their armies to their own territories, and undertaking at the same time to adopt a similar course himself. The allies declined this proposal, and war was formally declared. Sir Arthur Wellesley, brother of the Governor-General, advanced with an army from the south, while Lord Lake proceeded to Hindusthán. The fort of Ahmadnagar fell into the hands of the former. Sindhia made an attempt to plunder the Nizam's territories in the rear of the English army. But Sir Arthur Wellesley wheeled round and came upon him at Assai, where a battle was fought. The regiments, disciplined by De Boigne, fought with desperate valour to protect the guns. But the Márháttá army was unable to resist the charge of the British, and, after a well-fought battle, Sir Arthur Wellesley was completely victorious (August, 1803). He was engaged in many arduous wars in after life and became famous as Duke of Wellington; but it was at the battle of Assai, that he won his first laurels. In this battle Sindhia lost about 12,000 men, and nearly a third of the British army was killed. Shortly afterwards, Colonel Stevenson was despatched in pursuit of Sindhia. He stormed the fort of Asirgarh and occupied Burhánpur (October, 1804).

Battle of Assai.

Lord Lake, advancing from Cawnpur, stormed the fort of Koel, occupied Aligarh, and marched to Delhi defeating the Márháttá army which opposed him on the way. Delhi fell into his hands and the blinded emperor, after thirty years of suffering, again came under British protection. Agra shortly afterwards shared the fate of Delhi. A pitched battle was fought at Laswari on 1st November, 1803, between Lord Lake and Sindhia's French Generals, Bourquin and Dudrenec. The disciplined troops of Sindhia fought with conspicuous courage and performed

Delhi occupied.

Battle of Laswari.

wonderful feats of valour; but, though Lord Lake lost a great portion of his army, he was victorious. Orissa and Bundelkhund were conquered by the English in the same year, and Sindhia, being thus defeated both in the north and in the south, sued for peace. Lord Wellesley was willing to grant it only on condition that he should withdraw his troops from the east. To this Sindhia would not agree. A large portion of his army, with his famous park of artillery, was waiting at Argáon together with the entire army of Raghují Bhonslá. Sir Arthur attacked their combined forces at Argáon (November, 1803) and, after a short but well-fought battle, gained a complete victory. Gwailgarh and Nárnálá fell into his hands in quick succession. Alarmed at the successes of the English, Raghují made peace with them by the cession of Orissa and western Berar (December 30, 1803). He also relinquished all his claims upon the Nizam for *chauth*, *sardeśmukhi*, and *ghásdáná*. Shortly afterwards Sindhia also made peace with the English at Śirji Anjangáon by the cession of Hindusthán and Khándeś, and by relinquishing all his claims upon the Nizám, the Peshwa, and the Gaekwar.

Battle of Argáon.

Peace with Sindhia and the Rájá of Nagpur.

Between the capture of Ahmadnagar and that of Gwailgarh there elapsed only a period of four months. But during this short time the Márháttá power was completely broken. Daulat Ráo and Raghují were compelled to make peace by the cession of nearly half their territories, and thenceforth they lost all their prestige and influence. The English, who till then had been merely one of the great powers of India, became thus the paramount power (1804).

In the same year, old Nizám Ali, the Subadár of the Deccan, died and was succeeded by his son, Sikandar Jáh. The English were supreme at Hyderabad, and so there was no dispute about the succession. The Nizam's army had joined the English in the Márháttá war, and Lord Wellesley made over to him the portion of Berar ceded by Raghuji Bhonslá.

Holkar had kept aloof all this time and did not join his Márháttá brethren. Indeed, he plundered Sindhia's territory and did him great injury. All the disbanded soldiery obtained an asylum with Holkar. Early in 1804, he demanded the *chauth* of certain districts in Hindusthán from the English. But they rejected his claims with scorn, and Lord Wellesley now deemed it necessary to break the power of Holkar. War was formally proclaimed, and Colonel Murray from Guzerat and Lord Lake from Hindusthán simultaneously invaded his territories (1804). Colonel Murray's force had retired to their quarters before the rains. But not knowing this, Colonel Monson entered Holkar's territories with the view of joining him. Holkar pursued Monson with his whole army and harassed him greatly for two months, at the end of which he, with the wreck of his army, reached Agra. Holkar next occupied Mathurá and then seized Delhi. But as soon as Lord Lake made his appearance there, he fled to Bharatpur, the Rájá of which place, in spite of his treaty with the English, joined him. Monson and General Fraser attacked their combined armies at Dig and totally routed them (December, 1804). Lord Lake came upon Holkar's cavalry at Farakkabad and dispersed them. Holkar himself fled and the English besieged Bharatpur (February, 1805. It was a strong fort, and every attempt to carry it failed. The Rájá of Bharatpur, however, finding that there was no hope of receiving any succour from Holkar, sued for peace, which was granted. This event produced an impression, which was not dispelled till the fall of the place 21 years after, that the English could not take Bharatpur.

War with Holkar.

Lord Wellesley, though constantly engaged in arduous warfare, yet found time to carry out many social and administrative reforms. People, who had no children born to them up to an advanced age, often made a vow to cast their first-born into the Ganges at its confluence with the sea. This cruel

Administrative reforms.

custom was a fruitful source of infanticide amongst the Hindus, and it was Lord Wellesley, who put a stop to it. The Governor-General in Council was the highest appellate court for the natives of India. But, the Governor-General being engaged in many arduous duties, the hearing of appeals was often greatly delayed. Lord Wellesley, therefore, made over his appellate power to a number of able judges, and the Sadr Diváni Adálat was thus created anew. He also established the College of Fort William for the training of European officers of the Company. But the cost of its maintenance was so great that the Directors insisted on a reduction of the expenditure on it.

CHAPTER VII.

LORD CORNWALLIS, SIR GEORGE BARLOW, AND LORD MINTO (1805-1813).

Lord Cornwallis again.

ON receipt of the news of Monson's defeat, the Court of Directors sent out Lord Cornwallis a second time to assume the office of Governor-General, with instructions to establish peace and check the thirst of Englishmen in India for territorial acquisition. On reaching Calcutta, his Lordship wrote a letter to Lord Lake, directing him to return the whole of Hindusthán to Sindhia and to restore his ancestral possessions to Holkar. Lord Lake had, however, already entered into a new treaty with Sindhia. Lord Cornwallis, though very old, undertook a journey to the North-Western Provinces, but fell seriously ill at Ghazipur, where he died (1805).

Sir George Barlow.

The death of Lord Cornwallis placed Sir George Barlow, Senior Member of the Council, at the head of affairs. It was with great reluctance that he carried out the non-intervention policy formulated by the authorities in England. The Government of India was instructed not to interfere in the affairs of Native States, unless their own territories were actually invaded.

The consequence of this short-sighted policy was that the establishment of peace in Central India was delayed by the mutual jealousies, animosities, and quarrels of the Native States. Holkar compelled the Rájá of Jaypur to pay eighteen lakhs of rupees. The Rájá of Bundi suffered greatly at the hands of the eccentric Márháttá chief, Yaśovanta Ráo, who killed all his brothers, and at last died insane in the year 1811. The Nizam, too, began to form new schemes of conquest.

The Vellore Mutiny.

The descendants of Tipu Sultán had their residence fixed at Vellore in the Madras Presidency, where two sepoy regiments and a number of European soldiers were stationed. An order to the sepoys to wear a new head-dress, produced great discontent amongst them, and this being probably fomented by the descendants of Tipu, they mutinied and killed their European officers on the 10th July, 1806. But Colonel Gillespie, arriving with British troops from Arkot, quelled the mutiny, and Tipu's descendants were brought to Calcutta. On the arrival of Lord Minto as Governor-General (July, 1807), Sir George Barlow was appointed Governor of Madras.

Lord Minto.

Lord Minto adhered, as a rule, to the non-intervention policy. But, the Native Chiefs of Bundelkhund having created great disturbances by their mutual quarrels, he sent General Martindell to establish peace in these hilly tracts (1807). The famous fort of Kálanjara fell into the hands of the English about this time. Napoleon Buonaparte, the emperor of the French, sent an ambassador to Persia in order, if possible, to check the progress of the English. For the purpose of counteracting French influence, Lord Minto organised Embassies to Persia, Afghánisthán, and the Punjab, and established friendly relations with those States. The Sikh chiefs to the east of the Sutlej placed themselves under British protection in the year 1809 (*see* Book VI., Chap. IX.).

After the death of Yaśovanta Ráo Holkar, two parties were formed in the State, a Márháttá party and a Pathán party. Amir

Khán, who was the leader of the latter, gained the upper hand in the management of the State, and established a small principality for himself by despoiling the neighbouring weak chiefs. At last, he ventured to attack Jaypur. In this matter, also, Lord Minto interfered, but, being unwilling to act against orders from England he was unable to crush Amir Khán. The Rájás of Kolhápur and Sávantwari were great pirates in the Arabian Sea. Lord Minto put a stop to their piracies with a strong hand.

Amir Khán.

He made an attempt to put down *dacoity* in Bengal. He contracted no fresh loans; and, during his administration the credit of the Government of India was so high that he succeeded in reducing the rate of interest on the Public Debt. At the time of his return in 1813, he recorded his opinion that peace in India was not likely to be disturbed except by an eruption of the Pindáris from Central India.

CHAPTER VIII.

Marquis of Hastings (1813-1823).

The prophecy of Lord Minto was falsified. The Marquis of Hastings, on his arrival in India, found that the Rájá of Nepal had invaded British territories. Nepal had made itself a great military power by the conquest of the greater part of the Himálayan regions. The Nepalese occupied the villages of Bhutwal and Śivráj in Bengal in 1813. The English recaptured these places, and the Nepalese declared war against them. The Marquis of Hastings, then on tour in the North-Western Provinces, sent four distinct armies against Nepal, two of these, the western and the eastern, being commanded by Generals Ochterlony and Gillespie respectively.

The Nepal war.

The fort of Maloun, though garrisoned by the famous Gurkhá general, Amar Sinha Tháppá, and his men, fell into the hands of Ochterlony early in 1815. Almorá was next captured, and the Nepal Council sent proposals for peace, but Amar Sinha Tháppá, arriving about this time at Khátmándu, advised the Council to continue the war, and this advice being accepted, General Ochterlony marched straight from Behar to Khátmándu. Finding the usual route strongly defended, he marched by another road and appeared suddenly before the fort at Mukbanpur, which commanded Khátmáudu. The fort soon fell into his hands, and the Nepal Council sued for peace, which was granted. By its terms the English obtained possession of Kumáun, Garhwal, and the mountainous countries between the Jamuná and the Sutlej. The Rájá of Sikkim was taken under British protection, and the Gurkhás were thus completely isolated from the rest of India (1815).

The history of the Pindári and Márháttá wars during the administration of the Marquis of Hastings has been given in Book VII., Chap. VIII.

CHAPTER IX.

Lord Amherst (1823-1828).

Lord Amherst.

The Marquis of Hastings returned to England early in 1823, and Mr. Adam, the Senior Member of the Council, acted as Governor-General for a short time, during which he became unpopular owing to his interference with the liberty of the press. Lord Amherst was sent out to India in 1823.

The first Burmèse war.

The first event of his administration was the Burmese war. The Burmese had already occupied Assam and taken possession of Sáhpur, an island in the Bay of Bengal, belonging to the English. Lord Amherst retook Sáhpur; but the King of Burma vain-gloriously sent a golden chain with which to bring the Governor-General captive to Ava. The financial position of the Government at this time was very prosperous. Lord Hastings had left ten crores of rupees in the treasury, and the annual surplus amounted to two crores. But the Burmese war was, in one sense, the most difficult in which the English had engaged in the East. The route to Burma lay through unhealthy jungles and over difficult and unknown mountains; and so it was determined to begin by taking the town of Rangoon, at the mouth of the Irrawady, and to advance by the river. But there were difficulties about this plan also. The necessaries of European life were unavailable at Rangoon, and during the rains the whole country became a vast sheet of water. In spite of all these difficulties, Sir Archibald Campbell sailed from Madras and took Rangoon and Martaban with ease, while Captain Richard occupied Assam. The Burmese general, Mahá Bundlá, made vigorous preparations for war; but he was killed at the battle of Donábew (1824). Proposals for peace were made about this time; but, the rains having set in, no treaty was concluded, and two years passed without any sign of the war coming to a speedy termination. Immense sums of money were spent and a large number of English soldiers died of fever and starvation.

In the third year of the war, however, Sir Archibald Campbell reached Yandabu by the Irrawady, and this frightened the king into coming to terms. The English obtained a crore of rupees as a war indemnity and the cession of Assam, Arakan, and Tenaserim (1826).

In the same year, Durjanśál deposed his minor cousin, and the Rájá of Bharatpur declared himself Rájá, and began to make preparations for war. The native chiefs secretly encouraged him, and Lord Combermere was sent against Bharatpur. The fort had been regarded as impregnable since 1806, and Lord Combermere was able to enter it only after blowing up a portion of the fortifications. The minor prince was restored to the throne, and Durjanśál sent a prisoner to Benares, in 1826.

The Capture of Bharatpur.

CHAPTER X.

LORD WILLIAM BENTINCK. (1828-1835).

Lord William Bentinck.

LORD WILLIAM BENTINCK was a man of a peaceful disposition, and he spent the greater part of his time in endeavours to improve the condition of the people. During the seven years of his administration, he was, nevertheless, compelled to annex two small principalities, *viz.*, Coorg and Cachar, to the British Empire. The people of Cachar invited the English to take possession of their country, and, the Rájá of Coorg having committed several murders, it became necessary to depose him. The Rájá of Maisur attained his majority in 1811, and took the administration of the State into his own hands. But its affairs fell into disorder, and the people broke out in rebellion. The Rájá was, therefore, pensioned, and the State placed under British Commissioners. These, however, are the only instances in which Lord William Bentinck interfered in the affairs of native States.

Social reforms.

Lord William Bentinck abolished the *Sati* rite, by which Hindu women used to burn themselves on the funeral pyres of their husbands. Marriage in Rájput families of the higher class being very expensive, the Rájputs were in the habit of killing their infant daughters. This cruel custom of female infanticide was also suppressed in British territories by his Lordship, who exhorted the native princes to do away with it in their States. In the Northern Circars, the Khonds were in the habit of propitiating their great mother Earth with human sacrifices, and he adopted strict measures to put a stop to this cruel practice; but the Khonds, unable to appreciate his benevolent motives, rebelled, and it was with great difficulty that the rebellion was put down. The reclamation of savage tribes engaged his earnest attention, and the Khonds, the Kols, and the Mairs of Ajmir were greatly benefited by his exertions.

Reclamation of savages.

An important controversy was raised during this administration as to the best medium for imparting education to the people of India. The Orientalists advocated the cause of Arabic, Persian, and Sanskrit literature; the Anglicists were for giving an English education, and the Vernacularists were for improving and encouraging the Vernaculars. Lord William Bentinck, after patiently examining the arguments advanced on all three sides, decided in favour of English education, which has since conferred immense benefits on the people of India.

The Anglicists, Orientalists, and Vernacularists.

Colonel Sleeman, in an able report, drew the attention of Government to the existence in India of a class of assassins and robbers called *Thugs*, who decoyed travellers, killed them, and robbed them of their property. The prevalence of dacoity in Bengal has already been noticed. Lord William Bentinck organised a special department, called the Thugi Department for the prevention of these violent crimes.

The Thugs.

It has been already stated that Lord Cornwallis had left only two openings for natives into Government service, namely, the post of Dárogá and that of Munsif. The Government, however, was not financially in a position to entertain the services of a large number of highly paid European officers, and in almost every district arrears of work accumulated, to the great hardship of the parties concerned. Lord William Bentinck accordingly proposed the appointment of qualified Natives to the higher ranks of the Services. He abolished Persian as the Court language and substituted the vernaculars for it; established the Calcutta Medical College, and declared change of religion to be no bar to inheritance.

Admission of Natives into the Public Service.

The Charter of 1813 abolished the Company's monopoly of Indian trade, and the Charter of 1833 abolished the Chinese monopoly also. In the latter year, the Company obtained a Charter for a further period of twenty years only as rulers of India. By this Charter, Europeans obtained permission to acquire landed property in India, and natives to enter the higher ranks of the service. The North-Western Provinces were constituted a separate Presidency, with Sir Charles Metcalfe as its first Governor.

CHAPTER XI

LORD AUCKLAND (1836-1842)

Lord Auckland.

LORD WILLIAM BENTINCK left India in 1835, and was succeeded for a time by Sir Charles Metcalfe, whose short term of office was made memorable by the grant of complete freedom to the Press On the arrival of Lord Auckland, the North-Western Provinces were reduced to a Lieutenant-Governorship, and Metcalfe consequently left India

The first act of Lord Auckland's government was the passing of an Act by which native Judges were empowered to try civil suits in which Europeans were parties

Causes of the Afghán war.

Mahárájá Ranajit Sinha took Peshawar from the Afgháns in 1835 Dost Muhammad, the Amir of Kabul, applied to the Governor-General for assistance to recover the place, but without success Shortly afterwards, Lord Auckland sent an ambassador to the Amir for the purpose of concluding a commercial treaty with him Finding that the Governor-General was not inclined to further his views regarding Peshawar, Dost Muhammad began to show greater respect to Vicovich, the Russian ambassador at his court, and Lieutenant Burnes the British ambassador, wrote to the Governor-General to the effect that it was desirable to check the influence of Russia at Kabul Lord Auckland accordingly formed a triple alliance with Shah Shujá, the ex King of Kabul, and Ranajit Sinha, for the purpose of driving Dost Muhammad from Kabul and restoring Sháh Shujá to the kingdom of his ancestor, Ahmad Sháh Abdálí

The Afghán war.

A proclamation of war was issued from Simla in 1838, and Sir Willoughby Cotton appointed commander of the expedition Some of the Amirs of Sindh tried to oppose the passage of British troops through their territories, but they were coerced and compelled to make over the strong fort of Bakkar to the English, and the united British army from Bengal and Bombay entered Afghánisthán through the Bolan Pass. They obtained possession of Kandahár in May, 1839. Ghazní and Kabul fell into their hands in quick succession. Dost Muhammad tried to treat; but the English refused to listen to him. Sháh Shujá ascended the throne of his ancestors, and the Bombay army returned to India, capturing Khelat on the way.

The Sikhs.

Ranajit Sinha, the 'Lion of the Punjab', died on the 27th June, 1839. After the treaty of 1809, he never quarrelled with the English. At the time of his death he had 80,000 disciplined troops trained by French generals. He had conquered Káśmír and Ladak, and made the Sikhs a great military power. But there was not a single able man among his successors; and it was a further misfortune for the State that several eminent *Sardars* (chiefs) died, within five or six years of his death, by the hands of assassins, and the affairs of the State fell into great disorder in consequence. From the year 1840 the English were compelled, through sheer necessity, to keep a close watch over the proceedings of the Sikhs.

After the departure of the Bombay army, Sir William Macnaghten remained at Kabul as Resident, with a portion of the Bengal army. He allowed the Bala Hissar to be occupied by Sháh Shujá and removed the British camp to the plains below, where the British soldiers became involved in constant quarrels with the inhabitants. Dost Muhammad surrendered to the English and was sent to India on an ample pension. His banishment, however, did not establish peace in Afghánisthán. Sháh Shujá was very unpopular; and his supporters, the English, shared in his unpopularity. But the brunt of the rage of the Afgháns fell upon Sir Alexander Burnes. On the 1st November, 1841 the Afghán Sardars attacked his residence and killed him. The English were not in a position to punish the offenders. General Nott was unable to move from Kandahár owing to the roads being blocked with snow; and Sir Robert Sale was obliged to shut himself up in the fort of Jalalabad. The number of the rebels increased at Kabul and supplies began to fall short in the English camp. Akbar, the son of Dost Muhammad, assumed the leadership of the rebels. Sir William Macnaghten tried hard to secure friends amongst the Afgháns, but without success, and at last was assassinated by Akbar Khán. There were still 15,000 British soldiers in Afghánisthán; and they could have made a bold stand, but unfortunately they surrendered their guns and money to the Afgháns, on the promise of a safe passage to India. That promise was shortly afterwards violated and the whole army perished, either in the snow, or by the hands of the Afgháns. Only one Englishman escaped, to bring the news of this terrible disaster to Jalalabad, which Colonel Sale was defending with great resolution and spirit. Before the close of the war, however, Lord Ellenborough was appointed Governor-General.

Afghán treachery.

CHAPTER XII.

Lord Ellenborough (1842-1844).

On his arrival in India, Lord Ellenborough despatched General Pollock with a large army to Afghánisthán, with instructions to restore British prestige in Central Asia and return to India. He reached the Khaibar Pass, by forced marches and in a short time took the fort of Ali Masjid and relieved Sale at Jalalabad. Then the united British armies began their march on Kabul, levelling the forts on their way and conquering the intermediate places.

Lord Ellenborough's Afghán policy.

General England marched through the Bolan Pass and reached Kandahár, after much fighting. General Nott and he then marched on Kabul, which at once fell into their hands. The first endeavour of the English at Kabul was to effect the release of the English prisoners, and in this they succeeded, though not without effort. They levelled the bazar of Kabul to the ground, destroyed the fort at Ghazní, signally punished the rebels, and returned to India. The rebels had already killed Sháh Shujá and Dost Muhammad was allowed to return to Kabul to be its Amir again (1842).

Sindh war.

During the Afghán war, many of the Amirs of Sindh rendered great assistance to the British army, and, except at the commencement of the war, they put no obstruction in the way of the transport of arms, ammunition, and stores. The Amirs were independent of one another; but there was a nominal chief. After the close of the Afghán war, Major Outram, the Resident, was obliged to report against some of the Amirs, and Lord Ellenborough requested Sir Charles Napier to enquire into the matter. Sir Charles found all the Amirs guilty of corresponding with the enemies of the English, and they were compelled to submit to a treaty by which they ceded two-thirds of their territories to the British Government. The Baluchis, their subjects, however, rebelled and attacked the Residency. Though they fought with desperate valour and would accept no quarter, Sir Charles defeated them in two pitched battles, at Míyáni and at Dubbá (1843). Sir Charles next took Hyderabad.

As the sepoys of the Madras and Bengal armies refused to serve in Sindh, Bombay sepoys only were employed to garrison that country, and it is the opinion of some, as subsequently explained that this was one of the causes of the Bengal Sepoy Mutiny

Gwalior war.

Daulat Ráo Sindhia died in 1827, and his adopted son, Janakjí, in 1843. At the instance of the English, Janakjí's widow adopted a child, and there was a great dispute about the guardianship. The Mámá Sáheb and Dádá Sáheb were the rival candidates, and each had his own followers. The English supported the Mámá and the Rání, the Dádá. The English called upon the Rání to surrender the Dádá into their hands and threatened that otherwise the Resident would leave Gwalior. The influence of the Dádá becoming daily stronger, war was declared against Sindhia, and the Governor-General himself marched from

Agra to Gwalior. The Ráni sought his protection, but the rebels prevented her from proceeding to the English camp. Sindhia's army was twice defeated, at Mahárájpur and at Punnair, in 1843, and Sindhia entered into a subsidiary alliance, by which his army was reduced and his artillery limited to thirty-two guns, the English undertaking the protection of his State during his minority.

Lord Ellenborough left India in 1844, and Sir Henry Hardinge, a veteran warrior, was appointed in his place.

CHAPTER XIII.

LORD HARDINGE (1844-1848).

Lord Hardinge.

LORD HARDINGE had scarcely had time to devote his attention to other matters when the invasion of British India by the Khálsá army, compelled him to embark in one of the most arduous wars in which the English were ever engaged in India.

Disorders in the Punjab.

Kharga Sinha, the son and successor of Mahárjá Ranajit Sinha, died in November, 1840, leaving behind him his son, Neonehál Sinha, a young man of great promise. Neonehál Sinha, however, also died a premature death by accident, and Sher Sinha, the second son of Ranajit, ascended the throne with the assistance of the Rájá of Jamu and his brothers. The Khálsá army began to show signs of discontent, and there was no one in the Royal family, or among the Sardars, who was in a position to control them. After a series of assassinations too horrible to detail, they placed Dhuleep Sinha, the youngest son of Ranajit, on the throne left vacant by the murder of Sher Sinha (1843). Dhuleep was a minor, and his mother, Mahárání Jhindan, became Regent. The army was conciliated by advances of pay; but the soldiers rose in their demands, and put the Mahárání's brother to death.

Causes of the first Sikh war.

The Mahárání appointed Lál Sinha, her favourite, Prime-Minister, and it was agreed between the two that the turbulent Khálsá army should be induced to invade Hindusthán. They argued that, if the army succeeded in gaining its object, the Punjab would be rid of its presence, while, in case of a reverse, it would be rendered less formidable ; and so, with the intention of getting rid of her own army, the Mahárání prevailed upon it to wage an unprovoked war against the English.

The Khálsá army crossed the Sutlej on the 16th December, 1845, and advanced against the British cantonment at Ferozpur. The English commander at the place, Sir John Littler, was not in a position to dispute its passage. But the commander-in-chief, who was at Umbala, set out for Ferozpur with all his available troops by forced marches. He met Lál Sinha's division of the Sikh cavalry at Mudki, on the 18th December, and at once attacked, and defeated it, capturing 17 guns. The main army of the Sikhs was stationed at Ferozpur in an entrenched camp. The commander-in-chief, without loss of time, attacked this strong position on the 23rd, and Sir John Littler joined him with 5,000 men. The battle raged furiously during the whole day, and the night was passed in great uneasiness.

Battles of Mudki and Ferozpur.

The troops being so mixed up in the field that it was impossible in the darkness to distinguish friends from foes. Lord Hardinge, the Governor-General, who was in the camp, and Sir Hugh Gough, the commander-in-chief, made every effort to inspire their men with courage ; and in the morning they attacked the Sikhs and gained a complete victory. Tej Sinha, who had come to the field of battle with 20,000 cavalry, retired without firing a shot. Both sides lost heavily but the Sikh army became utterly disorganised and plundered the camp of Lál Sinha.

The English, though victorious, were unable to follow up the enemy, as their field-pieces, stores, and ammunition had not yet arrived from Delhi. In the meantime the strength of the Sikh army was increased by reinforcements from beyond the Sutlej. When, however, ammunition arrived, the English again attacked the Sikhs at Aliwal, on 28th January, 1846, and completely routed them. Large numbers fled beyond the Sutlej.

Battle of Aliwal.

Goláp Sinha, the Rájá of Jamu, who had in the meanwhile become Prime Minister at Lahore, sent proposals for peace. But the Governor-General consented to treat only on condition that the Khálsá army should be disbanded. Goláp Sinha saw that this was impossible; and the war was continued.

Battle of Sobráon.

For some weeks the Sikhs were busy in constructing defensive works at Sobráon to cover a bridge of boats which they had thrown across the Sutlej. But, on the arrival of their heavy guns, the English not only attacked the works and destroyed them, but completely defeated the enemy, who fled precipitately to the bridge. There they were subjected to a heavy fire from the British horse artillery, and nearly ten thousand of their number perished in two hours (February 10th, 1846). The British losses amounted to nearly 2,500 men. Thus, in less than sixty days, the only native military power that existed at that time in India was defeated and humbled by the valour of British troops and the skill of British officers.

Treaty of Mian Mir.

The English now crossed the Sutlej and pitched their camp at Mian Mir, a short distance from Lahore. Goláp Sinha again came forward with proposals for peace, and a treaty was made with the Lahore Durbar on the 23rd February, 1846, the conditions of which were that the Durbar should pay a crore and a half of rupees and cede the *Doáb* formed by the Sutlej and the Bias. As it was not in a position to pay the whole amount in cash, Káśmír was sold to Goláp Sinha for a crore of rupees. A subsidiary treaty was made on the 6th March, by which the English consented to remain at Lahore for a year to effect a re-organisation of the Lahore Government.

After a year, however, the Sikh Sardars requested the English to leave an army at Lahore with the Resident, agreeing to pay twenty-two lakhs of rupees a year for its maintenance. A Council of Regency was formed with the Resident for its President, and it was settled that this arrangement should continue till Dhuleep Sinha attained his majority. Lord Hardinge retired from India in 1848.

CHAPTER XIV.

Lord Dalhousie (1848-1856).

Lord Dalhousie

Lord Dalhousie reached India early in 1848, at the age of thirty-six. He possessed no knowledge of the country, but he was a statesman of keen insight and extraordinary energy, and in a short time he made himself master of the details of every department of the State. He had expected to rule in peace, but war was forced upon him within four months of his arrival in India.

The Second Sikh war.

Múlráj was the Governor of Multan. On his father's death, he had agreed to pay Rs. 1,80,000 to the Lahore Durbar for his succession, but, on one pretext or another, he had delayed payment. The English now demanded the money on behalf of the Durbar, and Múlráj resigned. The Resident appointed another person in his place and sent two European officers, Mr. Vans Agnew and Lieutenant Anderson, to escort the new Governor. At the time of their arrival at Multan, Múlráj, though apparently making all arrangements for the evacuation of the fort, was secretly engaged in maturing a plan for a rising. His soldiers attacked Agnew and Anderson, and killed them. No relief came from Lahore, and the number of the rebels increased.

Lieutenant Edwardes, an English officer, was engaged in the survey of the Deráját Division; and on the news of the mishap at Multan reaching him, he, with a small body of gallant soldiers, attacked Múlráj and, twice defeating him, compelled him to seek shelter in Multan. The Nawab of Baháwalpur sent timely help to

Edwardes, which was of great use to him. On the arrival of reinforcements with siege-guns from Lahore, Multan was besieged, on the 7th September, 1848; but the operations were delayed by the defection of Sher Sinha, the representative of the Lahore Durbar with the English army, who marched with the whole of the Sikh army towards the north to join his father, Chhatter Sinha, already in open rebellion.

Multan taken.

On the arrival of a force from Bombay at Multan the siege operations were resumed. The fort was a strong one. Nature and art had combined to make it a second Bharatpur. But it yielded to British energy and science (2nd January, 1849). The magazine caught fire and blew up, destroying a portion of the town. The outer and the inner fortifications were gradually reduced, and Múlráj was taken prisoner and died shortly after.

Chhatter Sinha entered into a treaty with Dost Muhammad, and agreed to make over Peshawar to him if he succeeded in driving the English from Lahore. Dost Muhammad was so anxious to regain Peshawar that on this condition he joined his inveterate enemy and sent him a large number of Afghán troops.

Battle of Chillianwala.

Sher Sinha had taken up his position behind a belt of forest, in the neighbourhood of Chillianwala, and there he awaited the advance of the English. Lord Gough pitched his camp on the other side of the forest, and between it and the village of Chillianwala. There the Sikhs opened a heavy fire on him on January 12th, 1849, and he advanced his infantry through the forest to attack them. In the action that followed, the British suffered heavy loss; several of their guns were captured; and, though they ultimately won the day, the result was for a long time doubtful. After the battle, Sher Sinha marched first to Rasul, where he was joined by Chhatter Sinha and a reinforcement of the Afgháns, and ultimately to Gujarát, where he took up his position.

Battle of Gujarát.

Thither Lord Gough followed him, being reinforced on the way by three brigades from Multan. The battle opened with a fierce cannonade from his heavy artillery, which was greatly superior in weight of metal and number of guns to that of the enemy. The Sikh artillery was silenced, and, unable to hold their ground, the Sikhs retired behind the line of villages in their rear. There Lord Gough launched his infantry against them, and, after a gallant resistance, they were driven from all their positions (February 27th, 1849). Cavalry and horse artillery were sent in pursuit, and these were followed by two columns, which pressed them so closely that, after some days, the entire Sikh army surrendered unconditionally.

Annexation of the Punjab.

By the Proclamation of March 29th, 1849, Lord Dalhousie annexed the whole country governed by the Lahore Durbar and granted a pension of Rs. 5,00,000 to Dhuleep Sinha, who became a Christian and lived for many years in England, where, after various reverses of fortune, he died not long ago. Lord Dalhousie was made a Marquis for his success in the second Sikh war.

Annexation of Satára.

The Rájás of Kerauli and Satára died about this time. Both had adopted children. Lord Dalhousie held that the State of Satára was created by the English, and, therefore, on the failure of the direct line they were not bound to give it to an adopted child. Kerauli was an ancient State, not created by the English, and accordingly he held that the succession there should be determined by ancient custom. The Court of Directors and the Board of Control agreeing with his Lordship, Satára was annexed to British India.

The second Burmese war.

After the treaty of Yandabu, relations between the English and the king of Burma again became very strained. The Resident, slighted on various occasions, had to withdraw. The position of the English merchants in Burma was far from being secure and became more and more fraught with danger. The Governor of Rangoon having ill-treated the English, the Governor-General sent a fleet to punish him, and he was removed from Rangoon.

But the new Governor was a man of still haughtier disposition and would not condescend to see Englishmen. Admiral Lambert consequently blockaded Rangoon and captured one of the king's ships. The Burmese kept up a fire from the fort, but it was ineffectual. War was shortly afterwards declared. Martaban fell into the hands of the English; Rangoon was captured; Bassein and Prome were occupied, and Pegu opened its gates after a long siege. The inhabitants prayed to be relieved from the turbulent Burmese officers and the English acceded to their request. The places captured became part of the British dominions. Those who apprehended that the English would encounter great difficulties if they advanced beyond India, have been agreeably surprised by the prosperity of the Burmese Provinces since 1852.

The Nizam of Hyderabad proved a bad paymaster, and the arrears of the subsidy amounted to 8,000,000 rupees. The Directors put pressure upon Lord Dalhousie to realise the amount, and after much acrimonious correspondence, the Nizam made over Berar, Naldurg, and the Raichar Doáb to the English. The last two provinces were subsequently returned to His Highness in reward for his services during the Sepoy Mutiny, but Berar still remains in the hands of the English.

Annexation of Jhansi and Nagpur.

Bájí Ráo, the ex-Peshwa, died in 1853, and his pension lapsed to the State. His adopted son, Náná Sáheb, made several efforts to get the pension granted to him also, but in vain. The Nawab of the Carnatic died about the same time, and his rank and pension were abolished. It was proposed to remove the descendants of Bahádur Sháh from the Imperial palace at Delhi; and the Rájás of Jhansi and Nagpur dying without issue, these States were annexed, and the adopted sons declared ineligible for succession to the State.

Annexation of Oudh.

The Nawabs of Oudh had been for a long time the protégés of the English, who had raised them to the dignity of kings. But their administration of the country had been always unsatisfactory.

Lord Hardinge had consequently written to the king, warning him that if it did not improve in two years, it would be taken out of his hands But even this did not bring the king to his senses, and in 1856 the Directors ordered the annexation of the country. Lord Dalhousie, though he did not approve of the measure, oyally carried out the orders of the superior authorities, and the State was annexed, Wájid Ali Sháh being brought to Calcutta, and a pension of Rs 1,200,000 settled on him The people of the country were greatly alarmed at these annexations

Lord Dalhousie's administration

Lord Dalhousie was a man of indefatigable energy During the seven years of his administration, he was much occupied with political and military affairs But, nevertheless, he found time to introduce and carry out various measures of improvement It is to his energy and political foresight that India owes the inauguration of her Railway system It is to him that she owes the network of Telegraphic wires that covers the whole face of country It is to him that she owes her Trunk Roads, her admirable Postal system, which carries letters from one end of the country to the other for only two pice, and her grand Irrigation Canals spreading fertility over large tracts of land. But the hard work of seven years so undermined his health that he returned to England in 1856, only to die

The Charter of 1853 constituted Bengal a Lieutenant Governorship, and Sir Frederick Halliday was appointed its first Lieutenant-Governor

CHAPTER XV

Lord Canning (1856-1862)

Lord Canning.

Lord Canning looked forward to a peaceful reign and had made up his mind to devote himself to works of improvement, but he was not without misgivings, as was shewn by a famous speech, delivered by him on the eve of his departure from England.

He was, in fact, grievously disappointed. The English became involved in war with China and with Persia in 1856. In both cases they were victorious, and the king of Persia was compelled by Major Outram, the commander of the British forces, to engage never to invade the territories of Dost Muhammad, the Amir of Kabul, who was a friend of the English.

Causes of the Sepoy Mutiny.

The Bombay sepoys were willing to go to any part of India when ordered; but the Bengal sepoys always refused to do so. They prided themselves on their high caste and would not consent to perform menial services in the regiments This contrast was shown in a very striking way in the Sindh war, in which sepoys from both Presidencies were employed. Sir Charles Napier often predicted that the Bengal sepoys would one day mutiny, and, when appointed commander-in chief in 1850, he framed strict rules for the prevention of such a calamity and rigidly enforced them These rules and regulations, however, did not meet with the approval of Lord Dalhousie, who reposed complete confidence in the fidelity of the Bengal army, and Sir Charles resigned.

But the spread of English education, the construction of railway and telegraph lines, and the passing of such measures as the Widow Re-marriage Act, created a suspicion in the minds of the ignorant people of the country that the English were bent on making India a second England, and there were designing men who propagated the idea that the whole population would be forcibly converted to Christianity.

The annexation policy of Lord Dalhousie had greatly unsettled the minds of the people, and, in spite of the harshness and unpopularity of the measure, it was resolved to remove the family of the great Mughal from the palace at Delhi. Náná Sáheb, too, and his co-adjutor, Azimullá, travelled through various parts of Upper India, spreading disaffection and organising resistance. The astrologers who, in the beginning of the native year, go from house to house, reading the Almanac and foretelling the events of the year, gave out that, as a hundred years had passed since the battle of Plassey, the Company's rule would come to an end. In 1857 *chapatties* were circulated from place to place, throughout Hindusthán, and the mysterious nature of the occurrence has not yet been satisfactorily explained. Some are of opinion that it was a call to arms. However, neither the people nor the princes were the first to strike the blow, which came from the sepoys.

Enfield rifles were introduced into the army early in 1857, and an impression got abroad that the cartridges were greased with the fat of hogs and oxen, and designed to defile the Hindus and Musalmans alike. Lord Canning had them examined by the best chemists, who pronounced them not to have been greased; but the impression nevertheless gained ground.

The first outbreak of the Mutiny.

The mutinous spirit of the Bengal army first manifested itself at Barrackpur, and then at Raniganj and Berhampur. A sepoy regiment at Raniganj having disobeyed the orders of the commanding officer, it was brought down to Barrackpur, disarmed and disbanded. On their way to their homes in Oudh, the men spread all sorts of calumnies against the English, and thus fomented the spirit of disaffection which had already shown itself.

Meerut.

The news of the proceedings of the sepoys at Barrackpur and Berhampur reached the Upper Provinces and created a great stir among the sepoys. Eighty-five sepoys at Meerut were ordered to be hanged for refusing to use the cartridges, and this incensed their comrades, who, after killing their officers and breaking open the jails, marched off to Delhi, a distance of 40 miles, and declared the re-establishment of the Mughal Empire. All this happened in so short a time and so unexpectedly that the officers commanding the English regiments at Meerut were simply bewildered. The example of Meerut was followed at Delhi, and the Musalmans there joined the mutineers.

It was subsequently ascertained, after a careful inquiry, that the 30th May had been fixed for a general rising of the sepoys from Peshawar to Benares; but the sepoys of Meerut broke out in open mutiny twenty days before the appointed date. In the Punjab, the sepoys at Lahore, Amritsar, Peshawar, Jalandar, Phillour, Mardán, and other places were kept in check by the Sikh and European regiments. But those at Ferozpur mutinied, and, after committing various acts of violence, marched to Delhi. One regiment only mutinied at Lucknow.

Mutiny at various stations.

The regiments of Moradabad, Bareilly, Saharanpur, Sháhjahanpur, Badáon and Almorá in Rohilkhund, Aligarh, Mainpuri, Fatehgarh in Hindusthán, Nasirabad and Neemuch in Rajputána mutinied, killed the English residents of those stations, plundered the treasuries, and, repairing to Delhi, saluted Bahádur Sháh as emperor. The Musalmans of Bareilly rebelled under the leadership of Bahádur Khán, a Rohilla chief. The mutineers at Cawnpur set out for Delhi, but were induced to return by Náná Sáheb. He professed friendship for the English, but suddenly joined the mutineers and became responsible for the treacherous and inhuman massacre of the European residents of the town. He promised them a safe passage to Allahabad by boats; but, when they were embarked, the mutineers fired upon them from the banks, and killed all of them but four who escaped and brought news of the disaster to Allahabad.

Sindhia despatched a portion of his army to Agra, to guard the person of the Lieutenant-Governor in the event of a mutiny of the sepoy regiments stationed there. But a part of this force mutinied. The Rání of Jhansi joined the mutineers, killed seventy Europeans stationed at that place, and recovered her State. The regiments at Naogáon, Bándá, Fatehpur, Chhatterpur, Hámirpur, and Jalaun also mutinied and marched to Delhi.

The Punjab, however, remained tranquil; the Sikhs were loyal, and the Rájá of Kapurthalá, Patiálá, Jhind, and Nabhá actively co-operated with Sir John Lawrence, the Chief Commissioner of the Punjab, who was thus enabled to send troops to lay siege to Delhi. There was very little display of mutinous spirit in either Madras or Bombay, or even at Hyderabad, and not a single native feudatory chief joined the mutineers; while many made every effort to suppress them. The only persons of consequence who joined them were the Rájá of Bándá, the Nawab of Fatehgarh, the Rájás of Amethi and Bánpur, and the Zemindar of Jagadíśpur in Behar. The people in general remained friendly to the English, and, even in the districts affected, showed no sympathy with the mutineers. Many of the Talukdars of Oudh and the inhabitants of Lucknow, however, joined the rebellion.

Who joined the Mutiny.

The ability, promptitude, and scientific skill with which the English suppressed the Mutiny, added greatly to their prestige in the popular estimation.

Capture of Delhi.

General Anson, immediately after receiving the news of the events of the 10th May at Meerut, started from Simla and marched with three regiments for Delhi, but died of cholera on the way. His successor, Sir Henry Barnard, reached Delhi on the 4th June, and took up his position on a amall eminence to the north-west of the city, from which the sepoys, with all their endeavours, were unable to dislodge him. But he refrained from making any attack on the city, as it was strongly fortified and manned by 30,000 disciplined troops, who had ample supplies of provisions. Sir Henry Barnard also died of cholera on the 4th July, and was succeeded by General Wilson. Reinforements reached Delhi from Lahore on the 14th of August, and on the 6th September siege-guns arrived from the same quarter. On the 13th September, a breach was effected in the city wall, and in ten days the English were masters, not only of the city, but also of the palace. The emperor was made a prisoner and transported to Rangoon with his Begum. Two of his sons, found with armed followers, were shot down.

On receipt of the news from Cawnpur, Lord Canning immediately sent Major Neill to releive that place. The first Indian railway had recently been opened as far as Raniganj. Neill on foot, suppressed the mutiny of some Sikh regiments at Benares, and relieved Allahabad, which was then besieged by the rebels. At Allahabad he was joined by Henry Havelock, and, shortly afterwards he defeated the sepoys at Fatehgarh. On the 15th July a battle was fought for the possession of the bridge over the Pándu river, in which Náná Sáheb himself commanded the sepoys. Náná's forces were completely routed, and he fled precipitately to Cawnpur, where as already stated he perpetrated a crime which produced a thrill of horror throughout the civilised world. He ordered the massacre in cold blood of two hundred European prisoners, many of whom were women and children, and had their bodies, the dying with the dead, thrown into a well The English army arrived at Cawnpur within two days of this event and occupied the place.

Capture of Cawnpur.

In the mean time, the state of affairs at Lucknow grew worse and worse Sítápur, Fyzabad, Azimgarh, and other places became scenes of violence. Sir Henry Lawrence took every precaution for the safety of the Residency at Lucknow, but he was killed by a shot from the rebel ranks on the 4th July. The mutineers, in great force, attacked the Residency; but they were repulsed. General Havelock advanced twice from Cawnpur for the relief of Lucknow and defeated the rebels at Unáo and Busaratganj. In September, Major Outram arrived at Cawnpur, and Havelock, Neill, and Outram marched to the relief of Lucknow. Neill entered the city on the 15th September, but, in passing through a narrow lane, was shot dead from one of the palaces. The relieving army reached the Residency, but it only added to the number of the besieged In November, however, Sir Colin Campbell succeeded in relieving them. Leaving Major Outram

Relief of Lucknow.

with a strong force at Dilkhusa, a garden, two miles from Lucknow he marched for Cawnpur, and, pushing on vigorously, occupied the bridge of boats thrown across the Ganges. The Gwalior contingent had in the meantime mutinied, under the leadership of Tántiá Topi, a Márháttá Bráhman, and marched on Cawnpur, where Major Windham was hardly in a position to cope with the mutineers. But the advance of Sir Colin compelled them to retire.

Capture of Lucknow,

Major Outram was twice attacked in great force by the mutineers: but, on both occasions, he succeeded in repulsing them. The Governor-General having ordered that the pacification of the province should be effected before the capture of Lucknow, no attempt was made by Sir Colin to relieve that place for two months. In March, however, he advanced on Lucknow and occupied the bridges over the Gumti. The northern quarter of the city was thus cleared of the enemy; but the capture of the city took several days, as every house had been converted into a fort and manned by the mutineers. In ten days, however, the Begum of Oudh fled from Lucknow, and the city fell completely into the hands of the British.

And of Bareilly.

Bareilly now became the headquarters of the rebels, and Prince Feroz, the Begum of Oudh, Náná Sáheb, and others assembled there. Sir Colin sent three columns from different directions against the place, so that none of the rebels might escape The city was easily captured, but all the rebel leaders fled. Captain Douglas was despatched to Behar, where he quelled the rebellion of Kumár Sinha, zemindar of Jagadíśpur, who was killed in an action.

Sir Hugh Rose.

The Bombay army, under the command of Sir Hugh Rose, occupied Saugor in January. The undertaking before Sir Hugh was an arduous one. He had to cross hills and mountains that had proved impassable barriers to the Mughal emperors for centuries, and he subjugated in three months hill tracts which they had never been able to take. He took Chanderi on the 17th

March, and on the 23rd laid siege to Jhansi. Tántiá Topi and the Rájá of Bánpur came with 20,000 men to the relief of Jhansi, but they were defeated and dispersed. The Ránì, in despair, fled with a few horsemen, and Sir Hugh occupied the place and halted there to rest his troops for a few days.

Tántiá Topi.

The army of Sindhia had shown a mutinous disposition at the very outset. But in November they broke out into open revolt, under the leadership of Tántiá Topi, who immediately joined Náná Sáheb and occupied Bithur. General Windham at Cawnpur was hard pressed by them, when, as already stated, he was relieved by the unexpected arrival of Sir Colin Campbell. Defeated there, Tántiá attempted to join the Rání of of Jhansi. Foiled again, he occupied Kálpi.

Gwalior taken.

Driven from Kálpi, where he had to abandon the fine park of artillery in which Sindhia's army took so much pride, he came secretly to Gwalior, where all the mutineers joined him. The Mahárájá and his minister, Dinkar Ráo, opposed him in the field, but were defeated and compelled to flee to Agra; and Gwalior, with Sindhia's treasury, magazine, and artillery, fell into Tántiá's hands. Tántiá now declared Náná Sáheb to be the Peshwa. But Sir Hugh advanced by forced marches from Kálpi and encountered the enemy at Morár, where he completely defeated them. He then advanced on Gwalior. In the attack on that place the Rání of Jhansi was killed. Gwalior was captured on the 18th June, and Sindhia came back to his capital. Tántiá tried to revive hostilities in the Deccan, but he was betrayed by one of his followers in April, 1859.

Náná Sáheb and those who were with him were driven from place to place by the flying columns. They attempted to escape to Nepal, but Jang Bahádur, the minister, had espoused the cause of the English in Oudh, and they found no asylum there.

Pacification of the country.

All opposition being at an end, the English proclaimed a general amnesty. Only those who had been actually implicated in killing Europeans were excluded from the pardon, while those who had helped the English were rewarded with titles, jágirs, and pensions. English opinion in Calcutta was loud in its condemnation of the leniency thus displayed by Lord Canning, and he obtained the derisive name of "Clemency Canning;" but the judgment of posterity has vindicated his action. The rest of Lord Canning's administration was spent in the pleasant task of rewarding those who had rendered signal services during the Mutiny; he confiscated the properties of the Talukdars of Oudh, with the exception of six who had been staunch friends of the English.

CHAPTER XVI.

THE ASSUMPTION OF THE DIRECT ADMINISTRATION BY THE QUEEN (1858-1895).

Assumption of the Direct Administration by the Queen.

One of the results of the agitation caused in England by the Mutiny was that the Queen assumed the direct charge of the administration of India. The East India Company was abolished; and the Governor-General of the East India Company became the Viceroy of the Queen. The Court of Directors and the Board of Control were abolished, and a Secretary of State was appointed solely for India, who was made directly responsible to the Queen and Parliament for the good Government of the country, while an India Council was organised, with fifteen members, to advise the Secretary of State in all important matters. The Viceroy was made responsible to the Secretary of State and the India Council for his actions in India. In 1858, a Proclamation was issued in India in the name of the Queen. By it, all existing dignities, rights, usages, and treaties were confirmed; all grounds of suspicion of tampering with caste or religious faith were removed ; and from the highest to the lowest ranks of society, a reliant spirit of calm assurance and acuiescence in its simple provisions was at once created

The Queen's Proclamation.

This Proclamation, which inaugurated a new era of progress, is regarded as the Magna Charta of India Provision was further made for admitting three native members to the Imperial Legislative Council, and native opinion began to be respected in the administration of the country At the same time the Supreme Court and the Sadr Diváni Adálat were abolished, and the High Court was established in their place. Universities were founded in Calcutta, Madras, and Bombay, with "the advancement of learning" as their motto and schools and colleges, supported and aided by Government sprang up in every direction After doing everything in his power for the pacification of the country, Lord Canning returned to England in 1862 He was firm and resolute, and at the same time sympathetic and benevolent. It is doubtful whether any other ruler could have tided over with more tact the difficulties that surrounded India at the time

Administrative Reforms.

LORD ELGIN (1862-1863) LORD LAWRENCE (1864-1869)

Lord Elgin

LORD ELGIN succeeded Lord Canning, but he died, soon after his arrival in India, at Dharmaśálá, in the Punjab On his death, Sir William Denison acted for a short time as Viceroy of India. Ultimately Sir John Lawrence, who had been the Chief Commissioner of the Punjab during the Mutiny, was appointed Governor-General One of the objects of his appointment was the suppression of the rising of the Musalmans of Sitáná on the Punjab frontier, and the first act of his administration was the despatch of Sir Hugh Rose, the commander-in-chief, to that place. The rising was put down, but with a great loss of men and money.

Sir John Lawrence.

The English entered into their first treaty with the Devaráj of Bhutan in the year 1772 In the interval there had been many political revolutions in that country The Dharmaráj was, in theory, the supreme ruler of the country both in religious and in temporal affairs He used to appoint a Diván for the management of temporal affairs, and this Diván was the Devaráj When a Dharmaráj or a Devaráj died search was made throughout the country for a boy with certain marks on his body, who, when found, was appointed to the vacant situation About the year 1860, two provincial Governors were very powerful They were Tanso Penlo and Pero Penlo The former was hostile to the English, and often led raiding expeditions into Assam and Bengal He appointed his own Dharmaráj and Devaráj, and occupied the Doárs in Assam These were the passes by which hillmen descended into the plains, and which had come into the possession of the English on the conquest of Assam The Bengal Doárs, too, had subsequently fallen into their hands, and they paid an annual subsidy for all these Doárs to the Bhutanese On Tanso Penlo's assuming an attitude of open hostility, the Government of Bengal sent Sir Ashley Eden as Ambassador to the Devaráj with whom the English were in treaty But the insolent conduct of Tanso Penlo defeated the object of the embassy, and there was no alternative left but war Two forts, Divángiri and Dalimkot, fell into the hands of the Engish, but, the country being very unhealthy, they concluded a peace by which the subsidy was increased by a few thousand rupees

The Bhutan war.

LORD MAYO (1869-1872)

DURING the administration of Lord Mayo, Kabul was convulsed by a war of succession Neither Lord Lawrence nor Lord Mayo had interfered in this struggle. But Lord Mayo invited the Amir to India and entertained him with great pomp at

Umbala. The Duke of Edinburgh, the second son of the Queen, visited India during his Viceroyalty, and the occasion was marked by a great outburst of loyal feeling throughout the country, the people of which were thus, for the first time, brought into personal contact with the Royal family. Lord Mayo was assassinated at Port Blair, in the Andaman Islands, by a Musalman convict, in 1872.

The Duke of Edinburgh in India.

Lord Northbrook (1872-1876).

Lord Mayo was succeeded as Viceroy by Lord Northbrook, whose policy was marked by wisdom and moderation. A severe famine breaking out in Behar about this time, His Lordship appointed Sir Richard Temple to organise measures of relief. In this Sir Richard Temple was eminently successful and shortly afterwards he was made Lieutenant-Governor of Bengal.

Malhar Ráo, the Gaekwar of Baroda, being accused of attempting to poison the Resident at his Court, was tried by a mixed Commission of Native Chiefs and English Officers, and deposed, and a scion of the family was appointed in his place.

The Baroda affair.

The Prince of Wales, the eldest son of the Queen and heir to the British throne, visited India, in the year 1875, and the preparations that were made for his reception on the occasion, were without a parallel for grandeur in the history of India.

The visit of the Prince of Wales.

Lord Lytton (1876-1880.)

Lord Lytton was appointed Viceroy of India in the year 1876. He was the son of a well-known English novelist and, politician and was himself a gifted poet and successful diplomatist. In 1877 the Queen assumed the title of Empress of India. Up to that time, though the Paramount ruler in India, she had possessed no distinctive title corresponding to this position, and her assumption of the new style was the formal declaration of her supremacy.

Assumption of the imperial dignity by the Queen.

In the same year, a terrible famine broke out in Madras. Lord Lytton became very unpopular with the Native section of the Indian Press, owing to the passing of the Vernacular Press Act, which interfered with its liberties.

The second Afghán war

Having received information that Shere Ali, the Amir of Kabul, was intriguing with Russia, Lord Lytton despatched Sir Neville Chamberlain as Envoy to Kabul; but the Governor of Ali Masjid refused to allow him to proceed, and war was consequently declared against Kabul for the second time. Shere Ali, defeated and dethroned, fled to Mádári Sherif, where he died; and the English placed Yákub Khán, on the throne. By the treaty of Gandamak (May, 1879), a British Resident wss stationed at Kabul. Yákub, however, was very unpopular; and no sooner had the English troops returned to India than the Kabulese rose and murdered Sir Louis Cavagnari, the Resident at Kabul, and those with him. This was the cause of the third Afghán war. Yákub abdicated and retired to Mussoorie.

The third Afghán war.

LORD RIPON (1880-1884).

BEFORE the conclusion of the third Afghán war, Lord Lytton left India, and was succeeded by the Marquis of Ripon, than whom a greater friend of the country never occupied the viceregal throne. Ayub Khán defeated a British brigade at Maiwand; but General Roberts shortly afterwards signally defeated him, near Kandahár. The English placed Abdur Rahmán, the present Amir, on the throne, and the British troops evacuated Afghánisthán. Lord Ripon next repealed the Vernacular Press Act, and introduced a system of Self-Government, by which the management of Local affairs was entrusted to Boards locally elected, but his attempt to invest Native Magistrates with the power of trying Europeans made him very unpopular with the English residents in India. He, however, took them into his confidence and entered into a *concordat* to satisfy all parties. He also appointed an Education Commission to devise measures for the further diffusion of popular education.

The Local Self-Government Scheme.

LORD DUFFERIN (1884-1

LORD DUFFERIN succeeded Lord Ripon in 1884. Shortly after his arrival in India, he entertained the Amir of Kabul at a grand Durbar at Rawalpindi. About this time a Delimitation Commission was appointed, with Sir Peter Lumsden as its President, for the purpose of fixing the boundary between Russia and Afghánisthán. But, owing to the overbearing conduct of the Russians, an affray occurred between them and the Afghâns at Panjdeh, and the relations between the British and Russian Governments became greatly strained in consequence. The Native Chiefs of India placed the entire resources of their States at the disposal of the British Government, to be used in case a Russian war should break out. But the tact and diplomatic ability of Lord Dufferin averted a conflict.

The Pindi Durbar

The King of Burmah entered into intrigues with the French and the Italians. He was unable to maintain order in his own country, where organised dacoity had become of constant occurrence. The Burma Trading Company was

The third Burmese war.

subjected to frequent losses owing to the disordered state of the country, which the Burmese King could not, or would not, prevent, and Lord Dufferin, on negotiations failing, declared war. A few English steamers ascended the Irrawady, took Mandalay without difficulty, and, having deposed the King, brought him prisoner to India. Lord Dufferin annexed the country by a proclamation dated 1st January, 1886.

The Restitution of Gwalior.

Shortly after this annexation, Lord Dufferin made over the fort of Gwalior to the Mahárájá Sindhia; an act of grace, which did much to inspire the Native Princes of India with confidence.

The Public Service Commission

In view of the agitation which prevailed all over India on the question of the appointment of qualified natives to the higher offices in the State, Lord Dufferin appointed a Public Service Commission, and thus set the question at rest. On Her Majesty's completing the fiftieth year of her reign, in the year 1887, a Jubilee was held with great pomp to celebrate the event. Lord Dufferin on his retirement was created Marquis of Dufferin and Ava (1888).

Lord Lansdowne (1888-1893).

The Manipur war.

One of the principal events of Lord Lansdowne's administration was the Manipur war, in 1891. Tikendrajit, the Senápati of Manipur, having murdered five Englishmen, including the Chief Commissioner of Assam, a British force was sent to Manipur. The Rájá was deposed and the Senápati executed. A minor of a distant branch of the Rájá's family was placed on the throne, and a British Commissioner appointed to rule the country for him during his minority. Lord Lansdowne, having completed his term of office, returned to England in 1893.

LORD ELGIN (1893—1899).

LORD LANSDOWNE was succeeded in the Viceroyalty by Lord Elgin, the son of that Lord Elgin who died at Dharmaśálá in 1862.

The period of his administration was marked by a series of grave calamities, among which widespread famine and pestilence, and a destructive earthquake were the chief. But, thanks to the wisdom and energy of the authorities and the generous aid of the people of England, the worst consequences of the famine were averted; while the ravages of the plague have been checked, and the damage caused by the earthquake has been quickly repaired.

During this administration the peace of the North-West Frontier was much disturbed. In consequence of an invasion of Chitral a military expedition was sent into that country, and ultimately a British garrison was placed there, and a road was made from Peshawar through the intervening tribal territories. These operations were followed by a succession of tribal risings, the most formidable of them being that of the Afridis, which led to a military expedition on a great scale being sent into that country.

In commemoration of the completion of the sixtieth year of of Her Majesty, the Queen Empress's reign, a Diamond Jubilee was celebrated throughout India in 1897.

On his retirement, in January, 1899, Lord Elgin was succeeded by Lord Curzon, the present Viceroy whose political training and high attainments justify the favourable hopes of his administration entertained on all hands.

CHAPTER XVII.

THE EFFECTS OF BRITISH RULE IN INDIA.

Abiding Peace.

BRITISH rule has given India what she never enjoyed before, namely, abiding tranquillity. Peace extends throughout the length and breadth of the country, and has lasted in many places for more than a century The din of battle has not been heard in Bengal and Behar since the days of Mir Kásim, or in Guzerat since the second Márháttá war. Southern India has enjoyed profound peace since the death of Tipu Sultán in 1799, and the Deccan and Central India, since the removal of Bájí Ráo and Appá Sáheb from their capitals, Poona and Nagpur. The Punjab and Sindh, Assam and Burma, have experienced very little disturbance since their conquest. Once only during the century was the peace of Hindusthán disturbed, by the Sepoy Mutiny, which, as we have seen, was promptly and effectually quelled in little more than twelve months. Two fruitful sources of unquiet, which greatly disturbed the Mughal empire, have altogether ceased to exist under British rule; namely, the individual ambition of provincial governors, and civil wars between rival candidates at every succession to the Imperial dignity. Wars of succession have been unknown in England for the last two centuries, and the admirable system under which Viceroys and Governors of provinces are changed every fifth year, and subordinate officers more frequently, checks ambition in high places, and tends to prevent any one from acquiring dangerous local influence. The wild tribes of India, who were a constant source of disturbance of the peace, are being rapidly reclaimed. The Gáros, Kukis, Khásiás, Nágás, Bhils, Kols, Rámusis, Santáls, Mairs, Minas, Gonds, and Orangs, have all felt the power of civilised rule, and are fast setting down as peaceful agriculturists and honest labourers. The mountain fastnesses of the Himálayas,

Reclamation of savages.

the Vindhyas, the Sahyádri, and the Nilgiries, which perpetually sent forth disturbers of peace into the plains, have now been completely brought under control, and these once barely accessible regions have offered sites for a number of resorts of health and pleasure, such as Simla, Darjeeling, Nainital, Mári, Shillong, Mussoorie, Mahábaleśvar, and Ootacamund.

Establishment of Hill Sanitaria.

Another blessing which English rule has conferred upon India, is facility of communication between different parts of the Peninsula. Nations that were not even known to one another by name, have now become friends and neighbours. By railway the remotest corners of India may be reached from the capital in the course of four or five days, and through the telegraph a message can be sent to any distance in half an hour. Formerly, while one part of India reaped a superabundant crop, and the people had no means of disposing of the surplus, another part was, perhaps, the scene of a devastating famine. But improved communications have facilitated the distribution of food-grains, and famine is becoming more and more rare.

Easy communication.

India has always required a strong government, and no government has been stronger than that of the English. It has not only secured India from foreign invasion, but it has checked all violent and organised crime. The Thugs, who, in the name of religion, committed the grossest atrocities on travellers, have been almost extirpated, and dacoits have been put down with a strong hand. The dacoits of Bengal, the Pindaris of Central India, and the various marauding tribes that lived by plunder and violence, have been compelled to take to peaceful occupations.

Suppression of violent crimes.

Pestilence was another scourge of India, which swept away millions at a time from particular localities. Ancient India stood aghast at these terrible visitations of Providence and sought reme-

Sanitations.

dies for them only in prayer and worship. The Bráhmans, indeed, laid down minute rules of conduct, called *Achâras*, by strictly observing which individuals might avert these calamities and attain to longevity. B it it was reserved for the British Government to grapple successfully with these periodical visitations by draining marshes, supplying the urban population with filtered water, and establishing organised systems of conservancy. No Government has ever bestowed so much attention on the task of securing the lives and properties of its subjects, not only from foreign and domestic enemies, but even from the visitations of Providence. But an enlightened Government does not rest content merely with protecting the lives and properties of its subjects. It endeavours also to make life endurable and enjoyable.

New industries.

British rule has, indeed, wrought a great revolution in the economy of the country. Industries which were the pride and glory of India, and all her fine arts, have dwindled into insignificance owing to British competition. The manufacture of cloth, whether woollen, silk, or cotton, and of cutlery, has fallen mainly into the hands of the English. This was a serious change, and one that was fraught with immense suffering to those whose occupations were thus taken away. But the evil has been more than compensated by the introduction of British capital, which has enabled India to undertake gigantic Railway works, and at a great outlay, to establish the Cotton, Jute, Tea, and Indigo industries, affording occupation to millions of the natives of India. The greatest glory of English rule in India, however, is the noble attempt that is being made to educate the masses. Education was, in all preceding periods, confined to the higher classes. The masses were steeped in ignorance and superstition. British rule has established vernacular schools in almost every village, affording opportunities to all classess of the people to improve their minds.

Mass education.

Popular education is given through the medium of the vernacular, and high education through the medium of English, and no distinction is made of caste, colour, or creed in the steps thus taken for the diffusion of knowledge. A great impetus has also been given to the study of the classical literature of India. Sanskrit classical works which had long lain buried in oblivion, are being searched for, published, studied, commented upon, and translated,—revealing the part which, for four thousand years, Indian civilisation played in the various departments of life ; while, at the same time, a prose literature has sprung up in almost all the vernaculars, which has a large field for improvement and usefulness before it.

Toleration.

The policy of strict neutrality in religious matters is another excellent feature of English rule in India. It has given rise to many new religions. Rájá Rám Mohan Ráy founded the Brahmo Samáj, the members of which are strict monotheists. His great successor was the late Keśav Chandra Sen, who carried the ideas of the founder a little further. Dayánanda Sarasvatí, who founded the Áryya Samáj, also believed in one God. The Musalmans also have developed a new reform under the name of *Farázi*. Christian Missionaries of various denominations have done much good in diffusing education, in recliming the hill tribes, and giving shape to their languages. The names of Schwartz, Carey, Marshman, Ward, and Duff deserve all honour from the people of India.

Political development.

The history of India is the history of mighty individuals. Its people are, to a very great extent, incapable of united action. But, under the fostering care of their present rulers, who are noted for their capacity for such action, they are being made to understand its value. The Government of India has recently given the people the privilege of electing representatives on Municipal and District Boards, and even in the Universities; and the Legislative Councils have lately been remodelled so as to include a number of representatives of the people.

Employment of Natives in the Public Service.

The policy of Lord William Bentinck, who was the first to admit the natives of India to responsible offices of the State, has undergone gradual expansion, culminating in the Public Service Commission, which has thrown open to them all the higher ranks of the Service with the exception of a few of the most important appointments, reserved exclusively for the members of the British race. Natives can now aspire to high office in the Administrative Service without going to England.

Under British rule, for the first time in India, it has been declared that every man is equal in the eye of the law, and the Indian Judiciary have obtained an honourable reputation for incorruptibility and judicial capacity. India understands and appreciates the value of British rule, and earnestly and sincerely desires its long continuance.

FINIS.

GENEALOGICAL TABLE OF THE MUGHAL EMPERORS.

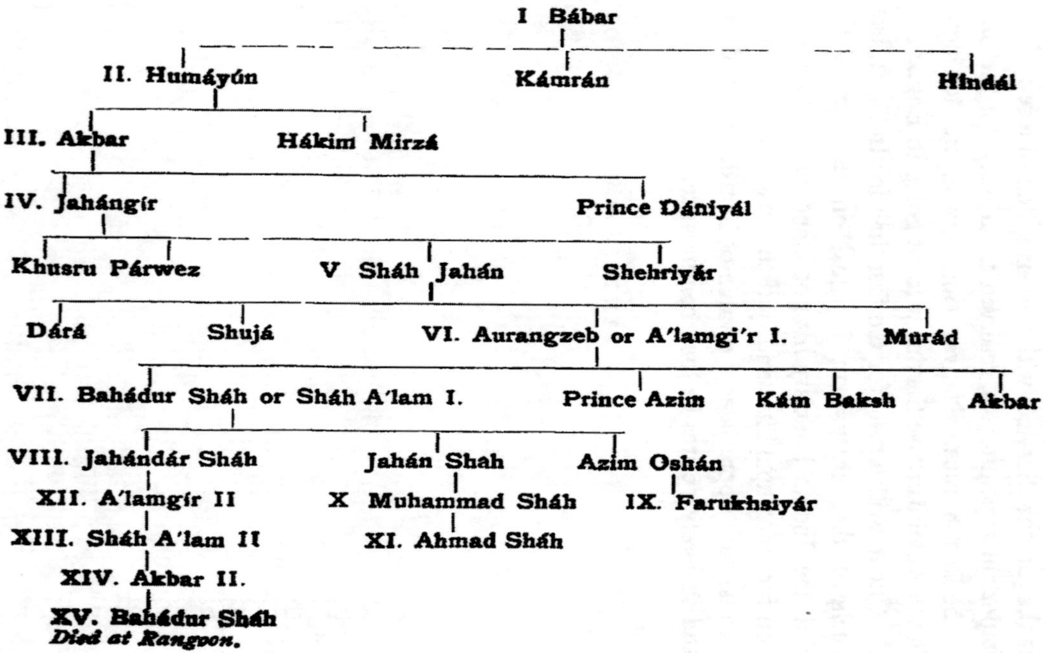

Genealogical Table of the Family of S'iva'ji'.

(Satárá Branch).

- **I. S'iváji'**
  - **II. S'ambhu'ji'**
    - **III. S'iváji' II.** **(Rájá Sáhu)** *After some years in the Mughal camp, became king again in 1708.*
      - **VII. Rám Rájá** *(Adopted son.)*
        - **VIII. Sáhu**
          - **IX. Pratáp S'iva** *Made Rájá by the English in 1818.*
          - **Rám Rájá**
          - **Sáhu**
  - **IV. Rájá Rám**
    - **V. S'iváji' III.**
      - **VII. Rám Rájá** *Became Rájá in 1748.*
    - **VI. S'ambhu'ji' II.** *Driven from Satárá, became Rájá of Kolhápur*

GENEALOGICAL TABLE OF THE PESHWAS.

- I. Báláji Biśvanáth Bhatta
  - II. Báji Ráo
    - III. Báláji' Báji' Ráo
      - IV. Mádhava Ráo
      - V. Náráyan Ráo
        - VI. Mádhava Ráo Náráyan
    - Raghunáth Ráo or Rághava
      - Amrita Ráo *(Adopted son)*
      - VII. Báji' Ráo II. *(Last Peshwa)*
        - Náná Sáheb *(Adopted son).*
      - Chimnáji A'ppá
  - Chimnáji A'ppá
    - Sadás'iv Ráo Bháo

A CHRONOLOGICAL TABLE OF THE PRINCIPAL EVENTS IN INDIAN HISTORY.

B. C.	
557	The Birth of Buddha.
521	Persian invasion under Darius.
477	Death of Buddha.
467	Death of Mahávíra, the founder of the Jaina religion.
327	Invasion of India by Alexander.
320	Chandra Gupta rises to power.
312	Chandra Gupta is made king.
312 to 307	Megasthenes at Pátaliputra.
292	The death of Chandra Gupta.
264	Bindusár dies and Aśoka comes to power.
260	Aśoka ascends the throne.
256	The Bactrian kingdom founded.
223	Aśoka dies.
181	The Sungas or Mitras become Emperors.
111	The Kánva dynasty usurp the Empire.
71	The Andhras conquer Magadha.
56	Starting of the Málava Era.
A. D.	
50	Gondopherus, king in the Punjab.
78	Kanishka becomes Emperor. Starting of the Śaka era.
249	Starting of the Chedi Era.
319	Starting of the Nepal or Gupta Era.
426	Kings of Valabhí known as Mahárájás.
468	The last mention of Skanda Gupta.
510	The last mention of Bhánu Gupta.
533	Yaśodharmadev expels the Húnas. The battle of Korur.
519 to 549	Gurjara kings of Látamandal
607	Harshavardhan ascends the throne of Kanauj.
627 to 642	Hiouen Thsang in India.
711 to 760	The first Muhammadan conquest under Kásim
736	The foundation of the Tomar kingdom at Delhi.
744	The fall of Valabhí.
746	The foundation of the city of Anahilpattan and of the dynasty of Chápotkatas.

672 A'ditya Sen of Magadha declares himself independent.
752 The Ráshtrakutas overthrow the Chálúkyas of Vátápi.
943 The Chápotkatas are overthrown. The Chálúkyas come to power in Guzerat
972 Chálúkya Tailapa overthrows the Ráshtrakutas of Mányakheta.
977 Subuktigín ascends the throne of Ghazní
997 Subuktigín dies and Mahmúd ascends the throne
1001 First invasion of Mahmúd.
1006 Bhoj becomes king of Málava
1008 Fourth invasion of Mahmúd
1710 Fifth invasion of Mahmúd
1023 Tenth invasion of Mahmúd and the annexation of the Punjab to the Ghazní Empire
1024 Twelfth invasion of Mahmúd.
1206 Mahmúd destroys the temple of Somanáth
1030 Death of Mahmúd
1036 Re building of the temple of Somanáth by Bhímadev of Guzerat
1062 Death of Bhoj
1066 Conversion of Tibet by Dípankar Srijnána
1081 Chola conquest of Orissa Building of the temple of Jagannáth
1119 Starting of the Lakshmana Sen Era
1151 The Chauháns conquer the Tomaras
1157 Chedi Vijjala conquers Kalyána.
1176 Muhammad of Ghor conquers the town of Uch in the Punjab.
1186 Muhammad of Ghor takes possession of Lahore.
1189 Yádava Bhillama conquers Kalyána.
1191 Muhammad of Ghor defeated by Prithví Ráy.
1193 Muhammad of Ghor completely defeats the Hindus under Prithvi Ráy, who is killed
1194 Muhammad of Ghor invades Kanauj, defeats Jay Chandra, and annexes Kanauj, and Benares
1197 Bakhtiyár Khilji conquers Behar.
1199 Bengal conquered by Bakhtiyár.
1202 The Bághelás expel Muhammadans from Guzerat and overthrow the Chálúkya dynasty.
1205 Muhammad Ghorí killed by the Gakkhars of the Punjab.
1232 Sultán Altamsh sacks Ujjayiní and destroys the famous temple of Mahákála.

1288	The fall of the Slave Kings. The Khilijis come to power.
1295	Aláuddín Khiliji ascends the throne of Delhi.
1297	Aláuddín Khiliji annexes Guzerat and Málava.
1310	Aláuddín Khiliji conquers the Deccan.
1316	Death of Aláuddín Khiliji.
1321	The end of the Khilijis. The Tughlaks come to power.
1325	Muhammad Tughlak ascends the throne.
1336	Foundation of the Hindu kingdom of Vijaynagar (Bukka Family).
1337	The rebellion of the Amirani Sada.
1345	Háji Iliás declares the independence of Bengal.
1347	The Deccan declares itself independent. The foundation of the Bahmaní kingdom.
1351	Death of Muhammad Tughlak, and the succession of Firoz Tughlak.
1394	Málik-us-Sharq declares himself independent at Jaunpur.
1396	Guzerat asserts its independence.
1398	Invasion of Timúr.
1401	Málava asserts its independence.
1412	The extinction of the Pathán Empire.
1424	Annexation of the Kákateya kingdom by the Bahmanís.
1478	Bahlol Lodí annexes Jaunpur.
1481	Assassination of Mahmúd Gáwán.
1487	Narasinha becomes king of Vijaynagar.
1489	Bijapur and Berar established as independent kingdoms.
1491	Foundation of the kingdom of Ahmadnagar.
1494	Annexation of Behar by Sikandar Lodí.
1494	Aláuddín Husain Sháh ascends the throne of Bengal.
1498	Vasco da Gama lands at Calicut.
1500	Foundation of Agra by Sikandar Lodí.
1512	Foundation of the Golkonda kingdom.
1516	Death of Sikandar Lodí.
1526	Invasion of Bábar. End of the Lodís. End of the Bahmanís. Bidar becomes an independent kingdom.
1526	First battle of Pánipat.
1527	Battle of Sikri.
1529	Conquest of Chitor by Bahádur Sháh of Guzerat.
1530	Death of Bábar and succession of Humáyún.
1536	Málava annexed to Guzerat.
1540	Humáyún defeated by Sher Sháh, who ascends the throne of Delhi.
1542	Birth of Akbar.

1555 Humáyún re-conquers Delhi.
1556 Second battle of Pánipat.
1557 Death of Bahádur Shàh of Guzerat.
1560 Akbar begins to reign independently.
1563 Sulaimán Kiráni establishes his independence in Bengal.
1565 Battle of Tálikot.
1565 Annexation of Orissa by Kálápáhár.
1568 Conquest of Chitor by Akbar.
1572 Berar ceases to be an independent kingdom.
1572 Guzerat made over to Akbar.
1575 Bengal annexed to the Mughal empire by Akbar.
1599 Establishment of the East India Company.
1605 Death of Akbar and succession of Jahángír.
1615 Arrival of Sir Thomas Roe in India.
1627 Death of Jahángír and succession of Sháh Jahán.
1627 Birth of Śiváji.
1636 Ahmadnagar annexed to the Mughal empire.
1639 Foundation of Madras.
1658 Battle of Ujjayiní and the defeat of Yaśovanta Sinha.
1659 Battle of Kajoá.
1659 Dárá betrayed into the hands of Aurangzeb and sentenced to death.
1659 Au. gzeb ascends the throne.
1664 Śiváji assumes the title of Rájá.
1666 Aurangzeb's treaty with Śiváji; and Śiváji's visit to Delhi.
1668 Bombay made over to the East India Company.
1670 Śiváji's war with the Mughals.
1671 Re-imposition of the Jizya.
1674 Śiváji assumes the title of Mahárájá.
1680 Death of Śiváji and the accession of Śambhúji.
1683 Aurangzeb marches to conquer to Deccan.
1689 Śambhúji sentenced to death and accession of Śiváji II.
1698 Fort William is built.
1698 The fall of Ginji.
1700 The death of Rájá Ram.
1704 Foundation of Murshidabad.
1707 Death of Aurangzeb; and accession of Bahádur Sháh.
1708 Release of Sàhu. Márhattá Civil War.
1708 Assassination of Guru Govinda.
1712 Death of Bahádur Sháh and accession of Farukhsiyár.
1712 Báláji Biśvanáth Bhatta founds the Peshwa family.
1717 Treaty of the Mughals with Rájá Sáhu.

1719	Death of Farukhsiyár, and accession of Muhammad Sháh.
1720	Bájí Ráo becomes Peshwa.
1721	The Nizam revolts.
1728	The Nizam makes peace with Bájí Ráo.
1730	Kolhápur made a separate kingdom. End of the Márháttá Civil War.
1731	Battle of Dubhoy.
1738	Bájí Ráo obtains Málava.
1739	Invasion of Nádir Sháh.
1740	Death of Bájí Ráo, and the succession of Bálají Bájí Ráo.
1740	Ali Vardi Khan becomes viceroy of Bengal.
1742	Invasion of Bengal by Raghuji Bhonsla.
1748	First invasion of Ahmad Shah Abdali.
1748	Death of Muhammad Sháh and accession of Ahmad Sháh.
1748	Death of Raja Sahu and removal of the Peshwa to Poona.
1748	Death of the first Nizam.
1751	Second invasion of Ahmad Shah Abdalí.
1752	Clive's defence of Arkot.
1752	Cession of Orissa to the Márhattas
1754	Death of Ahmad Sháh, and accession of Álamgír II
1755	Conquest of Guzerat by the Márháttás.
1756	Third invasion of Ahmad Sháh Abdálí.
1756	Death of Ali Vardi Khán and succession of Sirájud-daulá.
1756	The Massacre of Black Hole.
1757	The battle of Plassey.
1758	The Márháttás conquer Lahore.
1759	Loss of French influence in the Deccan.
1759	Fourth invasion of Ahmad Sháh Abdálí.
1759	Sháh Álam II. proclaims himself Emperor.
1759	Sadáśiv obtains Ahmadnagar.
1760	Clive returns to England.
1760	Hyder Ali becomes Sultán of Maisur.
1761	Capture of Pondicherry by the English.
1761	Third battle of Pánipat.
1761	Death of Bálájí Bájí Ráo and succssion of Mádhava Ráo.
1762	Sikh conquest of the Punjab.
1763	Mádhava Ráo proceeds against Hyder Ali.
1763	Battles of Udvánálá and Gheria.
1764	Battle of Baxar.
1765	Grant of the Diváni of Bengal, Behar, and Orissa to the East India Company.

1765	Sháh Alam II agrees to live under British protection
1759	Hyder Ali invades the Carnatic (First Maisur War).
1771	Bisvají Krishna invades Hindusthán Sháh Alam II renounces British protection and proceeds to Delhi
1771	Death of Mádhava Ráo and succession of Mádhava Ráo Náráyan
1772	Warren Hastings as Governor Náráyan Ráo murdered
1774	The Rohilla War
1775	First Márháttá War
1776	Treaty of Purandar
1779	Second Márhátta War
1779	Convention of Wargáon
1780	Hastings quarrels with Chait Sinha
1780	Second Maisur war
1782	Treaty of Salbai
1782	Death of Hyder
1783	Treaty of Mangalore
1774	Pitt's India Bill passed
1785	Hastings returns to England, and Sir John Macpherson becomes Governor-General
1786	Lord Cornwallis appointed Governor General
1787	Sháh Alam II blinded by Ghulám Kadir Sindhia supreme in Hindusthan
1790	Triple Alliance against Tipu Sultán
1792	Chinese invasion of Nepal
1790-92	Third Maisur War
1793	The Permanent Settlement and the return of Lord Cornwallis to England Sir John Shore Governor-General
1795	Battle of Kurdla
1795	Suicide of Mádhava Ráo Narayan and succession of Báji Ráo II
1798	Marquis of Wellesley, Governor General
1799	The policy of Subsidiary Alliance started
1799	Fourth Maisur War and restoration of the Hindu dynasty in Maisur
1800	Death of Naná Farnavis
1801	Ranajit Sinha assumes the title of Mahárаja
1802	Treaty of Bassein
1803	Third Márháttá war Battle of Assai
1803	Battle of Laswari

1803	Battle of Argáon.
1804	The English become the Paramount power in India.
1804	War with Holkar.
1805	Lord Cornwallis comes to India a second time.
1805	Death of Lord Cornwallis at Ghazipur. Lord Minto appointed Governor-General.
1806	The Vellore mutiny. Death of Sháh Álam.
1809	The Sikh chiefs to the east of the Sutlej place themselves under British protection.
1813	Lord Minto leaves India. The Marquis of Hastings appointed Governor-General.
1813—15	The Nepal war.
1817	Pindári war. Battle of Mehidpur.
1818	Fourth Márháttá war. Bájí Ráo overthrown.
1823	The Marquis of Hastings returns to England. Lord Amherst sent out as Governor-General.
1824	The first Burmese war.
1826	Cession of Assam, Arakan, and Tenaserim to the English.
1826	Capture of Bharatpur.
1828—1835	Lord William Bentinck, Governor-General.
1836	Lord Auckland, Governor-General.
1836	The first Afghán war.
1839	Death of Ranajit Sinha
1841	Sir Alexander Burnes killed
1842	Lord Ellenborough appointed Governor-General.
1842	Dost Muhammad returns to Kabul.
1843	The Sindh war.
1843	The Gwalior war.
1844	Retirement of Lord Ellenborough. Lord Hardinge, Governor-General.
1845	Battles of Mudki and Ferozpur.
1846	Battle of Aliwal
1846	Battle of Sobráon.
1846	Treaty of Mian Mir.
1848	Retirement of Lord Hardinge. Lord Dalhousie, Governor-General.
1848	The second Sikh war.
1849	Capture of Multan.
1849	Battle of Chillianwala.
1849	Battle of Gujarát.
1849	Annexation of the Punjab.

1852	The second Burmese war.
1853	Annexation of Jhansi and Nagpur.
1856	Annexation of Oudh
1856	Retirement of Lord Dalhousie: and the appointment of Lord Canning.
1856	English war with China and Persia.
1857	The Sepoy Mutiny.
1858	Assumption of direct administration by the Queen.
1858	The Queen's Proclamation issued.
1862	Lord Canning leaves India.
1862—63	Lord Elgin.
1864	Lord Lawrence appointed Governor-General.
1864	The Bhutan war.
1869	Lord Mayo appointed Governor-General
1872	Assassination of Lord Mayo.
1872	Lord Northbrook, Governor-General
1875	The visit of the Prince of Wales.
1876	Lord Lytton appointed Governor-General
1877	The Queen assumes the title of Empress of India.
1878	The second Afghán war.
1879	The Trenty of Gandamak.
1879—80	The third Afghán war.
1880—84	Lord Ripon
1884—88	Lord Dufferin.
1886	Annexation of Burma.
1887	Her Majesty's Jubilee.
1888—93	Lord Lansdowne
1891	The Manipur war.
1893	Lord Elgin, appointed Governor-General.
1895	Chitral Expedition.
1897-98	Tirah Expedition.
1897	Her Majesty's Diamond Jubilee
1899	Lord Curzon, the present Governor-General appointed.

BRITISH GOVERNORS GENERAL OF INDIA UNDER THE EAST INDIA COMPANY.

1774	Warren Hastings.
1785	Sir John Macpherson, (officiating).
1786	Earl (afterwards Marquis of) Cornwallis.
1793	Sir John Shore.
1798	Earl of Mornington (Marquis of Wellesley)
1805	Marquis of Cornwallis (second time).
1805	Sir George Barlow (temporary).
1807	Lord (afterwards Earl of) Minto.
1813	Earl of Moira (Marquis of Hastings).
1823	John Adam (officiating).
1823	Lord (afterwards Earl of) Amherst.
1828	Lord William Cavendish Bentinck.
1835	Sir Charles Metcalfe (afterwards Lord Metcalfe, temporary).
1836	Lord (afterwards Earl of) Auckland
1842	Lord (afterwards Earl of) Ellenborough.
1844	Sir Henry (afterwards Viscount) Hardinge.
1848	Earl (afterwards Marquis) of Dalhousie.
1856	Viscount (afterwards Earl) Canning.

VICEROYS UNDER THE QUEEN.

1858	Earl Canning.
1862	Lord Elgin
1863	Sir William Denison (officiating).
1864	Sir John Lawrence (afterwards Lord Lawrence).
1869	Earl of Mayo.
1872	Lord (afterwards Earl of) Northbrook.
1876	Lord (afterwards Earl of) Lytton.
1880	Marquis of Ripon.
1884	Earl of Dufferin (afterwards Marquis of Dufferin and Ava).
1888	Marquis of Lansdowne.
1893	Lord Elgin.
1899	Lord Curzon.

Transliteration of Indian Names.

Abhay Sinha, अभयसिंह ।
Abhidharma, अभिधर्म्म ।
Achalgarh, अचलगड़ ।
Áchára, आचार ।
Ácháryya Churámani, आचार्य्य-चूड़ामणि ।
Achyuta Ráy, अच्युत राय ।
Ádiśúr, आदिशूर ।
Ádityasen, आदित्यसेन ।
Adhvaryu, अध्वर्य्यु ।
Agastya, अगस्त्य ।
Agnimitra, अग्निमित्र ।
Ahalyá Bái, अहल्या बाइ ।
Ahluválá Misl, अहलुवाला मिसल ।
Ajátaśatru, अजात शत्रु ।
Ájívaka, आजीवक ।
Ánandí Bái, आनन्दी बाइ ।
Ananga Bhímdev, अनङ्ग भीमदेव ।
Ananga Pál, अनङ्ग पाल ।
Andhra, अन्ध्र ।
Anga, अङ्ग ।
Angirá, अङ्गिरा ।
Angria, अङ्गिया ।
Antyaja, अन्त्यज ।
Aparántaka, अपरान्तक ।
Ápastamba, आपस्तम्ब ।
Appay Díkshita, अप्पय दीक्षित ।
Áryya, आर्य्य ।
Áryyavata, आर्य्यभट ।
Áryyávartta, आर्य्यावर्त्त ।
Aśoka, अशोक ।
Asura, असुर ।
Aśvamedha, अश्वमेध ।
Áśvin, आश्विन ।
Atharvaveda, अथर्व्ववेद ।
Atharvavedí Bráhman, अथर्व्व-वेदी ब्राह्मण ।
Atri, अत्रि ।
Ayodhyá, अयोध्या ।

B

Bághelá, वाघेला ।
Bágri, वागड़ि ।
Bájí Ghorpare, वाजी घरपुरे ।
Bájí Ráo, वाजी राओ ।
Bálájí Bájí Ráo, वालाजी वाजीराओ
Bálájí Biśvanáth Bhatta, वालाजी विश्वनाथ भट्ट ।
Bálá Hissar, वाला हिस्सार ।
Ballál Sen, वल्लाल सेन ।
Balavanta Sinha, वलवन्त सिंह ।
Bánprastha, वानप्रस्थ ।
Banráj, वनराज ।
Bándá, वान्दा ।
Bánpur, वानपुर ।
Báppá Ráo, वाप्पा राओ ।
Bápu Gokla, वापु गोकले ।
Bargir Hangámá, वर्गिर हाङ्गामा ।

Bhadrabáhu, भद्रबाहु।
Bhagaván Dás, भगवान दास।
Bhágírathí, भागीरथी।
Bhakti Śástra, भक्तिशास्त्र।
Bharukachchha, भरूकच्छ।
Bháskaráchāryya, भास्कराचार्य्य।
Bhatáraka, भटारक।
Bhavabhúti, भवभूति।
Bhikshu, भिक्षु।
Bhillama, भिल्लम।
Bhrigu, भृगु।
Bhrigukachchha, भृगुकच्छ।
Bhuvaneśvara, भुवनेश्वर।
Bindusára, बिन्दुसार।
Biśvají Krishna, विश्वजी कृष्ण।
Brahmacharyya, ब्रह्मचर्य्य।
Bráhman, ब्राह्मण।
  Rigvedí, ऋग् वेदी।
  Yajurvedí, यजुर्व्वेदी।
  Sámavedí, सामवेदी।
  Atharvavedí, अथर्व्ववेदी।
Bráhmanábád, ब्राह्मणाबाद।
Brahmarshideś, ब्रह्मर्षिदेश।
Brahmávartta ब्रह्मावर्त्त।
Byaghrapallí, व्याघ्रपल्ली।

C

Chaitanya, चैतन्य।
Chakrapáni Datta, चक्रपाणि दत्त।
Chakravartí, चक्रवर्त्ती।
Chálúkya, चालूक्य।
Chálukya Vikram Samvat, चालूक्य विक्रम संवत्।
Chámundadev, चामुण्डदेव।
Chánakya, चाणक्य।
Chandáśoka, चण्डाशोक।
Chandeśvara, चण्डेश्वर।
Chandráditya, चन्द्रादित्य।
Chandrakírtti, चन्द्रकीर्त्ति।
Chápotkata, चापोत्कट।
Chastana, चष्टन।
Chaturvedí, चतुर्व्वेदी।
Chaube, चौबे।
Chauhán, चौहाण।
Chaurá, चओड़ा।
Chhanda, छन्द।
Chhatter Sinha, छत्तर सिंह।
Chimnájí Áppá, चिमाजी आप्पा।

D

Dádájí Kondeo, दादाजी कोण्डदेव।
Dalakeśvara, दलकेश्वर।
Dandaka, दण्डक।
Dantidurga, दन्तिदुर्ग।
Dayánanda Sarasvatí, दयानन्द सरस्वती।
Desádhikárí, देशाधिकारी।
Desapándya, देशपाण्ड्य।
Devaputra, देवपुत्र।
Ḍevaráj, देवराज।
Dhábári, धाबाड़ि।
Dhankataka, धनकटक।
Dhananjaya, धनञ्जय।
Dhánga, धाङ्ग।
Dharmapál, धर्म्मपाल।
Dharmarája, धर्म्मराज।
Dharmaśálá, धर्म्मशाला।
Dharmáśoka, धर्म्माशोक।

Dharmasútra, धर्म्मसूत्र ।
Dhritarashtra, धृतराष्ट्र ।
Dinemárdángá, दिनेमारडाङ्गा ।
Dipankara Srijnána, दिपाङ्कर श्रीज्ञान ।
Divángiri, देवीयानगिरि ।
Drávira द्राविड़ ।
Drirhaprahára, दृढप्रहार ।
Drishadvatí, दृषद्वती ।
Durjansála, दुर्ज्जनशाल ।
Duryodhana, दुर्य्योधन ।
Dváraká, द्वारका ।
Dvársamudra, द्वारसमुद्र ।

F

Fulkiá Misl, फुलकिया मिस्ल ।

G

Gadádhar Bhattácháryya, गदाधर भट्टाचार्य्य ।
Gáin, गांइ ।
Grámina, ग्रामीन ।
Gautamí, गौतमी ।
Ghásdáná, घासदाना ।
Ghatotkacha, घटोत्कच ।
Grahavarmá, ग्रहवर्म्मा ।
Grámádhikarí, ग्रामाधिकारी ।
Gritsamada, गृत्समद ।
Grihyasútra, गृह्यसूत्र ।

H

Hárít, हारीत् ।
Harapáldev, हरपाल देव ।
Harshacharita, हर्षचरित ।
Harshavardhan, हर्षवर्द्धन ।
Hemádri, हेमाद्रि ।
Hiranyabáha, हिरण्यबाह ।
Hoysálá Ballál, हयशाला बल्लाल ।

I

Ikshàku, इक्ष्वाकु ।
Indraprastha, इन्द्रप्रस्थ ।

J

Jagadís Tarkálankár, जगदीश तर्कालङ्कार ।
Jagannáth Tarkapanchánan, जगन्नाथ तर्कपञ्चानन ।
Jaimini, जैमिनि ।
Jamadagni, जमदग्नि ।
Janají Bhonslá, जनजी भोंसला ।
Jválámukhí, ज्वालामुखी ।

K

Kádamvarí, कादम्बरी ।
Kákateya, काकतेय ।
Kálápáhár, कालापाहाड़ ।
Kalinga, कलिङ्ग ।
Kalpasútra, कल्पसूत्र ।
Kálpí, काल्पी ।
Kalyána, कल्याण ।
Kamalákar, कमलाकर ।
Kámpilya, काम्पिल्य ।
Kanáda, कणाद ।
Kányakubja, कान्यकुब्ज ।
Karnasuvarna, कर्णसुवर्ण ।
Kathá Sarit Ságara, कथासरित् सागर ।
Kishkindhyá, किष्किन्ध्या ।
Kubja Vishnuvardhan, कुब्ज विष्णुवर्द्धन ।
Kumárila Bhatta, कुमारिल भट्ट ।

Kumbha, कुम्भ ।
Kunhají Bhonslá, कुन्हजी भोंसला ।
Kurukshetra, कुरुक्षेत्र ।

L

Lakshman Dev, लक्ष्मण देव ।
Lakshmídhara, लक्ष्मीधर ।
Lakhji Yádava Ráy, लखजी यादव राय ।
Lalitáditya, ललितादित्य ।
Látamandal, लाटमण्डल ।
Lingáyat, लिङ्गायत ।

M

Madají Panth Purandharí, मदजी पन्थ पुरन्धरी ।
Mádhavácháryya, माधवाचार्य्य ।
Mádhava Ráo Náráyan, माधव राओ नारायण ।
Madhyadeś, मध्यदेश ।
Mahábáleśvar, महाबालेश्वर ।
Mahá Bundlá, महाबुन्दला ।
Mahákála, महाकाल ।
Mahárájádhiráj, महाराजाधिराज ।
Maháráshtra, महाराष्ट्र ।
Mahavircharita, महावीरचरित ।
Maháyána, महायान ।
Mairáwárá, मैरावोयारा ।
Malakeśvar, मलकेश्वर ।
Málavasthityábda, मालवस्थित्यब्द
Mandaleśvara, मण्डलेश्वर ।
Mányakheta, मान्यखेत ।
Maukhari, मौखरि ।
Maurya, मौर्य ।
Milinda Praśna, मिलिन्द प्रश्न ।
Mímánsaka, मीमांसक ।
Mitákshará, मिताक्षरा ।
Mlechhadeśa, म्लेच्छदेश ।
Mugdhabodha, मुग्धबोध ।
Mulráj, मूलराज ।

N

Nágasena, नागसेन ।
Nahapána, नहपान ।
Naimisharanya, नैमिषारण्य
Nálanda, नालन्द ।
Nányadev, नान्यदेव ।
Narasinhadev, नरसिंहदेव ।
Narendravardhan, नरेन्द्रवर्द्धन ।
Navakrishna, नवकृष्ण ।
Neonehál Sinha, निओनिहाल सिंह
Nirukta, निरुक्त ।
Nirvána, निर्व्वाण ।
Niśápur, निशापुर ।
Nyáya, न्याय ।
Nyáyadriś न्यायदृश् ।

P

Padminí, पद्मिनी ।
Pakshadhara Miśra, पक्षधर मिश्र ।
Pálakápya, पालकाप्य ।
Pánálá, पानाला ।
Panchála, पञ्चाल ।
Panchavatí, पञ्चवटी ।
Pándya, पाण्ड्य ।
Paramabhattáraka, परमभट्टारक ।
Paramára, परमार ।
Paramardídev परमर्द्दिदेव ।
Paraśurám, परशुराम ।
Parichehárá, परिचेहारा ।

Pátanjala, पातञ्जल।
Patanjali, पतञ्जलि।
Paundra, पौन्द्र।
Paundravardhan, पौन्द्रवर्द्धन।
Pennákonda, पेन्नाकोण्डा।
Perumal, पेरुमल।
Pravákaravardhan, प्रभाकरवर्द्धन।
Prabhasa, प्रभास।
Prabodha Chandrodaya, प्रबोध चन्द्रोदय।
Práchí, प्राची।
Prahlád Nírají, प्रह्लाद नीरजी।
Pratinidhi, प्रतिनिधि।
Pratisthán, प्रतिष्ठान।
Prithví Ráy, पृथीराय।
Pulinda, पुलिन्द।
Pulumáyi Váśishthiputra, पुलुमायि वाशिष्ठी पुत्र।
Purandarpur, पुरन्दरपुर।
Purushapur, पुरुषपुर।
Purva Mímánsá, पूर्व्वमीमांसा।
Pushpamitra, पुष्पमित्र।

R

Raghují Bhonslá, रघुजी भोंसला।
Rághava, राघव।
Rájagriha, राजगृह।
Rájatarangíní, राजतरङ्गिणी।
Rájgarh, राजगढ़।
Rájmahendrí, राजमहेन्द्री।
Rájsuya, राजसूय।
Rámánanda, रामानन्द।
Ranjí Sindhiá, रणजी सिन्धिया।
Rání Bhavání, राणी भवानी।
Rásamálá, रासमाला।
Rashtrakúta, राष्ट्रकूट।
Rathor, राठोर।
Rigveda Sanhitá, ऋग्वेदसंहिता।
Rudradáma, रुद्रदाम।
Rup, रूप।

S

Sadáśiv, सदाशिव।
Sahyádri, सह्याद्रि।
Śaiva, शैव।
Śakadvípa, शकद्वीप।
Śákala, शाकल।
Śakári, शकारि।
Sáketa, साकेत।
Śákhá, शाखा।
Śálihotra, शालिहोत्र।
Sáma, साम।
Sámanta Sinha, सामन्त सिंह।
Śambhují, शम्भुजी।
Samudra Gupta, समुद्र गुप्त।
Sanátan, सनातन।
Sangama, सङ्गम।
Sangameśvar, सङ्गमेश्वर।
Sanghamitrá, सङ्घमित्रा।
Sangíti, सङ्गीति।
Śankarácháryya, शङ्कराचार्य्य।
Sànkhya, सांख्य।
Sannyásí, सन्न्यासी।
Saptaparni, सप्तपर्णी।
Sáradá, सारदा।
Śaśánka, शशाङ्क।
Śástra, शास्त्र।
Souman Rajput, सौमन राजपुत।

Sauvíra, सौवीर।
Sávantawarí, सावन्तवाड़ी।
Savitá, सविता।
Śikshá, शिक्षा।
Śílabhadra, शीलभद्र।
Śiláditya, शिलादित्य।
Sindhumátá, सिन्धुमाता।
Śiśunága, शिशुनाग।
Sitáná, सिताना।
Sítápur, सीतापुर।
Śivaráj, शिवराज।
Skanda Gupta, स्कन्दगुप्त।
Smriti Kalpataru, स्मृति कल्पतरु।
Someśvar, सोमेश्वर।
Srautasútra, श्रौतसूत्र।
Srávastí, श्रावस्ती।
Subarnabhúmi, सुवर्णभूमि।
Suddhodana, शुद्धोदन।
Sukarchakiá Misl, सुकारचकिया मिसल।
Súkta, सूक्त।
Súlvasútra, शुल्वसूत्र।
Súrasena, शूरसेन।
Súryyají Pisl, सूर्य्यजी पिसल।
Sushìma, सुषीम।

T

Tailanga, तैलङ्ग।
Tailapa, तैलप।
Tálikot, तालिकोट।
Tálukdàr, तालुकदार।
Telingá Mukundadev, तेलिङ्गा मुकुन्ददेव।
Tháneśvar, स्थानेश्वर।
Tikendrajit, टीकेन्द्रजित्।
Tirumalla, तिरुमल्ल।
Trailokyavarmá, त्रैलोक्यवर्मा।
Trigartha, त्रिगर्त्त।
Tryambakji, त्र्यम्बक जी।
Tukárám, तुकाराम।
Tungabhadrá, तुङ्गभद्रा।

U

Udayáditya, उदयादित्य।
Udayaji Pauyár, उदयजी पौयार।
Udgátri, उद्गातृ।
Udvánálá, उद्वानाला।
Upapuráṇa, उपपुराण।
Uttararámcharita, उत्तररामचरित।

V

Váchaspati Miśra, वाचस्पति मिश्र
Vaiśáli, वैशाली।
Vaiśeshika, वैशेषिक।
Vámdev, वामदेव।
Vána Bhatta, वाण भट्ट।
Varáhamihira वराहमिहिर।
Vararuchi, वररुचि।
Varendra, वरेन्द्र।
Vásava, वासव।
Vaśistha, वशिष्ठ।
Vasudev, वसुदेव।
Vátápi, वातापि।
Váyu वायु।
Vidarbha, विदर्भ।
Videha, विदेह।
Vidiśá, विदिशा।
Vihára, विहार।
Vijjvala, विज्ज्वल।

Vikramáditya, विक्रमादित्य ।

Vináyak Ráo, विनायक राओ ।

Viśáldev, विशालदेव ।

Vishnupáda, विष्णुपाद ।

Vishnuvardhan, विष्णुवर्द्धन ।

Viśvámitra, विश्वामित्र ।

Viśvás Ráo विश्वास राओ ।

Viśveśvar Bhatta, विश्वेश्वर भट्ट ।

Vitáśoka, वीताशोक ।

Vrihatdratha बृहद्रथ ।

Vrihadvala, बृहद्वल ।

Vrindávn, बृन्दावन ।

Vyása, व्यास ।

Yádava, यादव ।

Yájnavalkya याज्ञवल्क्य ।

Yama, यम ।

Yáska, यास्क ।

Yaśodharmadev, यशोधर्म्मदेव ।

Yaśovanta Sinha, यशोवन्त सिंह ।

Yati, यति ।

Yavana, यवन ।

Yonadeś, योनदेश ।

Yudhisthir, युधिष्ठिर ।

Yuvarája, युवराज ।

INDEX.

E

F

G

K

M

Q

R

S

T